NEW WORLD STUDIES

J. Michael Dash, Editor

Frank Moya Pons and Sandra Pouchet
Paquet, Associate Editors

Edwidge Danticat

THE HAITIAN DIASPORIC IMAGINARY

Nadège T. Clitandre

University of Virginia Press

Charlottesville and London

University of Virginia Press
© 2018 by the Rector and Visitors of the University of Virginia
All rights reserved
Printed in the United States of America on acid-free paper

First published 2018

ISBN 978-0-8139-4186-8 (cloth)
ISBN 978-0-8139-4187-5 (paper)
ISBN 978-0-8139-4188-2 (ebook)

9 8 7 6 5 4 3 2 1

Library of Congress Cataloging-in-Publication Data is available for this title.

In loving memory of
Mesilas Clitandre,
my paternal grandfather, and
Anna Rose Walter,
my maternal grandmother

I too yearn not for a singular authoritative voice on any particular event or subject, or disaster, but for a chorus of voices.
—Edwidge Danticat, *The Art of Death*

Contents

Preface

HAITIAN AMERICAN writer Edwidge Danticat (b. 1969) is one
of the most recognized writers in North America and around the world
today. She is also one of the most celebrated contemporary Caribbean
writers in the diaspora. She is indeed among the foremost of Haitian
writers writing in English and has been dubbed "the voice" of the Haitian
diaspora. After the publication of her debut novel, *Breath, Eyes, Memory*,
the *New York Times Magazine* named Danticat one of thirty artists under
thirty to watch. Danticat was a finalist (in fiction) for the National Book
Award in 1995 for her short story collection, *Krik? Krak!*, making her
the youngest nominee. Shortly after, she was awarded the Pushcart Prize
(1995) for "Between the Pool and the Gardenias" and the Granta award
for best young American novelist (1996) for *Breath, Eyes, Memory*. Two
years later, the novel was selected for Oprah Winfrey's Book of the Month
Club, springing Danticat into the national spotlight. In 1999, Danticat
received three prestigious awards for her second novel, *The Farming of
Bones*; the American Book Award for excellence in American literature
(1999); and the Super Flaiano of Literature Prize (1999), one of a set
of Italian international awards recognizing achievements in the fields of
creative writing, cinema, theater, and radio/television. In 2005, Danticat
became a finalist for the PEN/Faulkner Award and received the Anisfield-
Wolf Book Award, both for *The Dew Breaker*, which was published the
year before. The latter stands out as the only American prize that recognizes books that have made important contributions to our understanding
of racism and human diversity. The Dayton Literary Peace Prize, which
Danticat received in 2008 for her 2007 memoir *Brother, I'm Dying*, is also
distinctive in its recognition of US literary texts that contribute to the promotion of peace. Nominated for the National Book Award for *Brother,
I'm Dying*, Danticat was also bestowed the National Book Critics Circle

Award for autobiography in 2007 for *Brother, I'm Dying*. She is a recipient of the prestigious MacArthur Fellows Program Genius Grant, which she received in 2009. Most recently, Danticat made the 2014 Andrew Carnegie Medal for Excellence in Fiction short list for her novel *Claire of the Sea Light* and is the winner of the 2018 Neustadt International Prize for Literature, a lifetime achievement award that recognizes a writer's entire body of work in any language.

Danticat's work has been translated into French, Korean, German, Italian, Spanish, and Swedish, among other languages. She is the subject of hundreds of academic journal articles and dissertations, including my own, and numerous book chapters and articles published since the late 1990s. Her short stories have been anthologized profusely. A major contemporary American author with a BA in French literature and an MFA from Brown University (as well as two honorary degrees from Smith College and Yale University), Danticat has produced important works of fiction and nonfiction in diverse genres that merit full-length study. Despite the international recognition she has received and a plethora of important subjects and themes she takes up that dominate the fields of postcolonial studies, feminist studies, Caribbean studies, (African) diaspora studies, Haitian studies, literary studies, and global studies, Danticat's work, which now spans nearly a quarter of a century, has not until now received a single sustained full-length interpretive literary analysis. *Edwidge Danticat: The Haitian Diasporic Imaginary* offers a concentrated and extensive multidisciplinary analysis of the writings of Danticat at the intersection of various fields.

Heretofore, there was only one book devoted entirely to the work of Edwidge Danticat. Edited by Martin Munro, a prominent scholar of Francophone and Caribbean literature and culture, *Edwidge Danticat: A Reader's Guide* (2010) is a collection of fourteen essays by different authors and Danticat's contemporaries. The anthology concentrates on framing the work of Danticat in both its Haitian literary tradition and in the broader North American and Caribbean context. While it has been well received as both a great pedagogical tool and an important contribution to furthering serious scholarship on the prolific writer, it does not address why Danticat's work resonates worldwide or why a writer who homes in on the particular experience of Haitians in Haiti and the diaspora has such a global reach. Moreover, as Munro himself admits, the diasporic dimension of Danticat's work is not directly addressed in the anthology. In her review of the edited volume, Maria Rice Bellamy states, "There is a notable omission of [Danticat's] connection to the larger generation of diasporic, cross-cultural, immigrant writers."[1] This omission of the diasporic element, which includes the African diasporic literary tradition, the transnational contours of immigrant writers, and the intense articulations of displacement, makes it difficult to completely recognize Danticat's wide-ranging appeal and understand her overnight success in the late nineties, during a time when the very field of diaspora studies was established as a result of migration concerns and growing interest in dispersed ethnic populations. This book seeks to rectify this oversight of the missing diasporic element; it picks up where Munro's collection leaves off by emphasizing diaspora and offering a cohesive and overarching theme that is needed to comprehend Danticat's corpus and central preoccupation with the experience of displacement and its affective dimensions.

This book is an effort to explore the breadth and depth of Danticat's oeuvre through an examination of the relationships among nation, diaspora, and the imaginary in the contemporary moment, a relationship that many scholars have been scrutinizing for the past twenty-five years. Unfortunately, Danticat's influential ideas about the Haitian immigrant experience have not been comprehensively analyzed in the context of the diasporic imaginary. By focusing on Danticat's inscription of diasporic subjects and articulation of diasporic imaginary, I show that the diasporic component in Danticat's writings is a central tenet that cannot be ignored and indeed engenders Danticat's universal appeal well into the twenty-first century. The narratives of Danticat's diasporic subjects are foregrounded not only to tell the stories of fragmentation and difference but also to organize diaspora as a collective and diverse unit and to create an archive that can contain both national and diasporic histories, as well as old and new narratives of homeland and articulations of home as both geographical spaces that can be mapped and symbolic places that are imagined. Thus Danticat's diaspora, as I explore in this book, is a lived and imagined phenomenon that insists on both cultural and historical preservation and transformation and involves symbolic returns that can engender real returns and fruitful dialogic relations with the homeland.

Ultimately, I hope that this book demonstrates that a thorough study of the progression of one immigrant writer's literary treatment of displacement might bring us to a more layered methodological and theoretical approach to the dynamics of diaspora within historical, discursive, and epistemological evolution of globalization, a nuanced understanding of the relationship between diaspora and nation that dismantles and transgresses the binary and monologic framework, and more complex and diverse representations of the Haitian diasporic experience specifically and the migration experience more broadly.

Acknowledgments

IT HAS taken me a long time to complete this book. A number of people have guided me along the way and helped me stay the course. I must begin by thanking Edwidge Danticat, who is the impetus behind my scholarship and academic trajectory. I first read Danticat's work in the mid-1990s and met the author in person a few years later at a book signing event. Since that initial encounter, Edwidge and I have stayed in touch. Not all writers are as generous, modest, and open as Edwidge. I thank her for taking the time to answer my questions and supporting my work over the years. It is with utmost gratitude for her generosity and profound admiration of her work that I offer this book and these words of appreciation.

I am indebted to the person who has held my hand incessantly throughout the entire process of conceiving and writing this book. Claudine Michel has been my biggest cheerleader and has supported me and this project in many capacities, first as a committee member, then as a mentor, a sister-friend, a colleague, and now as an invaluable member of my family. It was Edwidge who brought us together when I was beginning the PhD program in African diaspora studies at UC Berkeley. I am immensely grateful for Claudine's guidance on all academic matters and her unwavering emotional and moral support throughout some of the most challenging moments in both my personal and professional life. I could not have completed this book without her support.

My scholarly work on Danticat began when I was an undergraduate student at Hampton University. I still owe a great deal of gratitude to the many professors who guided me along the way. I single out my senior thesis professor, Aimee Carmines, who taught me the craft of engaging theory through meticulous and rigorous close reading and critical analysis. I also thank her for remaining interested in my work. It gives me great joy to say that one of my college professors has read the manuscript and offered editorial support before the book went to production. My interest and research on Danticat did undergo another level of maturity at the University of Chicago, where I received my master's degree in the humanities. Being taught by renowned professors such as Homi Bhabha and W. J. T. Mitchell through the master of arts program in the humanities had a very positive impact on my intellectual growth.

At the University of California, Berkeley, where I completed my PhD, I must acknowledge the African American Studies Department for the training I received in the study of the African diaspora. Percy Hintzen and Michel S. Laguerre were members of my dissertation committee who pushed me to explore the socioeconomic factors at play in the formation and transformation of diasporic communities. My committee chair and advisor, Abdul R. JanMohamed, and member Donna V. Jones in the English Department asked important questions that placed my work in conversation with postcolonial studies and Caribbean studies. Classes offered in the African American Studies Department by Professors Ula Taylor, VèVè Clark, and Sylvia Winter were inspirational and meaningful. Other professors at UC Berkeley, such as Trinh T. Minh-ha, Paola Bacchetta, Charis Thompson, Karl Britto, and Gautam Premnath had an impact on the way I conceptualized and framed my dissertation project. I am also grateful for the friendships I developed at Berkeley. I thank Lisa Rollins for being a great friend, especially during some very difficult times in graduate school, as well as Robin Mitchell and Felix Germain for looking out for me. My little village at Berkeley was blessed by the presence of Natascha Cadet and Max Blanchet, two members of a very small Haitian community in the Bay Area.

At the University of California, Santa Barbara, where I am currently an assistant professor, I am grateful for the support of colleagues and friends. In Global Studies, my home department, I thank all my colleagues for pushing my work in ways that expanded the scope of the project beyond my imagination. I am particularly grateful to Giles Gunn, who read multiple versions of my manuscript and offered positive and constructive feedback as well as words of encouragement. His wise counsel over the years has been immensely valuable. I thank Paul Amar for understanding my work and use of the echo chamber. I am grateful to Aashish Mehta for checking up on me and for his honesty. The Center for Black Studies Research, where I am an affiliate and coordinator of the Haiti Projects, is a second home that feeds my soul and helps me to think critically about engaged scholarship and black knowledge systems and productions. A big thanks to Diane Fujino, Mahsheed Ayoub, Chryss Yost, Rose Elfman, Rosa Pinter, and Charles Nicholson, a friend of the center, for their moral support over the years. In the Department of Black Studies, where I am an affiliate, I thank George Lipsitz, who provided critical feedback on the book proposal, Chris McAuley, for the down-to-earth campus chats, and Douglas Daniels for having a way of putting everything into perspective. I have heartfelt appreciation of the late Clyde Woods, who supported the relief efforts at the Center for Black Studies Research during the aftermath of the earthquake in Haiti. I will never forget our time with a few students at Hotel Oloffson in Port-au-Prince, where we randomly ran into Edwidge Danticat. In the English Department, I have received guidance from Julie Carlson with writing self-assessments and navigating merit reviews and from Bishnupriya Ghosh, who was the advisor for my postdoctoral fellowship. Felice Blake and Swati Rana are colleagues and friends who understand the struggle. Felice and I began both our postdoctoral fellowships and our tenure-track positions at the same time. We would meet up on Fridays to decompress. Over the years, we have laughed, cried, gotten angry or sad together. It has been a blessing to emote with her without judgment. In Comparative Literature, where I am an affiliate, I appreciate the support of Catherine Nesci, chair of the program. In Feminist Studies, I thank Mireille Miller-Young for her friendship and for sharing her mother, Beatrice Miller, with a number of us, and Leila Rupp, for her sound professional advice. I thank Kum-Kum Bhavnani in the Department of Sociology for taking the time out of her busy schedule to check in, listen and offer guidance. I appreciate Melvin Oliver, former dean of the College of Letters and Science, for his support of my hire and professional growth. I also thank Zaveeni Kahn-Marcus, director of the Multicultural Center, not only for her support of our Haiti projects but also for her friendship and for recognizing the importance of making time for tea! Two members of the Haitian community in Santa Barbara, Raphaella Nau and Nancy Sterlin, have over the years become dear friends and enriched my life in Santa Barbara. I am grateful to Ella Turenne, Ralph Louissaint, Carine Fabius, and Marguerite Lathan, members of the Haitian community in the Los Angeles area for collaboration on projects relating to the promotion of Haitian culture and arts in California.

    A few scholars have helped me to broaden the scope of my research on the diaspora. I have to thank Manfred Steger for his critical insights and recognition of my work in the field of global studies, and Jana Braziel, for guiding me through the transition to a department of global studies. I am grateful to Jana for reading the dissertation, offering ideas for turning the dissertation project into a book, and understanding the importance of a monograph on Danticat. I also thank Francois Pierre-Louis for the feedback and questions that helped me "save" chapter 1 of the book while he was a visiting scholar at UCSB. Francois has become a big brother, and I appreciate his wisdom and expertise on navigating Haitian politics and culture. Sean Mills, whom I met at the 2017 Haitian studies conference in Louisiana, gave me a copy of his book, *A Place in the Sun,* which was immensely useful in helping me fill in some of the gaps in the section on the historical framing of the Haitian diaspora in Canada. I thank him for his work and generosity. I also thank Perle Besserman for giving me the brilliant idea of ending the book with an interview with Edwidge Danticat.

Scholarship on Haiti and its diaspora has been expanded by the Haitian Studies Association (HSA) and the impressive efforts of the association's founding members, who are leaving an institutional legacy for current and future scholars conducting research on Haiti. I thank in particular Marc Prou, former executive director of HSA and director of the Haitian Creole Summer Institute, for facilitating my first return to Haiti during the summer of 2000. I am grateful to other members of HSA, including Jocelyne Trouillot, who gave me my first teaching opportunity in Haiti, and Patrick Bellegarde-Smith, Legrace Benson, Florence Bellande-Robertson, and Marlène Racine-Toussaint for their moral support. I am also grateful for the camaraderie of Charlene Désir, Régine Michelle Jean-Charles, Marlene Daut, and Mark Schuller. I have heartfelt appreciation for my academic little sisters, Kyrah Daniels, Nathalie Pierre, and Eziaku Nwokocha, who represent a new generation of Haitianists who will take scholarship on Haiti to new intellectual heights.

The research for this book was made possible by numerous fellowships and grants: the Graduate Opportunity Fellowship, departmental fellowships at UC Berkeley, the Ford Foundation Predoctoral Fellowship, the Dissertation Fellowship in the Department of Black Studies at UC Santa Barbara, the University of California President's Postdoctoral Fellowship, two faculty career development awards that reduced my teaching course load, and the Faculty Research Assistance Program for the opportunity to work with talented and capable undergraduate students while I was completing the book. These undergraduate students, Maria Gomez, Alexander Brown, and Chloe Pan located and organized articles and interviews on Danticat in the research process and helped me complete the bibliography. They have made some of these tedious tasks in the final stages of the writing process much easier.

I am honored that this book is included in the New World Series at the University of Virginia Press. I am grateful to J. Michael Dash for immediately seeing the value in this book and encouraging me to submit a proposal. I can't thank Eric Brandt and the staff at the University of Virginia Press enough for their professionalism and responsiveness and for smoothly guiding the manuscript through the production process. I also thank my copyeditor, George Roupe, for doing such a great job editing the manuscript. Two anonymous readers offered meticulous feedback and constructive criticism that certainly made for a better book.

I must acknowledge publishers for reprints of very short sections of a few articles. I thank the Journal of Haitian Studies, the only refereed scholarly journal dedicated solely to scholarship on Haiti and Haiti's relations with the international community, for publishing my first article on Danticat back in 2001 when only a few scholars were writing about Danticat. Short selections from chapter 3 and 5 appeared in the *Journal of Haitian Studies,* "Body and Voice as Sites of Oppression: The Psychological Condition of the Displaced Post-colonial Haitian Subject in Edwidge Danticat's 'The Farming of Bones,'" Special Issue on Edwidge Danticat, vol. 7, no. 2 (Fall 2001): 28–49, and "Reframing Haitian Literature Transnationally: Identifying New and Revised Tropes of Haitian Identity in Edwidge Danticat's 'Breath, Eyes, Memory,'" vol. 9, no. 2 (Fall 2003): 90–110. Small sections of the epilogue appeared in "Mapping the Echo Chamber: Edwidge Danticat and the Thematic Trilogy of Birth, Separation, and Death," *Palimpsest* 3, no. 2 (2014): 170–90.

A big thank you to my family, particularly my parents, Pierre Andre Clitandre and Violette Clitandre. My father read earlier versions of the manuscript, provided words of encouragement when I experienced writers-block and offered very good advice and questions as I was preparing for the interview with Edwidge Danticat. I also thank my siblings, Don, who, in being proactive and present in our relationship, has more than made up for lost time, and Arabelle, for checking up on me and understanding the everyday struggle. My thoughts are always with my little sister, Tarah; I am hoping we will find our way back to each other again sooner than later. My nine nieces and nephews allow me to hold the title of aunt with great joy and pride. I consider four very dear friends, Chae D. Miller, Doris Pradieu, Safiya Dautricourt, and Tijuana Orr, members of my extended family. I am grateful to Chae and Doris for their long-lasting friendships and for believing that I could do it. I thank Safiya for always offering encouraging words that make me feel like a rock star and Tijuana Orr, whom I can always count on for real talk and laughter.

And last but certainly not least, I thank my loving husband, Roberde Madhere, who came into my life unexpectedly right before the earthquake in Haiti. What began as a friendship developed into this beautiful partnership I can only describe as home. I am in awe of his kindness and grateful for this enchanting and peaceful life we are building together.

Edwidge Danticat

Introduction

SINCE HER entrance onto the American literary scene of immigrant writers in the mid-1990s, Haitian American writer Edwidge Danticat has consistently oscillated unapologetically between real, imagined,
and spiritual place in her understanding of diaspora. She has been invested
in exposing the lived experiences of people who make up the Haitian
diaspora, in particular, by foregrounding not only how experiences of
displacement are lived and affectively perceived but also how they are
textually constructed, imagined, and reimagined by diasporic subjects.
The work of imagination for the writer involves a keen awareness of
histories and textual narratives as well as both liberating and oppressive
social imaginaries grounded in myths. But it is also fueled by a desire to
engender new imaginaries of identity, belonging, and home spaces that
transgress binaries, stable signifiers, and monologic truths that promote
absolutes and validate the geopolitical boundaries of nation-states and
their mythic narratives. These investments obviously expose Danticat's
conceptual framing of diaspora. But whether these new imaginaries produce revisionary tales, counternarratives, or completely new frames of
reference and mythic fantasies for alternative futures and places of belonging that take flight in new terrains of the imagination, they all emerge,
for Danticat, out of both individually embodied and disembodied experiences in historically specific and localized contexts that echo and recall
the nation—Haiti as homeland. Danticat's diaspora not only reframes the
concept of place but is also contingent on an empirical understanding of,
and attachment to, real and localized places that have been mapped, organized, and divided along natural and unnatural borders to form communities of belonging and regulate social relations. Thus Danticat's writings
do not efface the significance of local spaces and corollary notions such
as wholeness, culture, memory, community, ancestry, and reclamation

that traditionally reference the "stuff" of nations. Danticat redefines and reconfigures these notions diasporically. More than twenty years after the publication of her first book, *Breath, Eyes, Memory,* Danticat is still articulating, albeit more critically and insightfully, the world of diaspora and its multilocational, multihistorical, multinational contexts that reveal the mutually constitutive nature of nation and diaspora. Such a world exposes what black feminist scholar Carol Boyce Davies describes as a "consciousness of expansiveness" in black women's writing that involves a "dialogics of movement and community" along cross-cultural, transnational, translocal, and diasporic perspectives to traverse geographical and national boundaries and experiences of marginality and exclusion.[1]

This book explores the ways in which Edwidge Danticat's literary articulations of the experience of displacement reveal a diasporic imaginary that insists on a dynamic and dialogic relationship between nation and diaspora, one that attends as much to the history and to the experience itself as to the fruitful aesthetics and liberatory possibilities it offers. By diasporic imaginary, I mean the creative domain of the displaced subject's imagination and his or her ability to perceive, interpret, and reimagine the world from a diasporic lens. Danticat's diasporic imaginary, and by extension that of her diasporic subjects, is shaped by a diasporic consciousness, the writer's self-reflexive awareness and embrace of identity as diasporic, knowledge of oral and textual narratives of migration and displacement, and understanding of the work of the imagination in transgressing borders, disrupting binaries, and reclaiming or engendering alternative visions and different ways of existing to accommodate the plurality and productive contradictions and complex ambivalence of diasporic subjectivity. In this sense, I evoke Mikhail Bakhtin's conception of the dialogical principle in his theory of literature and the novel as the recognition of the complex web of multiple voices against ideological monologism,[2] and Kobena Mercer's appropriation of Bakhtin's theory to foreground the "critical dialogism" of the diaspora perspective as a practice that overturns binary relations by "multiplying critical dialogues within particular communities and between the various constituencies that make up the 'imagined community' of the nation."[3] I also conjure post-structuralist scholars of literary theory, such as Julia Kristeva and Roland Barthes, who stress the link between dialogism and intertextuality to explore the contours of literary imagination and the practice of writing.

Building on the work of a number of scholars who theorize diaspora and examine questions of displacement, I argue that Danticat, oscillating between fiction and reality, inscribes the experience of displacement through a diasporic consciousness that is both a deterritorialized and reterritorialized form of social, political, cultural, and aesthetic transformation at the local, transnational, and global level. This diasporic consciousness involves the workings of a diasporic imaginary that produces descriptions of home spaces that are both real and fantasy, rooted and floating, spiritual and physical. But unlike theoretical articulations of diaspora consciousness and formations that are foregrounded to problematize the notion of the nation-state and celebrate a postnational imaginary,[4] Danticat's diasporic consciousness does not privilege diaspora at the expense of the nation and its localized narratives. It does not adhere to a nation/diaspora binary.[5] Nor does it cling to a kind of intellectualization or elitist vision of diaspora[6] in ways that efface the circumstances of marginalized individuals and their mundane or dangerous lives. Instead, as I argue in this book, Danticat calls for a deconstruction and reconstitution of nation through a diasporic imaginary that informs the way ordinary and everyday people who experience displacement view the world (past and present), experience the dynamics of globalization both positively and negatively, and imagine more liberatory and alternative futures.

In Danticat's diasporic imaginary and consciousness, nation and diaspora, like the local and global, are relational and mutually constitutive, particularly as they connect to the notion and rewriting of home in the context of migration experiences and their transnational components. This reconstitution of the relation between nation and diaspora involves an understanding of the intertwined nature between the local and the global in the dynamics of globalization, as scholars such as Roland Robertson, Anthony Giddens, and Arjun Appadurai argue.[7] Globalization is a complex phenomenon, and there are different ways to approach the concept. My interest here is in the question of closeness, exchange, and exposure. As Danticat herself asserts, globalization makes villages "come closer together. And it also makes it possible for writers to read other writers, to be aware of what other writers are doing." This, Danticat continues, makes the question of national literature "harder to pin down."[8] Thus I am using the term *globalization* to stress what Robertson calls "the compression of the world and the intensification of a consciousness of the world as a whole"[9] that makes the world a single place in both thought and action and what Giddens defines as "intensification of worldwide social relations."[10] As Arjun Appadurai explains, this global dynamic is formed by the global cultural flows that constitute historically situated and intertwined imaginary landscapes and create complex transnational practices and exchange.[11] Manfred Steger's understanding of globalization insists on a "thickening of global consciousness," a growing awareness of global connectivity, that has resulted in the decline of a national imaginary.[12] Taking up the question of the relation between the national and the global in discourses of globalization, Saskia Sassen asserts that the global and national are not mutually exclusive domains.[13] Building on the work of these scholars, who explore the cultural dimensions of globalization in this manner, this book looks at the way Danticat, as immigrant writer, reformulates the interplay between nation and diaspora to offer new and more nuanced ways of thinking about ourselves, our interconnection, and our relation to place in a globalizing world. It is an exploration of one writer's evolving contemplation of the meaning of diaspora in relation to the bind of displacement, immigrant identity, and the (re)writing of home in diaspora under the conditions of globalization, marked by increasing migration of peoples that bolster interconnectedness, cross-cultural communication, linguistic diversity, and transnational exchange.

But Danticat's understanding of globalization also highlights what Jana Braziel and Anita Mannur call the "hegemonic, homogenizing forces of globalization" that influence international patterns of migration and the phenomenon of diaspora.[14] These uneven forces and processes of globalization for Danticat are tied to histories of slavery, colonialism, imperialism, and transnational flows of global capital that both produce and negatively affect economically disadvantaged communities. They also undergird the racialized and marginalized experiences of immigrants and ironically engender a desire for national insularity. In my own interview with her, which I offer as the appendix to this book, Danticat states: "Rather than borders falling away now, we see more coming up and the poorest of the poor being locked on the other side. That's of course the negative impact. That money, as the late Édouardo Galeano has written, can cross borders, and human beings cannot." Danticat's work exposes both the positive and negative impact of globalization. The present study is not about celebratory definitions and narratives of globalization or realizing a fixed and determinate definition of diaspora, nor is it about positioning diaspora in opposition to nation—as homeland—in the field of diaspora studies, postcolonial studies, or global studies. Transgressing disciplinary limitations, this book offers a transdisciplinarity that is invested in destabilizing homogenous and outdated notions and representations of nation, nationhood, and the nationalist rhetoric of identity and community that relies on a monologic, totalizing framework and claims of authenticity; it is about breaking down the dichotomy between empirical place and conceptual place in ways that complicate our understanding of the experience of displacement and the dynamics of diaspora.

Echo Chamber

A main objective of this book is to examine specific reading practices and textual strategies that are central to the diasporic imaginary and the process of writing diaspora not only as an experience of displacement but also a "consciousness of expansiveness," plurality, and multiplicity. This book offers a unique reading of Danticat's work by introducing a fresh trope, that of the echo, to critically approach her treatment of the nation/diaspora and its local/global dynamics in ways that navigate between the reality of diasporas and imaginative opportunities that diasporas produce. In her collection of essays, *Create Dangerously: The Immigrant Artist at Work,* which was originally published eight months after the catastrophic earthquake in Haiti on January 12, 2010, that killed an estimated 300,000 people, Danticat writes: "Maybe that was my purpose, then, as an immigrant and a writer—to be an echo chamber, gathering and then replaying voices from both the distant and the local devastation."[15] Building on Danticat's own self-description as "echo chamber," I contend that the echo trope is a consistent strand that binds the selected texts analyzed in this book. I concentrate on the metaphor of the echo and trope of echo chamber to home in on the way in which Danticat works, interprets, deconstructs, and rethematizes both the local/global and nation/diaspora opposition through her preoccupation with voice and intertextual relations. Exploring the echo as central narrative thread, I show the ways in which Danticat's texts present the nation as the source of the echo, the diaspora as the reverberation of the echo (echo recalled, repeated, refracted, relayed) with a difference, and the immigrant writer as the echo chamber that preserves, deconstructs, reconstructs, and proliferates narratives of both nation and diaspora with ambivalence. In Danticat's diasporic imaginary, the nation is not disavowed or elided; it becomes implicated in the same relational process of formation, deformation, and reformation of the subject in diaspora.

I further contend that Danticat's preoccupation with voice and self-description as echo chamber reveals a tropic permutation of *echo* grounded in the Greco-Roman myth of Echo and Narcissus. The Oxford dictionary defines an echo in the following ways: As a noun, the echo is a sound or series of sounds caused by the reflection of sound waves from a surface back to a listener; it is also the repetition of an idea or feeling. Synonyms include *reverberation, reflection, repetition, double, duplicate, replica.* As a verb (*echoes, echoing, echoed*), it means to repeat a sound after the original sound has stopped; to repeat someone's words; to be reminiscent of or have shared characteristics with an object, movement, or event. It is beyond the scope of this book to explore the uses of *echo* as acoustic phenomenon in popular music and in the literature of architectural and acoustic design that explores the relationship between natural sound and space, though this book encourages literary scholars to consider Gilles Deleuze's notion of territory and deterritorialization in Danticat's work through critical analysis of Danticat's position as echo chamber.[16] What is important to note here is that echo, as sound, is not only the product of an auditory imaginary but a physical phenomenon and product of space.[17] Echo travels in space, time, and language. Echo sounds are ambiguous and unstable, as the original utterance is difficult to trace. As such, they disrupt the unity and uniformity of voice, body, and subjectivity.[18]

Echo as figurative phenomenon and imagery of voice is central to my reading of Danticat's texts. In Greek mythology, Echo is a nymph who loved the sound of her own voice and was able to distract others with long entertaining stories. However, Echo was punished for her trickery by Juno and could only repeat the voice of another, words from another source.[19] Indeed the metaphor of the echo has a history grounded in classical texts. However, it is not the intention of this book to provide insights into how the myth is used in Western literary narratives over the ages.[20] A few scholars have rightly pointed to the significance of Greco-Roman myths in Danticat's work, but they home in on the myth of Persephone, particularly in their analysis of Danticat's *Breath, Eyes, Memory.*[21] This is not surprising, as the myth centers on the complex relationship between mother and daughter, issues of abduction, and the trauma of rape, themes central in Danticat's bildungsroman. The mother/daughter theme is potent in African Caribbean women's literature and is often presented through the mother/motherland/mother country trichotomous relationship.[22] Ingrained in a collective unconscious, African Americans also appropriate and revise these myths to narrate the black female experience and in effect create a tradition of African American women's classical revision of female (sexual) oppression.[23] I attend to this revisionary strategy in my analysis of *Breath, Eyes, Memory* in chapter 3 and explore Danticat's recentering of African diasporic mythology in the novel to subvert master narratives of displacement as well as reclaim Haitian women's voices through the trope of the Marassa.[24] In my reading such destabilization entails dialogic engagement that necessitates rereading of Western myths and their tropic permutations. Other Greek myths, such as Sophocles's *Oedipus the King* and *Antigone,* as I explain in chapter 5, emerge in Danticat's work as master texts that must be deconstructed.

But no one has thoroughly scrutinized the figure of Echo to examine the diasporic imaginary and Danticat's treatment of themes of silence, dislocation, exile, and loss, certainly not beyond Danticat's first novel. In this book, I ask: What can the myth of Echo and its transmutations reveal about Danticat's self-description as echo chamber specifically and the process of writing diaspora more broadly? In what way does the myth of echo tease out certain elements that are critical to the way we read diaspora as an experience of displacement and to the way we read texts by African diasporic women writers to understand the gendered contours of diaspora? How does it foreground Danticat's concern with voice and the preservation of diasporic narratives? Or Danticat's nuanced meditation on the relation between the oral and the written? How do the qualities of echo speak to the relation between nation and diaspora and regimes of silence? In what way does Danticat induce the echo trope to articulate perpetual silence as threat? How does Danticat magnify voice in diaspora to counter this threat? Can we conceive of diaspora as the magnification of the female voice or the magnification of voices that form and forge subjectivities? In my analysis of Danticat's texts, I answer these questions by looking at the tropic formation and permutation of Ovid's figuration of Echo as the feminine voice/storyteller in his most famous work, *Metamorphoses.* I do so to present Danticat's characters as Echo-like subjects who face the threat of silence through state-sanctioned violence and patriarchal monologism. Working through and defying silence, Danticat's diasporic subjects, as Echo-like subjectivities, participate in the recall of Haiti's silenced histories to tell their own stories. Danticat, as author who doubles as storyteller, is implicated in this practice of recall. As I will show, this is the case not only in *Breath, Eyes, Memory* but also in the other four texts I analyze in this book: *Brother, I'm Dying; Create Dangerously; The Dew Breaker;* and *The Farming of Bones.*

Diasporic Imaginary and Relational Poetics

The term *imaginary* is quite complex and carries a variety of meanings. Jacques Lacan's psychoanalytic notion of the imaginary involves the subject's early identification with images, which are formed out of a struggle to obtain an imaginary coherence with the external world and an illusory sense of self as whole.[25] This desire for wholeness propels an imaginary image of totality in the mirror that works against the primordial experience of fragmentation. In Benedict Anderson's understanding, for example, the nation, as imagined community, is part of an organized cultural system that relies on a national imaginary. Such an imaginary produces and reproduces set images and practices tied to a particular understanding and commitment to organizing, conceptualizing, and unifying the nation and its people through fixed ideas of cultural roots, land, home, blood ties, fraternity, and kinship.[26] Charles Taylor, building on the work of Cornelius Castoriadis uses the term "social imaginary" to focus on the way ordinary people in the modern world imagine their social surroundings and express these imaginings through images, stories, and legends. These imaginings give people a sense of shared group life.[27] Manfred Steger suggests a "rising global imaginary" born out of a new sense of denationalized identity and intensifying relation with the world now perceived as a single place. These global identities are fostered not only by transnational corporations and global flows of capital and goods but also by the production and dissemination of images, metaphors, myths, symbols, and spatial arrangements of globality.[28]

Rather than relegate discourses of wholeness, ancestry, unity, and collective consciousness to a national imaginary, I ask: What if we looked at diaspora, and by extension, diaspora imaginary not as a concept at odds with ideas such as "collectivity" and "wholeness"[29] but in relation to them? In his work *Poetics of Relation,* Martinican writer, poet, and literary critic Édouard Glissant defines the imaginary, his translator reminds us, as "all the ways a culture has of perceiving and conceiving of the world."[30] The imaginary, Glissant asserts, "helps us to grasp the (not prime) elements of our totality."[31] Glissant, perhaps the foremost theorist of relation, positions the imaginary as part of a system of relation and "aesthetics of rupture and connection" between the local and the global.[32] Glissant's imaginary encompasses the totality of diverse narratives that form a poetics of cultural diversity and praise opacity. Building on the work of Glissant, I use the term *diasporic imaginary* in this book to home in on a reservoir of images and narrative strategies in literary texts by diasporic writers who engender an echoing relation between nation and diaspora, one that centralizes the significance of voice. I assert that diasporic writers like Danticat who are themselves displaced subjects rely on a diasporic imaginary to produce and conjure images, forms, patterns, and narrative strategies that help organize and unify the diaspora and diasporic characters and actors beyond idealized unity. Danticat does so through an intertextual play among the reader, writer, narrator, and characters that calls for a rereading and subversion of Manichaean notions of duality, double, and doubling predominant in Western philosophy and mythic imaginaries. This desire for unity and wholeness is a compensation for the primal separation experienced as lack, loss, disintegration, and alienation, as in the case of Sophie in the novel *Breath, Eyes, Memory*. Danticat revisits this idea of wholeness in *The Dew Breaker* by exploring the primal experience of fragmentation in processes of identification and disidentification on the one hand and the process of writing and rewriting on the other. In doing so, Danticat makes a distinction between the desire for wholeness never quite fulfilled and the illusion of wholeness sustained in the symbolic order and by the semiotic process.

Glissant offers a theory for understanding what he defines as a consciousness of relation, a totality of the world[33] and the entanglements of a worldwide relationship that presents itself most visibly in the Caribbean.[34] This totality of the world consists of a "detour that leads away from anything totalitarian" and the "totalitarianism of any monolingual intent."[35] Diaspora is presented as a place of relation marked by global dynamics that involve the practice of "self-break and reconnection."[36] As Glissant asserts, relation involves things joining without conjoining and contains knowledge of particularity.[37] This practice helps us understand the relational nature between the homeland and its diaspora more broadly and the African diasporic experience in the New World more specifically. Centered on the Caribbean and its creolized collective presence, Glissant's global vision of relating carries a polyphonic element that privileges an auditory imagination.[38] What fascinates me most for the purposes of this book is Glissant's idea of "*échos-monde*" (world echoes) as expression of confluence, of things relating and resonating with one another in ways that navigate between an individual consciousness and a collective consciousness, local and global realities, as well as particular and universal frames of reference.[39]

Glissant asserts that échos-monde are created by individuals and communities "to cope with or express confluences" and the plurality and unities of interacting consciousness.[40] I invoke Glissant's concept of échos-monde to highlight the polyphonic element of Danticat's diasporic imaginary critical to understanding and reading the dynamic relation between nation and diaspora through the echo trope and its mythic foundations. Glissant's écho-monde concept complements not only my framing of the trope of the echo as metaphor that delineates the relational nature of nation and diaspora in the diasporic imaginary that I want to foreground in this book but also Danticat's own investment in displacing and disrupting the single authoritative and totalitarian voice in favor of polyvocality. As I show in chapter 4, this instance of echoing against totalitarian regimes of silence is most evident in *The Dew Breaker,* which recalls the autocratic regime of François Duvalier and his son Jean-Claude Duvalier, a regime of terror and censorship that lasted for twenty-nine years.

At the dawn of the twenty-first century, Danticat has emerged as the "voice of a community" for her artistic ability to evoke the myriad histories of Haiti and its most dispossessed people and for her commitment to articulating the experiences and sensibilities of the Haitian diaspora and its transnational contours in the United States. But as her work reveals, and as she herself has expressed, Danticat's intention has always been to uncover silences and recall untold and unheard stories in order to memorialize lives. In the process, Danticat's body of work proliferates and reverberates the diverse voices of Haiti and its diaspora in ways that contribute to the endless knowledge of relation within the world's totality and projects that attempt to destabilize all totalitarian structures of thought that insist on uniformity and univocality.

Metaphors and Tropes of Diaspora: The Exile/Diaspora Binary

Diasporic imaginaries engender tropes; tropes are part of textual strategies and reading practices in migrant, emigrant, immigrant, and diasporic literatures that focus on the experience and affective dimensions of displacement. One of the long-standing tropes in the writing of immigrant experiences and the discourse of displacement is that of exile. Unfortunately, theoretical framings of exile create a dichotomized relationship between the literature of exile and that of diaspora. This ultimately confines the trope to outdated formulations constrained by nation-state language. In postcolonial discourse, some scholars and writers present exiles, refugees, tourists, and émigrés simultaneously as both figures and tropes of displacement because of their sense of nonbelonging and liminality.[41] These figures live in the in-between space and locale of cultural displacement that trouble fixed and essentialized notions of identity and destabilize the nation-state framework. Homi Bhabha describes this as the "third space," which allows for the reconsideration of the boundaries of the nation and the breakdown of binaries such as inside/outside, self/other, center/periphery, and production of new hybrid identities.[42] Edward Said, for example, presents exile as both a model for and metaphoric condition of the restless and unsettled intellectual, novelist, or political activist who breaks down barriers and dares to represent change.[43] He asserts, "The essential privilege of exile is to have, not just one set of eyes, but half a dozen."[44] Simon Gikandi views exile as an opportunity to question the colonial situation, recenter the colonial subject, and deconstruct the colonial text to develop new consciousness.[45] He argues that the discourse of displacement in modern Caribbean literature in particular is a revisionary strategy that deconstructs colonial history and offers writers of the Caribbean diaspora an opportunity to inscribe the colonial condition in their own terms.

Yet Carine M. Mardorossian points to a paradigm shift and movement from exile to migrant literature in postcolonial writing for a second generation of Caribbean writers such as Danticat who challenge what she describes as "literary criticism's traditional reliance on that experience [of exile] as the 'basis' of explanation in literary analysis."[46] This movement away from exile to the privileging of the terms *migrant* and *immigrant* is evident in transformations in immigrant literature during the 1990s.[47] Indeed, Danticat does not position herself as an exile writer. When asked to make a distinction between exile and immigrant in a 2010 interview with Jennifer Ludden Danticat responded, "Well, I am probably the child of, you know, of that exile generation for my particular group of people, for the—for Haitian-Americans. So I am what exiles perhaps eventually become or what their children become, as the gentleman was talking about earlier. And in exile, I'm able to go back to Haiti, and I have been able to for as long as I can remember. So I don't consider myself an exile. I'm probably closer to an immigrant than an exile."[48] When asked specifically if she considers herself an exiled writer in a later interview by Nadève Ménard, Danticat replied, "No, not at all. And I have never called myself that because I can go back whenever I want. Exiled writers cannot do that."[49] But this distinction that specifies a historical moment does not mean that Danticat fully adheres to an exile/diaspora binary. Furthermore, both Ménard and Danticat believe that the trope of exile should not imply a lack of creative expression in the homeland or be limited to a debilitating pathos of writers outside the homeland.

Theorists of Haitian literature and exile in particular contribute to articulations of the literary trope of exile that describe the cultural and literary production of Haitian writers both inside and outside the homeland. Yanick Lahens states that "exile is certainly one of the dimensions which, along with resistance and syn-cretism, give Haitian culture its coherence."[50] Making a distinction between interior exile and exterior exile, Lahens redefines exile as a "metaphor for the writer's retreat wherever he finds himself."[51] Myriam Chancy finds it necessary to read the novelistic tradition of Haitian women through the lens of personal and communal exile. The experience of Haitian woman, Chancy argues, is "defined by exile within her own country."[52] For Chancy, exile, which can be self-imposed, is "what makes remaining in the homeland unbearable and untenable."[53] More recently, Martin Munro reads the work of a number of Haitian writers including Danticat to present exile as master trope in post-1946 Haitian fiction. For Munro, exile is a fluid but constant referent and floating signifier of semantic displacement in Haitian texts of the latter half of the twentieth century that points to the emergence of a new wave of consciousness that complicates notions of home and defines the Haitian diaspora today.[54]

Both Lahens and Chancy highlight the gendered distinctions of the exile experience and their articulations in Haitian literature specifically and a Caribbean literary tradition more broadly. In *Making Men,* Belinda Edmondson asserts that in the West Indian literary canon, the term *exile* demarcates a male intellectual literary space of authority and individuality: "Unlike 'exile,' the term 'immigrant' carries with it a different, arguably feminized, status to the metropole; one associated with physical, not intellectual, labor. The place from where the 'immigrant' writer speaks, therefore, cannot carry with it the same authority of intellectual tradition."[55] The term *exile* is loaded with gendered connotations of the experience of self-imposed exile and effaces the experience of displacement in the lives of everyday individuals. Certainly, the relationships among internal/external exile, notions of home, the diasporic experience, and questions of gender are crucial to understanding Danticat's female characters and feminist/feminized reading of Haitian history and narratives.

There is a large body of scholarship on the discourse of displacement that either critiques the trope of exile or completely abandons it to embrace new symbols and aesthetics of displacement. Caren Kaplan sees the trope of exile as one of many that bolster the ideology and discourse of displacement as artistic production and aesthetic gain in Euro-American theory of dislocation.[56] Immigrants, refugees, exiles, nomads, and homeless people, she argues, become tropes in modernist constructions of authorship and not historical producers of the discourse of displacement.[57] As a result of a paradigm shift in migration politics of the 1990s, wherein diaspora increasingly becomes a signifier for a nation outside the borders of the homeland for political support and mobilization, particularly in postcolonial studies and cultural studies journals and work of black British scholars of the period, diaspora also emerges as a new trope against the old trope of exile in what Kaplan perceives as the modern world's discursive play and aestheticization of displacement. Consequently, like the trope of exile, diaspora becomes a "catch-all phrase" for all movements and types of dislocations.[58]

Diaspora and Aesthetics of Displacement

Indeed, since the 1990s diaspora has become the privileged trope of displacement and symbol for the articulation of new discursive and aesthetic spaces. Attending to the question of historical contextualization that Kaplan highlights in her analysis of various articulations of displacement, Paul Gilroy and Stuart Hall, who examine the black settlers in Britain and emergence of black British cultural production in the 1980s and 1990s, both position diaspora as a new configuration of displacement against exile as an old configuration. Gilroy asserts that the term diaspora "lacks the modernist and cosmopolitan associations of the word 'exile' from which it has been carefully distinguished."[59] For Gilroy, a "simple unambiguous exile" is part of a nation-state spatial and temporal ordering of diaspora.[60] Gilroy later writes that old formulations of "enforced exile" get "repossessed" and "reconstituted" as the basis of a privileged standpoint.[61] Diaspora, as a new framework for the articulation of black expressive cultures in Britain, emerges as an alternative to different varieties of absolutism that confine culture in "racial, ethnic, or national essences."[62] It is a "new vocabulary"[63] that "identifies a relational network."[64] Homing in on the relationship between the Caribbean imaginary and new articulations of home, Hall also asserts that diaspora becomes a metaphor and experience of the New World against the old nation-state framework. Exile in this new framework becomes a particular space in the complex workings of diasporic experiences. Hall's diaspora disrupts a national imaginary and exposes its limitations; it creates new infinite imaginaries that produce a "diaspora aesthetic" grounded in an understanding of difference, heterogeneity, and diversity.[65] Though this "new world presence" that is the beginning of diaspora gives rise to desire for return, the idea of "homeland" becomes, as Stuart Hall asserts, a "symbolic imaginary" that contains these traditional concerns with essence and purity and offers a "backward-looking conception of diaspora." Such conception reinforces, Stuart asserts, national fantasies that can result in ethnic absolutism.[66] What unites black British scholars of the 1990s, such as Gilroy and Hall, is an insistence on a diasporic paradigm of cultural identity, imaginary, and production that deconstruct the nation-state framework of identity and its monologic forms of (artistic) expression.

This antiessentialist move in the work of these scholars is critical to understanding Danticat's framing of diaspora.

The distinction between old and new configurations of displacement offers insights into articulations and narratives of the homeland and its relationship to memory and the diasporic imaginary, which emerges more succinctly as a result of a move toward the aestheticization of diaspora. In the work of Vijay Mishra, who uses the term "diasporic imaginary" specifically, it is not the celebration of the new that is most critical; rather, it is the understanding of how old and new diasporic subjects create their own "fantasy structures of homeland" out of the trauma of displacement in ways that demarcate different triggers of the imagination and, in effect, produce different diasporic archives.[67] Mishra differentiates between "old" archives marked by an earlier pattern of migration and "new" diasporic archives affected by the more recent process of globalization to avoid the trend in presenting new diasporas as the "self-evidently legitimate archive with which to explore diasporic subjectivities."[68] Overall, the literature on diaspora in the 1990s that delineates a distinction between old and new diasporas also broadens the definition of diaspora into what Rogers Brubaker describes as "semantic, conceptual and disciplinary space."[69] Danticat's framing of diaspora moves through conceptual and empirical space. For Danticat, diasporic subjects' narratives are foregrounded not only to tell the story of fragmentation and difference but also to organize diaspora as a collective unit and to create an archive that can contain both national and diasporic histories, as well as old and new narratives of homeland and articulations of home as both geographical spaces that can be mapped and symbolic places that are imagined. This is not just a matter of aesthetics and representation; it is also about cultural preservation and symbolic returns that can engender real returns and fruitful relations between homeland and its diaspora.

However, there are drawbacks to the metaphoricization and aestheticization of diaspora as trope of displacement that home in on the imaginary, as many scholars have already exposed.[70] Indeed, the attention to diaspora, its proliferation, explosion, and tropic figuration has resulted in serious challenges in defining the term.[71] Instead of focusing on the concern with the metaphoricization of diaspora that results in "decontextualization" and "semantic dissolution,"[72] it is more fruitful to examine the ways in which diasporic imaginaries engender a set of tropes and what these tropes reveal about the process of writing diaspora for immigrant writers in a moment of heightened globalization. As Danticat's writing exposes, diaspora cannot be reduced to an aesthetic exercise or universal figuration that eschews historical particularities of diasporic communities. Thus I intentionally do not position diaspora as a trope of displacement in my analysis of Danticat's works; rather, I find it more useful to contemplate the very tropes Danticat persistently evokes in all her writings to narrate the everyday lived experiences and historical traumas of people who make up the Haitian diaspora. As Jonathan P. A. Sell asserts, studying metaphors that contribute to literary transcription of diasporic imaginaries helps increase knowledge of "how the diasporic subject conceptualizes the world it lives in and the experience it has of it."[73]

In this book I suggest that we read Danticat's preoccupation with memorializing individual lives and their voices not in the context of diaspora as a distinctive trope (against the trope of exile) but through tropic permutations of echo and the myth of echo that both evoke and engender other tropes of displacement. The centrality of the echo trope figure for diasporic consciousness and imaginary helps us to refigure diaspora as an open-ended phenomenon of global expansiveness. This way, we can attend to the relation between voice, subjectivity, and gendered constructions of home in literary articulations of experience of displacement. In focusing on tropes of diaspora and their transformations as opposed to the idea of diaspora as trope, this book, much like Danticat's own writings, praises the postmodern literary production and performance of diaspora[74] but avoids the pitfalls of restricting diasporas to a state of mind (Brah),[75] imaginary landscapes (Said) in literary praxis,[76] or an "intellectual commodity of a theoretical enterprise" (Brennen)[77] that frames and privileges the condition of emigrant elite intellectuals (Chow)[78] and saturates the field of postcolonial studies. The move away from privileged experiences of diaspora to a focus on ordinary people and everyday practices is key to understanding Danticat's diasporic narratives. In this book, I am interested in what Danticat's narratives tell us about the particular dynamics of the diasporic imaginary in the everyday lives and narratives of diasporic subjects. The narrative of the everyday disrupts the intellectualized language and discursive space of diaspora that privilege and give authority to narratives of displacement by privileged male writers.[79]

(African) Diaspora as Feminist Category

In a 2017 interview, Edwidge Danticat stated, "Black women certainly are at the center of my stories. I think part of this is from my personal experience of growing up with women who are very powerful—to me—but very vulnerable in their society."[80] Diasporic women writers like Danticat usher in a new diaspora politics and consciousness that critique nationalist and paternalist discourse in ways that attend to the specificities of women-centered experiences and spaces. In doing so, their narratives offer reconfigurations of ideas of home, motherhood, and kinship that are inclusive and expansive. This is paramount for Danticat, whose influences are not only the women storytellers of her youth but also black women writers like Maya Angelou, Toni Morrison, and Paule Marshall. As I explore in later chapters, especially in my analysis of *Breath, Eyes, Memory* and *The Farming of Bones,* Danticat shows that a focus on women's individual experiences offers a different way of looking at kinship ties, motherhood, and relationships to homeland and nation, one that moves beyond blood relations, nonpolarized dualities, and patriarchal articulations that are produced to control women's lives and their bodies. Danticat's women-centered diasporic spaces provide a more inclusive approach to understanding and redefining Haitian identity. Her work displaces the singular voice of male authority and counters the inherently masculinist vision of home, family, and nation.

Furthermore, in foregrounding the relationship between historical silences, the construction of female subjectivity, and representation of female voice, Danticat offers a feminist revisioning of Haitian history from a diasporic lens, one that exposes the way in which Haitian history and the lived experiences of women within this history are presented as silent and silenced subjects/objects of investigation. But Danticat amplifies the multiple histories of Haiti and the diverse voices of Haitian women not only to offer counternarratives to male-centered history but also to reevaluate our understanding of diaspora, its gendered contours, and its relationship to state-sanctioned violence and repression against women. As I show in chapter 1, Danticat's inscription of the Haitian diaspora, and women's experiences within it, cannot be decoupled from the twenty-nine-year dictatorial family regime of François Duvalier and his son, Jean-Claude Duvalier. The regime's rhetoric of the nation and its citizens reframed traditional nationalist discourse that define women as "mothers of the nation." In her examination of the development of Haitian women's organizations in North American, Carolle Charles asserts, "In contrast to the other dictatorial regimes of Latin America that appeal to the image of the suffering, self-sacrificing, patriotic mother who has no place in the political arena, the Duvalierist state focused on a 'patriotic woman' whose allegiance was first to Duvalier's nation and state. Any woman who did not adhere to these policies became an enemy subject to political repression."[81] Danticat's work "disposes of the concept of 'mothers of the nation'"[82] by exploring the ways in which Haitian women have been undoubtedly subjected to multiple forms of abuse, including sexual violence by nationalist regimes. It also reconstructs Haitian female identity and offers the possibility of alternative notions of womanhood and motherhood that resist patriarchy.

Danticat's emphasis on the relationships among diaspora, Haitian women's experiences, and nation-state violence contribute to black feminist critical thought on diaspora and subjectivity. Black feminists expose the imperialist, elitist, and gendered elements of the diasporic model of black subjectivity and political consciousness of the twentieth century. Carole Boyce-Davies asserts, "Any articulation of a critique of home for black women has to begin with an examination of the totalizing nature of nationalist (African-diaspora) discourse." She further states that the ideologies of Pan-Africanism, black/African nationalism and Afrocentricity are "'totalizing discourses' which can tolerate no different articulation and operate from a singularly monolithic construction of an African theoretical homeland, which asks for the submergence or silencing of gender, sexuality, or any other ideological stance or identity position which is not subsumed under Black/African nationalism."[83] Similarly, Angeletta K. M. Gourdine explains, "The male intellectual emphasis on the race-as-family model has left women particularly silent. Male-centered diaspora narratives have underwritten the role of women as well as the effect of homosocial contracts between men."[84] Black nationalist rhetoric has been produced in isolation from critical discussions around gender and sexuality. Indeed, the politicized ideology of black nationalism and the diasporic model for black subjectivity, as black feminist writers like Audre Lorde, Barbara Smith, Alice Walker, Michele Wallace, Patricia Hill Collins, and bell hooks assert,[85] form heteropatriarchal norms that exclude the black female subject, who experiences a double othering as the "other of the other" along lines of gender and sexuality.[86] Danticat's stories highlight the relationships among emigration, politics, and the black female subject. As she states, "[Migration] stories come in bodies. And for me, it's often a black female body like mine."[87]

Since the foundational structure of the field of African diaspora studies positions women on the margins, black women feminists call for a reevaluation of diaspora studies and consciousness that centers the black female subject and her cross-cultural and migratory experiences. For example, to explore the intricate relationship between eighteenth- and nineteenth-century Western constructions of blackness, the twentieth-century intellectual tradition of African diasporic counter-discourses of black subjectivity, the discourse of diaspora, and the ideology of nation, Michelle Wright raises the question, "Does the black subject belong to the nation or the diaspora?"[88] Wright's work exposes the ways in which black male intellectual discourse and the search for alternatives to the nation alienate "active black women in the nation."[89] And yet, as Michel Stephens astutely remarks, "As both the new national state and the older imperial governments get figured as masculine 'fatherlands,' women remain, seemingly contradictorily, the figures of more open-ended sentimental, affective, and relational dimensions of both imagined national and diasporic communities—the imaginary homeland as motherland."[90] Black women scholars like Wright and Stephens insist that the complexities of home and belonging that emerge as a key issue in African diasporic and denationalized subjectivities are often explored in black women's literature. In a more recent work on the relationships among race, gender, and diaspora aesthetics, Samantha Pinto examines the role of black women's writing in imagining, designing, defining, and "disordering" diaspora.[91] As she astutely states, "Black women's writing is no longer compartmentalized as an addition, supplement, or appendix to male-centered theories of the diaspora." To the contrary, they call for a remapping of diaspora scholarship, destabilizing male-centered themes of diaspora, to position diaspora as feminist category.[92]

I build on the work of these scholars but offer a more transdisciplinary perspective that homes in on how an examination of the Haitian diaspora and the diasporic imaginary might bring us to a particular understanding of Haiti's history of displacement and a reading of absence and silence in that history. One of my intentions throughout this book is to show that Danticat's fictional texts uncover the silenced, displaced, and disavowed histories of Haitian people in general and Haitian women in particular in ways that not only recalibrate our understanding of diaspora but also foreground its very relationship to gender struggles and forms of gender oppression, as well as paternalist discourses and nationalist regimes that attempt to define, confine, and essentialize Haitian women's identities and lived experiences.

Diaspora Consciousness and the Double

Diaspora is often presented as a rich figure of doubleness, and double consciousness is embodied in the image of diaspora.[93] Thus the conjunction of diaspora, metaphors of doubleness, and double consciousness is not new. But much like the critique of the term *diaspora* as a loose buzzword for the postmodern era, strategies and metaphors of doubling in literary texts get consumed by discourses of hybridity and postcolonial investment in the enduring Manichaean ethos of the colonial world that orders society in terms of binary categorizations.[94] Moreover, doubleness, the performance of it, and double writing as a mode of inscription are viewed as narrative disruptions and deformation of the construction of nation that is more imagined than real. Presenting a more dynamic relationship between nation and diaspora, one that concentrates on both separation and reconnection à la Glissant, this book highlights metaphors and strategies of doubleness and processes of doubling that are not only literary modes of inscribing diaspora but also real strategies and coping mechanisms of a nation's displaced and violated subjects. In both postcolonial and Caribbean literature, doubling functions as a recurring trope in the writing and representation of sexual trauma.[95] This book maintains a distinction between the double as narrative strategy and the act of doubling as coping mechanism and strategic form of survival, or cultural and spiritual practice of healing, but examines them in relation to each other.

Both the figure of the double and practice of doubling exemplify Danticat's subversion and reworking of the Western imaginary-grounded Cartesian duality and the Hegelian dialectic of self/other, her attentiveness to indigenous paradigms and folk tradition, and her call for alternatives that speak to the emergence of new (diasporic) subjectivities. They also expose the ambivalence that defines Danticat's subjects and narrative style, which in its double-voiced[96] discourse, gives way to the recognition of linguistic diversity, as I discuss in chapter 5. This ambivalence results from what James Clifford calls the positive and negative constitution of diaspora consciousness that involves the lived tension of entanglement and separation, as well as loss and hope.[97] Here diaspora consciousness is less about the intellectualization of an existential tradition[98] and more about the ambivalence formed out of the collision and dialogue of cultures. In her articulation of diaspora, Danticat does not spend time contemplating a "Haitian problem" per se. She is, however, invested in presenting characters who express ambivalence to the homeland. Danticat articulates this ambivalence by working through and transgressing masculininst Western dualities that construct artificial borders. As I show in chapter 5, perhaps the most ambivalent of Danticat's characters is Amabelle Désir in *The Farming of Bones,* a novel that reminds us that interactions between cultures and relations between people in spaces of cohabitation are not always peaceful, harmonious, and celebratory. In fact, they can lead to a split consciousness or sense of twoness in an internal struggle to reconcile two cultures, as in W. E. B. Du Bois's double consciousness of African

American subjectivities or, far worse, the genocide of an ethnic community at the border between two nations arbitrarily and unnaturally split into nation-state projects. Thus the dedication of *The Farming of Bones* to Metrès Dlo, the Haitian vodou god and mother of the rivers, and Amabelle's silent address to her is a doubling that reveals Danticat's notion of the border as both a porous zone of multiple interactions and a site of mourning and memorializing the dead bodies that inhabit that site.

This book navigates between literal and metaphorical conceptions of diaspora to break down the binary of real and imagined. My basic premise, then, is that tropes of diaspora emerge out of a diasporic imaginary and diasporic consciousness grounded in physical diasporas and their social forms, what Regine Jackson calls the geographies of diaspora that make it possible to "engage diaspora as an imagined space or subjective state without crowding out concern for the details and mechanisms linked to geography or place" in the production and reproduction of diasporic consciousness and their local meanings.[99] In my analysis of Danticat's work, I subscribe to the definition of diaspora that "refers to the double relationship or dual loyalty that migrants, exiles, and refugees have to places—their connections to the space they currently occupy and their continuing involvement with 'back home.'"[100] This double relationship is induced by a transnational network that includes the homeland.[101]

Haiti, the United States, and the Dynamics of Dyaspora and Haitian Transnationalism

Danticat is a proud member of a Haitian diasporic community in the United States with a history that began in the latter half of the twentieth century. In the beginning the Haitian community in the United States was divided along class, political, social, and religious differences. In the 1960s, with efforts to promote a model of cultural pluralism in the United States, Haitians began to understand their collectivity as an ethnic community and were aware of the advantages of maintaining an ethnonational consciousness. At the same time, the political and organizing consciousness of the Haitian community was being affected by the promotion of cultural nationalism and the black power movement in the United States. While a decline in ethnic organizing in the 1970s ensued as emigrants were being scapegoated for the rapid growth of unemployment in the United States, Haitians opted for alternative forms of group identification.[102] Evoking the biblical imagery of diaspora, the term was first used in in the 1980s by Haitian fathers steeped in the international liberation theology moment to describe the Haitian community in New York.[103] Influenced by the Freirian concept of social awareness that engendered the groupman movement and a number of structured associations in rural Haiti during the 1960s,[104] the Haitian fathers wanted to organize the Haitian immigrant community against the Duvalier dictatorship. These efforts at unification and solidarity of the Haitian community were based on nationalist or ethnic identities.[105]

Later, Haitians born or raised outside of the geographical boundaries of the Haitian nation would embrace and creolize this term as *dyaspora* or *djaspora* to invoke a new collective identity and political consciousness that muddled traditional notions of nation and ethnicity. *Dyaspora* simply means Haitians living abroad. But in both Haiti and in the United States, where the term is widely use, *dyaspora* is a marker of difference between Haitians living in Haiti (*moun peyi*) and those living abroad (*moun andeyo*). In Haiti, *dyaspora* can be used pejoratively to alienate Haitians no longer living in their native land.[106] It is also used to describe returnees who go through the process of dediasporization, that is, reincorporation into the homeland.[107] In the United States, dyaspora is a productive space to assert a syncretic identity formed out of the experience of physical displacement and distance from Haiti. Dyaspora is also the liberatory space that questions traditional perceptions of Haitian identity that marginalize Haitians along class lines and challenge certain cultural traditions that are used as tools of oppression. Haitians in the United States also claim this position to articulate the many issues they face collectively as a marginalized group in the United States. These varied articulations of the Haitian diaspora necessitated a reconceptualization of the migration and settlement of Haitians in the United States, a reconceptualization that foregrounded the transnational contours of the migration experience and the dual allegiance of transmigrants.

Edwidge Danticat began writing at a moment when Haitians were claiming a diasporic identity that acknowledges multiple home spaces and identities.[108] When Danticat's acclaimed 1994 novel *Breath, Eyes, Memory* was published, the concept of transnationalism had already emerged to describe the social, political, and economic cross-border practices of new immigrant populations. Diasporas became "emblems of transnationalism."[109] Marking a clear distinction between immigrants and diasporas, Clifford asserts that diaspora is a distinct version of modern, transnational, and intercultural experience. Although *diaspora* is not simply a signifier of transnationality and movement, diasporas are "deployed in transnational networks built from multiple attachments, and they encode practices of accommodation, as well as resistance to, host countries and their norms."[110] As Basch, Schiller, and Blanc show, Haitian diasporic subjects, particularly in the United States, are part of a transnational social field that connects them simultaneously to two or more nation-states.[111] The term emerged in the 1990s as a new analytical paradigm that describes both an "interconnected social experience"[112] and a political process.[113] New conceptualizations of transnationalism in the 1990s emerge as a result of changes in labor patterns and shifts in households and family structures. It is in this context that *Breath, Eyes, Memory* "explores the complexities of Haiti's transnational space by presenting female characters that must come to terms with the complex consequences of emigration and exile."[114]

The crossings of geographical, cultural, and political borders would lead to what Appadurai describes as complex "transnational construction of imaginary landscapes."[115] Literary scholars use Danticat's work to interrogate the formation and articulation of transnational identities as well as the transnational contours of women's experiences. Indeed, Danticat's fictional texts contribute to the formation of cross-cultural, transnational, and global alliances that are part of what Grewal and Kaplan call "feminist transnational practices."[116] However, more recently, scholars are paying attention to Danticat's works of nonfiction to explore the political and economic dynamics of Haitian transnationalism. For example, Danticat has been described as an "eloquent witness to the psychological and social effects of Haitian transnationalism."[117] As some scholars argue, Danticat participates in transnational forms of global social justice activism.[118]

I look at the ways in which Danticat's writings strive to transgress racialized, gendered, and class-based violence that is implicated in nation-state formations and the (black) national imaginary through transnational practices of diasporic communities and global articulations of political and ethical consciousness. I am interested in how these practices and articulations form and inform not only the contours of the Haitian diaspora, which include communities in the Dominican Republic, Canada, and the Bahamas, among other places. But since Danticat migrated to the United States at the age of twelve and has spent most of her life in New York, I home in on the experiences of Haitians in the United States, where close to one million Haitian Americans reside, and how the presence of these communities shape relations between Haiti and the United States.

I begin with a historical analysis of the evolution of the Haitian diaspora to examine how Haitian diasporic formations expose the way Haiti and the United States are intertwined and the dual relationship between Haiti and its diaspora. I offer the case of Haiti and the historical particularities of the Haitian diasporic experience in North America that began with the migration of the Haitian intelligentsia in the 1960s as a case example of complex dynamics of the diaspora phenomenon and its ties to transnationalism and processes of globalization. This necessitates an understanding of Haitian migrants' incorporation into the politics of North American definitions of ethnic community in the 1970s, the scapegoating of racialized migrant bodies during a recession in the United States during the 1980s, and the transnational political participation of the Haitian diasporic communities in the 1990s as a result of a massive movement toward democracy in Haiti after the fall of the Duvalier dictatorship. The historical formation of the Haitian diaspora informs not only Danticat's evolving definition of diaspora but also her own political consciousness of the plight of immigrant communities in the United States.

The Structure of This Book

In her work on the relationship between gender and the nation, Nira Yuval-Davis asserts, "Of particular significance in the global/local relations is the existence of diasporic communities."[119] In order to be cognizant of these global implications, we must pay attention not only to what the writing of diaspora offers to our understanding of a diasporic imaginary in the twenty-first century but also how such imaginary contributes to the "global imaginary." These forward-looking imaginings can only be contextualized in relation to the emergence and dynamics of economic, political, and cultural processes of globalization in the twentieth century, their impact on the political sphere and social imaginary of the nation and its citizens, and their influence in shaping the way we read histories and material conditions of disenfranchised local communities at home and abroad and their geopolitical restructuring of space as a consequence of economic restructuring. Chapter 1, "Recall: The Echo Effect of Historical Silences," delineates significant historical moments pertinent to an understanding of the Haitian diaspora and its global contours. I explore the way in which reinscription, for Danticat, is linked to a commitment to unearthing the silences in Haitian histories of migration and displacement. I argue that if Haiti's silenced histories are the sources of an echo, then the recall of these histories, in diaspora, is a strategic form of echoing what can never be completely retrieved, only repeatedly re-membered, and returned, in the diasporic imaginary.

In chapter 2, "Echo Chamber in *Create Dangerously,*" I develop the trope of the echo chamber as a central narrative reading strategy for analyzing Danticat's preoccupation with silence and voice and their relationship to narratives of both the Haitian nation and the Haitian diaspora. Focusing on the collection of essays on the role of the immigrant writer, *Create Dangerously: The Immigrant Artist at Work,* I examine Danticat's preoccupation with recalling, recording, and registering diaspora subjects as subjects that have an echoing relationship with the nation. I highlight the Greco-Roman myth of Echo and Danticat's tropic permutations of the myth to discuss the polyphonic element of Danticat's diasporic imaginary. I do so by revisiting a less well known but more violent story of Echo that involves the god Pan in the pastoral poem account of *Daphnis and Chloe,* the first pastoral prose romance and only known work by Greek author Longus. I explore how the relationship among echo, the centrality of voice, and experience of dismemberment as punishment that is revealed in Longus's version of the Echo story relates to Danticat's rendition of Alèrte Belance's story of survival and resistance in "I Speak Out" as a modern Echo. Furthermore, I argue that Danticat's collection of essays reveals her conscious awareness of the need to create a diaspora archive that preserves the narratives of nation and constructs new narratives of diaspora.

In chapter 3, "Haitian Echoes: Tradition and Nation in *Breath, Eyes, Memory,*" I offer an analysis of Danticat's debut novel, *Breath, Eyes, Memory* (1994), a semiautobiographical narrative that explores the struggles of the character Sophie, a young emigrant girl coming into her own identity in New York City. In this chapter, I focus on the idea of echo in relation to narratives of nation tied to the dissemination of cultural values and traditions. My question in this chapter is, How do women echo and recall the nation in ways that both enforce and unsettle male-centered narratives of displacement and notions of home? I examine Danticat's preoccupation with the practice of storytelling and its evocation of "secrets" and cultural rites of passage into motherhood and womanhood. I argue that Danticat presents oral culture and the art of storytelling as the source of what I am calling Haitian echoes, the local tropes Danticat uses to subvert the Western imaginary and its literary authority. These local tropes, like the figure of the Marassa, reveal the double and doubling as a function of narrative strategy of textual preservation and creative strategy of resistance and survival. They offer alternative notions of dualities and twoness. I also discuss the ways in which Danticat articulates multiple echoes of this original source by tapping into the oral and textual residues of the African tradition, the African American tradition, and the African diasporic tradition to develop new diasporic mythologies. Lastly, I offer a reexamination of the classic myth of Persephone, Demeter, and Hades that centralizes two thematic concerns in Danticat's novel: the violence of patriarchy and the contours of matrilineal diaspora.

In chapter 4, "*The Dew Breaker* as Écho-Monde," I argue that Danticat's *The Dew Breaker* (2004) explores the evolving transnational and pluralistic contours of Danticat's diasporic subjects in ways that foreground a poetics of relation, in the Glissantian sense, and its instance of écho-monde, wherein the art of echoing is presented as a polyphonic narrative weaving and confluence of intertexts, voices, thematic repetitions, repetition of phrases, temporal moments, and spatial orientations. Echo here is presented as repetition, revision, and double. Offering a Lacanian psychoanalytic reading, I argue that this relational double is presented in the way Danticat articulates the dialogic between the nation and the diaspora in *The Dew Breaker* as a matter of a shared obsession with genealogy, preservation, and the anxiety of separation. I further propose that we read *The Dew Breaker* as a textual genealogy of the Haitian diaspora that disorders, redefines, and expands our very understanding of genealogy itself beyond the linear national masculinist frame. The relational double is used as a way for Danticat to both master and transgress the binaries that maintain a monistic ordering of the national imaginary and its corollary narratives of origin, family and ancestry, history, wholeness, unity, and community. But the process of transgression in the diasporic imaginary for Danticat is not a disavowal of traditional narratives of the nation but rather a self-reflexive rewriting that necessitates mastery, deformation, and reformation of these narratives in a relational and dialogic manner. Such rewriting exposes and unsettles not only the monological world as master signifier but also the inherent dialogue involved in the process of writing. Danticat recalls, recovers, and unveils literary predecessors to engage in a dialogue and magnify the multiplicity of the intertextual field that grounds the relationship between the reader and the writer. In expanding the field to incorporate oral narratives, Danticat also highlights the primacy of voice and the relationship between the listener and the speaker. Through a complex intertextual play between different voices, words, phrases, themes, and texts, Danticat, in *The Dew Breaker,* I argue, retains ideas of origin, wholeness, unity, family, ancestry, history, and community to reenact them as "the stuff" of both nation and diaspora but also to disentangle them from ideological frames and totalitarian absolutes that hinder heterogeneous, pluralistic, and liberatory possibilities of imagining the world, our place in it, and our relationship to each other.

In chapter 5, "Voices from beyond the (Unmarked) Grave in *The Farming of Bones*," I focus on the workings of a diasporic imaginary in the formation of diasporic subjectivities at the border. I examine Danticat's 1998 historical novel, *The Farming of Bones*, a love story that follows the experiences of Amabelle and her relationship with her lover Sebastien, to explore what I see as Danticat's strategic attempt to echo Haiti through the recall of a particular moment in history that reminds the readers in diaspora of silenced and suppressed traumatic stories that bear on Haiti's relationship with its neighbors, both close and distant, today. This silenced circular history must be excavated through witness testimony that aims to record the traumatic event. Danticat privileges collective memory and individual remembering in the process of recovering, recalling, and retelling such histories. Danticat's masterful fictional retelling of the 1937 massacre of thousands of Haitians at the border of Haiti and the Dominican Republic is also an examination of the power of speech and voice as threat in colonial, postcolonial, and neocolonial contexts. Like the nymph Echo, Haitians are silenced by the perversion of language as phonetic marker of sameness and difference. In this novel, the tongue, as representation and most important articulator of speech, is symbolically slashed by the machete of Dominican soldiers. As in *Breath, Eyes, Memory*, the relationships among silence, dismemberment, and nation building are foregrounded. But this silencing is not meant to curtail speech as in the case of Echo; it is a death sentence, an execution intended to alter or obliterate an other's speech and existence. Moreover, Danticat's evocation of this particular historical moment also gives insight into the idea of the neighbor as symbolic mirror of both the self and the other and the dialectic between the two. Here the echo trope functions as the other who imposes violence on his or her neighbor but also as the abject mirror image and double of the gendered national self. This self/other Hegelian dialectic produces the systematic production and reproduction of Haiti as contagion and contamination. Thus, in echoing a particular site of bloody border conflict between "twin" nations that share the same island and interlocking histories, Danticat critiques the pitfalls of nationalist ideology and discourse that completely efface the lived experiences of multiple border crossings that engender new unrecognizable, unreadable subjectivities. In doing so, she not only exposes the falsity of linguistic singularity purity but also considers, and in fact honors, the spaces beyond language—that is, the space of communion with the dead, with shadows, revenants, and ghosts.

In the epilogue, I return to the question of voice and voicelessness by examining how the particular image of the voice box that emerges in one of the stories in *The Dew Breaker* and in Danticat's memoir, *Brother, I'm Dying,* elucidates both Danticat's preoccupation with voice and use of the echo chamber trope.

In the appendix, I offer an interview with Edwidge Danticat to reflect the breadth and depth of her work. The interview was conducted through numerous email exchanges that began in July 2017 and was completed in early August 2017, around the time President Trump endorsed the Reforming American Immigration for Strong Employment Act. The bill, which creates a merit-based immigration system that privileges English-speaking visa applicants, aims to reduce levels of immigration by 50 percent over the next ten years. In the interview, Danticat does not shy away from expressing her opinions of the Trump administration's immigration policies. She also discusses her latest book, *The Art of Death: Writing the Final Story,* which chronicles the death of her mother, Rose, from ovarian cancer in 2014.

1 Recall

The Echo Effect of Historical Silences

> For historians, echo provides yet another take on the process of es-
> tablishing identity by raising the issues of the distinction between
> the original sound and its resonances and the role of time in the
> distortions heard. Where does an identity originate? Does the sound
> issue forth from past to present, or do answering calls echo to the
> present from the past? If we are not the source of the sound, how can
> we locate that source? If all we have is the echo, can we ever discern
> the original? Is there any point in trying, or can we be content with
> thinking about identity as a series of repeated transformations?
>
> —Joan W. Scott, "Fantasy Echo"

THE HISTORICAL, social, and political dimensions of the Haitian diaspora are the crucible of real and imagined geographies that are
constitutive elements of Haitian diasporic imaginary and consciousness.
What gives birth to and stimulates Edwidge Danticat's diasporic imaginary
and anchors her work is a complicated history of Haitian migration and
its literary (mis)representations. Certainly, it is impossible to explore, for
example, the character Martine and her psychological state resulting from
past trauma in *Breath, Eyes, Memory* without an awareness of the context
of the Duvalier regime, which fundamentally transformed migration patterns in Haiti during the latter half of the twentieth century. How can we
tease out the affective dimensions of Amabelle's experience of displacement
in the Dominican Republic in Danticat's historical novel, *The Farming of
Bones* (1998), without a keen sense of the historical relationship between
the two countries or the border culture that is formed out of the historical
circumstances that brought Haitians to the Dominican Republic in the
early twentieth century as migrant laborers on sugarcane plantations and
the traumatic consequences of a pivotal moment in Haitian history, the
1937 massacre at the border that exacerbated relations between the two
nations? We understand the limbo state and deterritorialized social identities of Danticat's tragic characters in the opening story of *Krik? Krak!*

(1995) most succinctly when they are situated simultaneously within the context of the plight of Haitian boat people in the 1980s who attempted to escape the dictatorship for better lives in the United States and the tribulations of African slaves during the Middle Passage that remains a powerful symbol of the transatlantic slave trade in the African diasporic imaginary. We effectively engage the ethical and human rights questions raised in Danticat's memoir *Brother, I'm Dying* (2007) only to the extent that we become familiar with pre- and postdiscriminatory immigration policies against Haitians in the United States. We are pushed to reflect on the multiple dimensions and contradictions of Haitian (diasporic) subjectivities in *The Dew Breaker* when we recognize Danticat's investment in deconstructing master tropes of political violence in Haiti that elide the intricacies and nuances of people's everyday lives. We are transfixed by the powerful stories of immigrant artists in *Create Dangerously* because we sympathize with their predicaments under regimes of silence that create climates unfavorable to artistic production and its dissemination.

James Clifford asserts that we must insist on the routing of diaspora in specific maps and histories. When historicized, "diaspora cannot become a master trope or 'figure' of modern, complex or positional identities."[1] For Danticat, invocations of diaspora in displaced Haitian communities and articulations of Haitian diasporic subjects are historically situated in time and tied to real geographies, specific maps, and physical sites located in specific space. Danticat's fictional characters point to the histories, political realities, and lived experiences that frame the writer's understanding of a collective but multidimensional and polyphonic Haitian diasporic community. Danticat's work makes it impossible for any astute reader of her text to fully escape the historical dimensions of migration and displacement that not only form what is now known as the Haitian diaspora but also produce the affective dimensions that Danticat is invested in inscribing and reinscribing. In this chapter, I ask, In what way do literal experiences of migration and displacement and their effects in the particular context of Haiti's history reframe our understanding of the relationship between history and the echo phenomenon in Danticat's work? How does Danticat work through historical silences in her understanding of diaspora to foreground individual and collective experiences of diasporic subjects in her literary inscriptions? What are the local, national, transnational, and global contours of the histories that Danticat recalls, excavates, and recovers in her work? How do the politicized histories Danticat foregrounds expose the relation between silence and authoritarian regimes?

It is my contention that diasporic subjects have an echoing relationship with the homeland and its histories. Echo repeats what came before.[2] It hears original sounds and attempts to capture source signals. Echoes are sounds of the past that "represent a sound or a signal that has already been deployed and is in decay."[3] Echoes travel in time and space. Echo, as a product of space, also puts history back in place. Danticat, like her Echo-like diasporic subjects, participates in an echo effect induced by the recall of silenced histories. But in the practice of recall and recollection, the histories, written out of historical records and perceived as loss, resonate incompletely. They can only be returned and restored as fragments of memory, fragmented memory that bears a semblance to history.[4] Danticat uses these fragmented memories to generate narratives that can become part of a diaspora archive that preserves recollected stories and memorializes individual lives within the historically specific frames, references, contexts, and backgrounds that make up the central focus of this chapter. Reinscription, for Danticat, is linked to a commitment to unearthing the silences in Haitian histories of migration and displacement. If Haiti's silenced histories are the sources of an echo, then the recall of these histories, in diaspora, is a strategic form of echoing what can never be completely retrieved, only repeatedly re-membered, and returned, in the diasporic imaginary.

Historical Silences and Echo

While Danticat is well known for writing masterfully about Haiti's history, it was the publication of her historical novel, *The Farming of Bones*, in 1998 and its powerful recall of the 1937 Haitian massacre at the border of Haiti and the Dominican Republic that exposed this talent. Two years after the release of the book, Eleanor Wachtel asked Danticat in an interview about what she found when she made the visit to the Massacre River that inspired her to write about the genocide, also known as the Parsley Massacre, which killed as many as twenty thousand people. Danticat responded:

> I think it was what I didn't find there that most moved me. I had heard so much about the Massacre River, going from the first massacre of the colonists in the 19th century to this present massacre. And I think I had built up in my mind this angry, raging river, this body of water that just did not forget. And I felt that, as soon as I got there, I would sense the history, that I would see it as though unfolding on a screen. But when I got there, it amazed me that

there were people washing clothes, that there were children bathing, that there were animals drinking. The ordinariness of life was striking to me. There's a line in the book that says that "Nature has no memory" and it struck me in a great sense that it's both sad and comforting that nature has no memory, that things go on in spite of what's happened before. That the tree will grow, that there will be weeds and that the river will flow. So it was the lack of event that inspired me, that made me want to recall the past and write about this historical moment.[5]

Lack of an event, a nonevent, not only inspires; it points to silences and generates narratives. All narratives, as Michel-Rolph Trouillot asserts in his influential work *Silencing the Past,* impose silences. The historical narrative, for Trouillot, "is a particular bundle of silences, the result of a unique process, and the operation required to deconstruct these silences will vary accordingly."[6] These silences "enter the process of historical production at four crucial moments: the moment of fact creation (the making of sources); the moment of fact assembly (the making of archives); the moment of fact retrieval (the making of narratives); and the moment of retrospective significance (the making of history in the final instance)."[7] These sources and archives contain "presences and absences" that are "neither neutral nor natural" but created.[8] Consequently, Trouillot argues, two tropes in modern historiography emerge: formulas of erasure and formulas of banalization. These formulas of silence explain the general silencing of the Haitian Revolution as a nonevent specifically[9] and "narratives of global domination" more broadly.[10] Like the Haitian Revolution, the Parsley Massacre, as Danticat reveals, is a nonevent of the twentieth century, one of the least remembered genocides of the period. But for Danticat, the massacre is just one example of a plethora of historical silences that need to be excavated. In all her work, Danticat pulls from a number of nonevents to recall specific moments in Haitian history tied to patterns of migration. This recall extends not only to the reclamation of the past but to the recovery of the individual self and forgotten lived experiences that must be memorialized.

Many scholars of Haitian studies in the humanities and social sciences who examine historical and political realities of Haiti and its diaspora follow, or build, in some form or fashion on Trouillot's argument to critically investigate the silencing of the Haitian Revolution specifically and Haitian history more broadly.[11] Susan Buck-Morss differentiates between two silences, one past and the other present.[12] Sibylle Fischer examines how the "disavowal" of the Haitian Revolution in historical and cultural records is central to an understanding of Western modernity.[13] Literary critics of Haitian literature both within Haiti and in the diaspora insist that Haitian literary history is about working through these silences and absences. J. Michael Dash argues that Haiti was relegated to a zone of negativity and absence in nineteenth-century literary texts.[14] Nick Nesbitt explains that a certain image of Haiti was presented to silence a global vision of black sovereignty and displace Haiti as symbol of universal freedom.[15] Nesbitt views Danticat as a writer who reconstitutes exceptional events of the past to reanimate life, and "recover something of the life lost."[16]

As a result of the intentional discursive silencing of Haiti, traditional Haitian literary texts are viewed as aesthetic modes of recuperating the idea of the Haitian Revolution idea of 1804.[17] But such recuperation embodied in male figures and tropes of the revolutionary hero displaces and effaces the role of women in Haiti's revolutionary history. Indeed, as Jana Braziel asserts, with the exception of Dédée Bazile, popularly known as Défilée-La-Folle, revolutionary heroines "have remained obscured within literary, historiographical and hagiographical narratives from this era."[18] Myriam Chancy asserts that Haitian women's culture and the revolutionary dimensions of Haitian women's literature are defined through a consciousness of absence and silence, not as a negative space of lack but as a space of nothingness through which identity is affirmed and transformed. She defines this space as a cultural lacuna that accounts for the presence of absence.[19] Haitian women's vision, Chancy further asserts, describes this cultural space as "one that embraces its own silencing even as it contests it."[20] But as Chancy makes clear in her critical work on Haitian women writers, this only appears to be the case because "women have consistently been written out of both the historical and literary records of Haiti."[21] This erasure applies to the broader Caribbean literary tradition, wherein the literature of women writers and their representation of new Caribbean female subjects threaten patriarchal literary authority and master narratives of colonialist discourse.[22] Thus in Caribbean women's literary tradition, femininity, the idea of giving voice to women's histories is not only paramount but engenders tropes of female vocal agency and mastery of voice.

Regimes of Silence, the Duvalier Dictatorship, and Peak Migration

A particular era in Haitian history replete with its own silences is the Duvalier regime in Haiti that began in 1957 and ended in 1986. Many novels by Haitians in the 1970s and 1980s were produced in North America by what Haitian writer and literary critic Yanick Lahens describes as the "lost generation," a generation of exile and censorship with an unyielding memory of the Duvalier regime period in the 1960s.[23] A large majority of Haitians from this generation, many of whom were writers, journalists, politicians, and professionals of the elite and educated class, emigrated during this period to escape state-sanctioned persecution and violence. Edwidge Danticat, who was born in 1969, at the tail end of this decade, is particularly haunted by historical moments of this period. In her collection of essays, *Create Dangerously*, the subject of the next chapter, Danticat discusses her obsession with the story of the public execution of Marcel Numa and Louis Drouin on November 12, 1964, and explains how this nonevent affects her writing and identity as an emigrant writer: "All artists, writers among them, have several stories—one might call them creation myths—that haunt and obsess them. This is one of mine. I don't even remember when I first heard about it. I feel as though I have always known it, having filled in the curiosity-driven details through photographs, newspaper and magazine articles, books and films as I have gotten older."[24] The individuals, writers, artists, and texts Danticat foregrounds in *Create Dangerously* become voices that fill in the gaps of a historical moment that is partially recalled through oral transmission. The diasporic subjects of Danticat's book are heavily affected by an emigration pattern that began to emerge when François "Papa Doc" Duvalier came to power in September of 1957, just a few years before this event. François Duvalier established himself as president for life in 1964 and on his deathbed handed over power to his nineteen-year-old son, Jean-Claude, in 1971, prolonging decades of autocratic rule that came to a halt with the downfall of the regime on February 7, 1986.

Danticat's recall of Papa Doc Duvalier in *Create Dangerously* relies on a myriad of tangible source texts that she collected over the years. She also depends on intangible sources, borrowed recollections, and transmitted testimonies and memories of families, friends, and acquaintances. But the memory of Jean-Claude "Baby Doc" Duvalier, who succeeded his father when Danticat was about two years old, includes her own testimonies: "A lot of us *must* remember. I remember a great deal of silence, people being afraid to say anything. You didn't trust your neighbor because you didn't know who might turn you in for whatever reason. . . . There's a proverb that says 'yesterday is always better' but it was really a difficult time. A lot of people would just vanish overnight, or they would go into exile, or they would run."[25] The question of silence and censorship under the Duvalier regime is the overarching subject of *Create Dangerously*. But it also consumes all of Danticat's work in some form or fashion.

Duvalier's regime of silence was emboldened and sustained by his secret police, formally named Milice des Volontaires de la Sécurité Nationale (Militia of National Security Volunteers) but popularly known as the Tonton Macoutes. This Haitian paramilitary police force was founded in 1958 to defend the autocratic regime. While Danticat's first two publications evoke the consequences of Macoute violence on the lives of its victims, Danticat returns to this historical and politicized moment in history more intricately in her second collection of short stories, *The Dew Breaker,* the subject of chapter 4. The intertwined stories in the collection are about the life of a Haitian torturer, a member of Duvalier's Tonton Macoutes, raising a family in New York, and the individuals and victims who are connected to him directly or indirectly. In an interview with Terry Hong about the book that moves between the genre of the novel and the short story cycle, Danticat recalls, "I've always wanted to write about the Duvalier era and about the aftermath of the 29 year Duvalier dictatorship because it's really the last period I spent in Haiti—the last time I lived there. I wanted to write about what people make of that time period and the realities of migration and the idea that you have this mixture of people who were victims of the dictatorship and those who were perpetrators of it now living in New York."[26] With the exception of *The Farming of Bones,* which recalls the Parsley massacre of 1937, all the texts discussed in this book involve individuals, real and fictional, whose lives in Haiti and in the diaspora have been affected by Duvalier's regime of terror.

The Duvalier dictatorship, as Danticat reveals in her work, engendered massive emigration. Delineating the history of the Haitian diaspora in the United States in his work *Diasporic Citizenship,* Haitian social anthropologist Michel Laguerre asserts that there have been uninterrupted streams of Haitian emigration into the United States with high, low, and dormant periods. He describes the high periods as three major peaks of migration that go even further back to the nineteenth century: "The three periods of Haitian immigration to the United States roughly corresponds to the Haitian revolutionary era and its aftermath (1791–1810), the period of the US occupation of Haiti (1915–34), and the Duvalier and immediate post-Duvalier era (1957–94)."[27] Laguerre describes the border-crossing practices and developing economic, social, and political significance of Haitian emigrants who fled the Haitian Revolution to places like Baltimore, New York City, Chicago, Philadelphia, Charleston, and New Orleans and contributed to the development of those cities. Laguerre argues that the earliest diasporic communities in the United States sustained these practices to maintain relations with the homeland.[28] These early instances of migration began to change the social landscape of both Haiti and the United States. The US Immigration and Naturalization Service, which did not begin recording Haitian immigration separately until 1932, reveals that during the US occupation only a couple of hundred Haitians from urban areas of Haiti left the country, presumably to escape the atrocities of the occupation.[29] From 1932 to 1950 only 5,544 Haitians entered the United States as immigrants.[30] However, as Laguerre asserts, the Duvalier regime marked a peak of Haitian migration that would completely transform the social structure of the two countries and the relationship between Haiti and its diaspora population: "The Dynastic Duvalier regime (1957–1986) brought about major transformation in the social structure of society characterized by massive rural-urban migration and emigration to the United States, the downgrading of the military, the paramilitarization of the system, a sustained effort at controlling dissidents through state violence, the primacy of the capital city, the burgeoning of slums in the margins of the city, and the diaspora's disbursement of remittances all over the country."[31]

Indeed, the majority of Haitians in the United States, including Danticat's family, emigrated during the Duvalier period. Between 1950 and 1970, 8 percent of the Haitian population emigrated.[32] Flore Zéphir highlights the climate of this period in Haiti as one example of multiple debilitating political, economic, and social climates all over the world that have transformed immigration patterns in the United States: "The post 1965 flow of immigration was quite different from previous flows in the sense that the majority of immigrants came primarily from Asia, Mexico, Latin America, and the Caribbean."[33] Zéphir specifies the year 1965 as a significant moment in immigration patterns because it points to the Immigration Act of 1965, which opened the doors for immigrants. The passing of the Immigration Act was, as Zéphir asserts, a direct result of the civil rights movement of the 1960s, which called for a reevaluation of US positions on issues of race and ethnic minorities. In contrast to previous restrictive immigration policies enacted in the late nineteenth and early twentieth centuries, the new immigration policies of the 1960s were attractive to emigrants.[34] Interestingly, Danticat's recall of the 1960s and other periods in Haitian history puts a spotlight on individuals affected by problematic immigration policies in the United States. She does this with the hope of generating awareness and empathy. The retelling of the story of her uncle dying while detained at Miami's Krome Detention Center in her 2007 memoir, *Brother, I'm Dying*, is a thoughtful reflection on the relationships among the Duvalier regime, emigration of Haitians in the latter half of the twentieth century, and post-9/11 immigration policies.

Canada, the Haitian Intelligentsia, and the Question of Exile

Although Danticat's work largely focuses on the experiences of Haitians in Haiti and the United States, it is important to discuss first the migration of the Haitian intelligentsia to Canada and its impact on Haitian literature, the question of Haitian identity, and the concept of exile during this period. Indeed, Haitian emigrants were attracted to tolerant immigration laws in Canada during the 1960s. But they were also more inclined to see Canada as a place of refuge than the United States, which occupied the country by military invasion for nineteen years in the early part of the twentieth century.[35] The image of the United States as an occupier resurfaced when the United States invaded Santo Domingo in 1965 with forty-two thousand troops. This occurred at the height of the American civil rights movement, which exposed racial segregation and discrimination rooted in the history of slavery in the country. Adverse conditions in Haiti also resulted in massive Haitian emigration to Canada, which transformed relations between Haiti and Francophone Canada as well as the social landscape of Quebec. In *The Haitians in Quebec,* an early examination of Haitians in Canada published in 1980, Paul Dejean traces the relationship between Quebecois and Haitians to the arrival of Canadian citizens in Haiti during the 1940s: "The Quebecois presence in Haiti appeared in the early forties with the arrival of missionaries who were subsequently followed by businessmen, entrepreneurs, technical assistance personnel and tourists. Haitians have been drawn to Quebec through this complex of influences."[36] Dejean describes two distinct stages in the pattern of Haitian migration since the 1940s: "From the 1940s to the late 1960s, an elite Haitian group numbering a few hundred individuals settled in Quebec and assimilated quickly into the society due to their high degree of education and the need for their skills in the medical, educational, and technical fields." Dejean points to 1967 as the year new regulations and policies on immigration were put into effect in Canada. These immigration policies preceded the formation of the Quebec Ministry of Immigration in 1968 and coincided with the international exposition of Montreal. In 1968, Haiti was not considered one of the fifteen countries that were the main sources of emigration to Quebec. By 1969, however, Haiti was number ten on the list. From 1974 to 1976, it was recognized as the first source of emigration to Quebec, surpassing France, the United States, and Lebanon.[37] Haitians were attracted to Canada as an alternative to the repressive Duvalier regime because of an already established Canadian presence in Haiti, the positive image of Canada as a hospitable country with tolerant immigration laws, and Canadian investment in cheap labor.

However, in *A Place in the Sun: Haiti, Haitians and the Remaking of Quebec,* the most recent book on the history of Haitians in Quebec, Sean Mills dates the first notable exchange and "initial contours" that forged the relationship between Haiti and French Canada and twentieth-century Canadian discourses about Haiti to the 1930s, specifically to 1937, during the Congress on the French Language in Canada, which included a small delegation of intellectuals from Haiti, such as Dantès Bellegarde.[38] Mills asserts that the delegation reinforced ties with Canada by highlighting the "special connection" between the two societies, which promoted cultural solidarity and reinforced the idea of a universal French culture in the Americas.[39] The 1937 event was the impetus to other delegations, as well as university student exchange activities and large-scale entry of French Canadian missionaries and Catholic intellectuals into Haiti.[40] But when Haitians began to migrate to Canada decades later, the intellectual, political, and social landscapes were undergoing radical transformations as a result of a global atmosphere of revolt and anticolonial sentiment of the 1960s. Miller explains, "When they landed in Quebec, they arrived in a society undergoing an important transformation and in this environment their literary and political sensibilities found a welcome home. At this moment when they arrived, Quebec's intellectual structures were beginning to crumble under the weight of new radical ideals, some generated locally and others inspired from movements of Third World decolonization."[41] By 1965, the presence of two thousand Haitians in Quebec marked the first wave of Haitians penetrating the avant-garde intellectual scene.[42] This first generation of Haitian migrants whose academic credentials were recognized presupposes the reality of a brain drain crisis that became evident by the end of the decade.[43]

In his essay "Uprooting and Uprootedness: Haitian Poetry in Quebec (1960–2002)," Vincent Desroches states that the first Haitian writers to settle in Montreal in the 1960s were members of Haïti Littéraire, a collective of five young Haitian poets founded in 1960 in Port-au-Prince. These included Anthony Phelps, who arrived in Montreal in 1964; Serge Legagneur, who moved to Montreal in 1965; Roland Morisseau, who joined Phelps and Legagneur in Montreal; and René Philoctète. (Marie Chauvet, who was the only female member of Haïti Littéraire and held an open house in Bourdon on Sundays for the group's literary gatherings, was living in New York after the publication of her triptych *Amour, colère et folie.*) Serge Legagneur and Roland Morisseau joined Phelps in an apartment they shared in Carré Saint-Louis, downtown Montreal. Gérard Étienne and Émile Ollivier, other well-known Haitian Canadian writers of the same generation, also migrated to Montreal around this time. These writers were part of a developing Haitian literary scene in Montreal that included weekly poetry readings at Perchoir d'Haiti, a literary café in downtown Montreal, in 1964 and 1965. Desroches argues that this literary scene was "the occasion for fructuous encounters with Quebecois nationalist poets. . . . These friendly contacts had a direct influence on the poésie du pays (poetry of the country), exposing Quebecois poets to Caribbean authors such as Aimé Césaire and René Depestre." However, major anthologies of Quebecois literature from the 1960s did not include these authors until much later. Yet Haitian poets in Quebec tended to publish in a small number of publishing houses, such as Nouvelle Optique (renamed Humanitas), Triptyque, and Éditions du CIDIHCA (Centre International de Documentation et d'Information Haïtienne, Caribéenne et Afro-Canadienne).[44] The poetry of the period that glorifies Haiti's historic past and promotes a national soul is a response to racialized notions of blackness. Migrating a decade later to Montreal, Dany Laferrière would depart from this trend and become the most well-known Haitian writer writing in French.[45] But when Laferrière arrived in the 1970s, new patterns of Haitian migration emerged: Haitians coming to Quebec were poor and worked in manufacturing, and the domestic service industry was dominated by female Haitian migrants. These less skilled migrants experienced heightened racism and were targeted for deportation.[46]

Canada, which is currently home to a little over 200,000 members of the Haitian diaspora, most of whom are located in Quebec, was a natural destination for French-speaking writers. Quebec was particularly attractive to the Haitian intelligentsia, primarily because of the commonality of Francophone language and culture. Dejean observes, "In the artistic and literary field, the fact that the Quebec and Haitian intelligentsia share a common language has certainly favored an initial pattern of exchanges and fruitful links."[47] Distinguishing between the immigrant workers and the artists and writers who migrated to Quebec during these distinct periods of migration, Dejean alludes to the different class status and migration experiences of Haitians forced to leave for political or socioeconomic reasons. In spite of these differences, Dejean states that because of this collective reality of forced migration resulting from a repressive regime, the mentality of the Haitian community in Quebec by the time of his study is closer to that of the exile than the immigrant.[48]

With the onset of a large migration of writers that followed the emigration of doctors, lawyers, and engineers in the 1950s and the mass migration of the middle class in the 1960s, the experience of exile in the United States and French-speaking Canada became an overwhelming thematic concern in Haitian literature and framed the development of Haitian literature abroad. Haitian writers like René Depestre, Jean F. Brierre, Félix Morisseau-Leroy and Anthony Phelps articulated a consciousness of exile, wherein the experience of being elsewhere almost always meant the nostalgia for an "idealized" and authentic home one desires to return to, the question of Haitian identity in a strange land, and the struggle of self-redefinition resulting from displacement and deterritorialization.[49] Return was not possible. While writers living abroad during this period narrated their experience with exile differently, they all began to deal with the complexities of the self as Haitian within an insider/outsider framework in response to the patriarchal and patronizing authority of the Duvalier regime, which enclosed Haiti from the rest of the world and turned exiled Haitians abroad into enemies of the nation. During the 1960s and under the authority of François Duvalier, those who left would have their passports revoked, assets expropriated, and return visas refused. *Expatriate* was a pejorative expression in Haiti,[50] and those who returned often faced violent deaths.

All in all, the Duvalier dictatorship incited an exclusivist nationalist rhetoric that identified Haitians in exile as individuals who had abandoned the nation and taken up another nationality. Yet it was the Duvalier government that abandoned these Haitian citizens by first marginalizing them as outsiders because of their political position against the dictatorship and to strip them of their citizenship and rights. Exile for these Haitian writers was an experience of denationalization that led to the rearticulation of their own commitment to the Haitian nation, a process that they believed would ultimately end in return. As a result, writers who emigrated in the 1960s began to articulate an exilic sensibility that informed Haitian nationalism, albeit differently from Duvalier's rhetoric. Their exile was a transit place to strategize for the overthrow of Duvalier.[51] Their extended exile posed a challenge to traditional articulations of Haitian identity and authentic reenracination to Haitian land for a renewed sense of self and commitment to the country's development. These writers began to call into question the nationalist beliefs of literary antecedents, which I discuss in my analysis of *The Dew Breaker* in chapter 4. As exiles of the Duvalier dictatorship, Haitians living outside the country became both an inclusive exclusion and an exclusive inclusion that grounded Haitian national identity politics at the time and influenced the development of Haitian diasporic identity politics. But by the 1970s and 1980s, the Haitians in exile living in major cities like Paris, Montreal, Quebec City, Chicago, Boston, and New York City were confronted with the obstacles of return. They began to settle in their adopted countries but held on to the dream of return. Their settlement led to the growth of a new generation of Haitians born outside of the homeland. For Danticat these early migration patterns are the genesis of a global diaspora that is "very layered because it encompasses many generations, many decades now of migrations and different levels of assimilation and return to the community."[52]

Haiti, Industrialization, and the Global Economy

The migration of the Haitian intelligentsia in the 1960s is also a consequence of global trends toward industrialization and global division of labor that began at the dawn of the twentieth century. These trends had a major impact on the Haitian working class. From the 1960s to the present, thousands of working-class Haitians, essentially motivated by the prospect of employment and economic improvement, immigrated to Quebec. During this period, Western powers turned to decolonizing states and developing nations for trade partnerships, while developing nations were enticed by market-driven development strategies from Western industrial nations. These development strategies included manufacturing and the creation of export processing zones (EPZs) that produce apparel, sporting goods, and toys. In 1960, Haiti established the first Caribbean export processing factory in Port-au-Prince. EPZs became the centerpiece to Jean-Claude Duvalier's "economic revolution."[53] As Paul Farmer states, "Duvalier's Haiti offered enormous benefits for offshore assembly—generous tax holidays, a franchise granting tariff exemptions, tame unions, a minimum wage that was but a tiny fraction of that in the United States."[54] As a result, dozens of EPZs were established in the 1970s. By the 1980s, an estimated 240 multinational corporations operated in Haiti.[55] While Haiti modernized in this fashion, agriculture stagnated as a result of deregulation policies. The reduction in domestic food crop devastated local farmers, who had to compete with the importation of corn, millet, and rice from the United States. This was the price paid for US financial support that came in the form of loans and structural adjustment programs (SAPs) designed and guided by international financial institutions such as the World Bank and the International Monetary Fund to encourage international investment in assembly sweatshops. These programs required the adoption of free market measures, such as removal of tariffs on foreign goods, deregulation of markets, and privatization of state enterprise and public utilities. The goal was to make Haiti the Taiwan of the Caribbean.[56] These measures also influenced the migration of the Haitian peasant population into the Dominican Republic to find work in rice fields and on coffee and cocoa plantations. They replaced the Dominicans who were also migrating to find work in international free trade zones and factories in New York.[57] As Corten and his coauthors assert, "The human labor force is uprooted and abandoned elsewhere, obeying not the logic of accumulation but a logic based on the destruction of human resources."[58]

Instead, the removal of trade barriers left Haiti, like other countries in the Caribbean that accepted SAPs, even poorer and economically dependent on foreign aid. With a per capita annual income estimated at $253 in 1980, Haiti entered the decade as the poorest country in the Western Hemisphere.[59] As Terry Buss asserts, Haiti now depends more heavily on foreign assistance than any other nation in the Caribbean region.[60] The efforts toward industrialization and their negative impact on agricultural production in the countryside have created what Saskia Sassen describes as new geographies of centrality and marginality that completely reconfigured urban spaces as either global cities or global slums.[61] Thus Haitian migration is a microcosm of major global economic, cultural, and political changes that began to take effect after the Great Depression, became salient in the 1970s, and completely altered systems and structures by the 1980s. Political instability in the latter half of the twentieth century was exacerbated by the restructuring of the world economy that led to the economic crisis in Haiti during the 1980s.[62] The literature of the Haitian diaspora in the 1990s written by a generation born in the early 1970s in Haiti but raised in the diaspora is formed by these textual and real signs and consequences of internal and external migrations that would result in Haiti's multidimensional territorial and extraterritorial transformations. Danticat's work pays specific attention to the way these transformations exacerbated the plight of the Haitian working class, in particular the conditions of Haitian peasants in rural communities, as a result of a declining economy. Danticat's inscription and reinscription of the Haitian working class involves strategic literary affiliation and dialogue with classical literary novels on the subject, such as Jacques Roumain's 1944 novel *Gouverneurs de la rosée* (*Masters of the Dew*) and Jacques Stephen Alexis's 1955 novel, *Compère Général Soleil* (*General Sun, My Brother*).

The 1970s global financial crisis that led to the embrace of neoliberal agendas and the global economic restructuring of the time included the internationalization of capital. The United States, for example, promoted the vision of Haiti as a low-wage product assembler.[63] This vision coincided with falling profits from the US economy and led to outsourcing of production overseas, where free trade treaties and agreements were upheld. Corporations relocated to third world countries for cheap labor. This of course led to displacement of US workers, stagnation of wages, massive loss of high-paying jobs, and the decline in manufacturing known as deindustrialization. This capital restructuring and its debilitating consequences for the US economy led to the spread of right-wing domestic conservative ideology in the 1970s, spearheaded by President Richard Nixon, that attacked welfare, education, and other state-based social programs in the United States;[64] anti-immigrant sentiments and scapegoating of foreigners ensued in the 1980s.

Migrating in Droves: The Media's Boat People

Anti-immigrant sentiments would manifest in the representation of Haitians as "boat people" in the 1980s, an image developed through media coverage of Haitian emigrants entering the United States by boat and being intercepted on the shores of South Florida. The media portrayal of Haitian migration in the 1980s in the United States is ingrained in the developing diasporic consciousness of a young Edwidge Danticat, who moved to New York from Haiti at the age of twelve to be reunited with her parents in 1981. In one of her early essays, "AHA!," Danticat writes:

> Every night on the six o'clock news, you could see dead, bloated bodies washing up on Miami beaches. This was often followed by some type of report on AIDS, still a fresh news topic then, too. Both items would keep all the members of my family anxious. The boat people, because coming from a poor Haitian family, any of those faces could have been one of our relatives. So we watched the television screen with great interest as the Coast Guard's white sheets were thrown over the dark, dead faces, already half buried in the Florida sand. And we watched with great interest those who had survived the boat journey to America and were able to walk away, only to be processed into detention centers in New York and Miami. We leaned in to observe their gait, their height, their body type, and we searched for traces of ourselves in them.[65]

As a teenager, Danticat spent her Sunday afternoons with her father in detention centers, where she listened to the stories of asylum seekers.[66]

The influx of refugees to South Florida by boat in the 1970s and 1980s led to the idea of Haiti as an unsafe place and substantially devastated the tourist industry in the country. Deepening poverty, famine, progressive deforestation, violence, instability, and human rights violations in Haiti during the 1970s and 1980s changed migration patterns, resulting in the large presence and established networks of Haitians in North America. These changes in the migration pattern are embodied in the image of Haitian emigrants as boat people.

Derogatorily defined as boat people, the plight of Haitian refugees fore-grounded external migration to the United States in the 1970s through the 1990s. In *Haitian Americans,* Flore Zéphir observes, "Scores of other Haitians fleeing political persecutions decided to make their 700-mile sea journey to the South Florida Coast in small rickety boats. They became known as the boat people, and it is estimated that 40,000 Haitian boat people arrived as early as 1980–81."[67] Increased emigration to Florida began when the Bahamas, previously a common of destination for Haitian emigrants, reversed its tolerant immigration policies of the 1960s.[68] Zéphir provides the example of the *Haitian Times* 2001 fiscal report on US Coast Guard interdiction and the media coverage of the interception of a boat carrying 167 Haitians on December 3, 2001, to link the media image of boat people in the US consciousness to the continuous emigration of Haitians to Florida by boat and the powerful media coverage and promulgation of these interceptions.[69]

The phenomenon of boat people is a direct consequence of the plight of peasants in Haiti under Jean-Claude Duvalier's government and the deteriorating economic circumstances of the time. Many have argued that the emigration of peasants is a direct result of the slaughter of local Haitian pigs replaced by foreign pigs, a slaughter imposed by the US government allegedly to prevent African swine fever from reaching US shores.[70] The economy plummeted with the withdrawal of foreign investment and the US embargo on Haiti as a result of anti-Haitian sentiment and negative publicity and political instability within the country.[71] With the emigration of peasants to the shores of Florida, economic prospects were recognized by the United States as the motivating factor for emigration. Haitian immigrants, unlike Cuban immigrants from the Mariel boatlift in 1980, who were welcomed and granted asylum because of US anticommunist sentiments, were not seen as political immigrants: the fact that these economic circumstances were intrinsically linked to the oppressive Duvalier regime and subsequent political chaos was ignored. Even though the Cuban-Haitian entrant program established in 1980 under the Carter administration to curb differential treatment accorded to Haitians and Cubans, discrimination against Haitian refugees by US Immigration and Naturalization Service continued. When Ronald Reagan assumed the presidency in 1981, his administration established a harsh policy of interdiction at sea. Between 1981 and 1990, during Reagan's two-term presidency, 22,940 Haitians were interdicted at sea, and only 11 Haitians qualified for asylum.[72] If Haitians were not repatriated, they were held indefinitely in detention centers such as Krome Service Processing Center, a federal detention facility that looms ominously in the imaginations of Miami's Haitian community. When Krome became overcrowded, they were sent to detention centers in New York, West Virginia, Texas, and Puerto Rico.[73]

The plight of Haitian boat people is a consequence not only of an oppressive regime within the country but also of the 1970s global financial crisis that led to the embrace of neoliberal agendas mentioned above. During this period, Haitians were targeted and confronted with xenophobic hostility. By the 1980s, North American and international media capitalized on sensationalizing images of Haitian boat people. The American media also collaborated in publicizing allegations that Haitians were the source of AIDS after the Centers for Disease Control named Haitians as one of four groups, and the only ethnic group, considered to have the highest risk of contracting AIDS.[74] An estimated fifty to eighty thousand Haitian Americans came together as a community to protest the CDC and stigma by crossing the Brooklyn Bridge with Haitian flags on April 20, 1990. Though the Haitians were removed from the list on April 8, 1985, Haitians continued to be stigmatized through bad press, television shows, and Hollywood films that portrayed Haitians as drug dealers, zombies, cannibals, and devil worshippers.[75] The 1991 novel *Passages* by Haitian Canadian writer Émile Ollivier is a literary representation of the plight of Haitian boat people in cities such as Miami and Montreal.[76] Danticat's first collection of nine interconnected short stories of tragedy and survival, *Krik? Krak!*, published a few years later in 1995, opens with the fictitious story of refugees on a sinking boat fleeing state-sanctioned violence, including a fifteen-year-old Celiane, who delivers a baby girl, the product of gang rape by Tonton Macoutes, on the boat, only to throw her dead baby overboard and then herself.

Haitian Migration in the 1990s

By the 1990s, when the discourse of diaspora boomed and new forms of transnational exchange began to emerge, Haitians in the diaspora were no longer seen as temporary sojourners. Haitians born in North America could articulate a Haitianness that did not negate their citizenship in the host country. Ironically, during this period, Haitians in the diaspora simultaneously faced the possibility and challenges of return. The departure of Jean-Claude Duvalier for France in 1986 resulted in a series of political movements, coups, and shifts in government that both advanced and stifled the prospects of democracy. These included Operation Dechoukaj (Operation Uprooting), an mission aimed at cleansing the country of Tonton Macoutes and the traces of Duvalierism by a military junta led by General Henry Namphy that began in 1987.[77] Haitians in the diaspora were defined by the Haitian government in the late 1980s under General Henri Namphy as external to the nation. During this period, acts of retribution were made against the Tonton Macoutes, and the Conseil National de Gouvernement, which ruled Haiti under Namphy, agreed to authorize legal proceedings against the secret police.[78] Namphy's control did not endure for long, as he was deposed by yet another repressive military government under the control of General Prosper Avril, who held power between 1988 and 1990. Avril's departure on March 12, 1990, was followed by the appointment of Ertha Pascal Trouillot as interim president of Haiti, the first female to hold that office.

A back-to-Haiti movement emerged after the fall of the Duvalier regime but was stilted by strikes and civil unrest. With the emergence of the Ti Legliz, a liberation theology movement in Haiti, and the Lavalas political movement, both spearheaded by Jean-Bertrand Aristide, the back-to-Haiti movement was revived with the first democratic election of Aristide in 1991, who won with 67 percent of the vote. The movement was stilted again with the subsequent overthrow of his government just seven months into his presidency as a result of a coup led by Lieutenant General Raoul Cédras. In his analysis of the refugee crisis between 1991 and 1994, Patrick Gavigan asserts, "The surprise coup in September 1991 opened the refugee floodgates."[79] Indeed, the coup drove more than 100,000 Haitians into exile. The wave of military repression that ensued after the coup led to the creation and development of a refugee diaspora located in nearby Caribbean nations such as the Dominican Republic, Haiti's closest neighbor, which received about twenty-five to thirty thousand Haitians after the coup. Haitians reluctantly migrated to the Dominican Republic, a country with a history of anti-Haitian sentiments and practice of arbitrary deportation and expulsion of Haitians, typified by the massacre of Haitians at the border in 1937, which I discuss further in chapter 5. In June 1991, just a few months before the coup, the Dominican government forcibly and inhumanely began to round up and expel Haitians and Haitian Dominicans.[80] Danticat's 1998 historical novel, *The Farming of Bones,* which recalls the 1937 Haitian massacre of Haitians on sugarcane plantations near the border, is a reminder of the fraught relationship between Haiti and the Dominican Republic prolonged by active state-sanctioned and state-condoned discrimination against Haitians and Haitian descendants in the Dominican Republic throughout the twentieth century. The coup also created an internally displaced population of 300,000.[81]

There was a large-scale exodus of boat people heading to the United States after Aristide was overthrown. In 1991 alone, sixty-seven thousand Haitians were intercepted on the coast of Florida.[82] By November of that year, the United States sought the support of other nations such as Belize, Venezuela, and Honduras to house Haitian refugees.[83] But this massive emigration into the United States did not subside and was met with George H. W. Bush's forcible expatriation of Haitian refugees, which was adopted by the Clinton administration in 1993 after Clinton had promised Haitians refuge during his campaign for the presidency.[84] During this time, Haitians were indeed in need of refuge. The Front pour l'avancement et le progrès Haïtien (FRAPH) was organized by Emmanuel "Toto" Constant to brutalize, torture, and kill Aristide supporters. The death toll reached five thousand by 1994. Danticat evokes this historical moment subtly in *The Dew Breaker* through the mention of the "Wanted for Crimes Against the Haitian People" flyers printed and circulated by a community group in the story "The Book of Miracles" and more directly in *Create Dangerously* through Danticat's recall of the story of Alèrte Belance, who was kidnapped and tortured by FRAPH but survived to tell her story.

Jana Braziel notes that US policies toward Haitian refugees under the Carter, Reagan, Bush, and Clinton administrations were shaped by racist attitudes against Haitians. Their status as "liminal citizens" raised questions about Haitian citizenship and the Haitian nation-state as well as immigration laws and border control policies in the United States.[85] While in the 1950s and 1960s racial tensions and ethnic politics in the United States encouraged Haitians to maintain their ethnic status and resist the African American label,[86] racial discrimination against Haitian boat people in the 1980s and 1990s created alliances between Haitian Americans and African Americans. The personal protest of African American dancer and anthropologist Katherine Dunham against deportation of Haitians is a most notable manifestation of this alliance at an individual level: in February 1992, Dunham began a forty-seven-day fast at the age of eighty-two to protest deportation of Haitian refugees.[87] At a collective organizational level, civil rights activists in association with organizations such as the NAACP, the Congressional Black Caucus, and human rights organizations collaborated to contest discriminatory programs of deportation that favored Cuban refugees over Haitian refugees. These coalitions with African Americans would later resurface around the time of intense police brutality against black immigrants in New York City typified by the Abner Louima case in 1997 and the murder of Patrick Dorismond in 2000.[88] Danticat uses these stories as historical backdrop in *The Dew Breaker;* they are echoed by voices on radio stations, voices that are heard by diasporic characters whose lives navigate between two countries, Haiti and the United States.

Aristide's Diaspora, the Tenth Department, and Diasporic Political Consciousness

On December 7, 1995, a year after the publication of her first novel, *Breath, Eyes, Memory,* Edwidge Danticat presented a lecture at the Inter-American Development Bank (IDB). Entitled "Haiti: A Bicultural Experience," the talk was part of the IDB Cultural Center's lecture series.[89] Danticat divided her talk into four subsections that frame her understanding of biculturalism and her own process of identity formation and transformation in the United States. In the first section, "AHA," Danticat discusses her discovery of a new label, African Haitian American, to call herself, through an encounter with a young man at a bookstore in Miami. In the second section, titled "1981," referring to the year she moved to the United States, Danticat offers an autobiographical sketch of her first experiences in the United States, wherein the social imaginary of Americans included discriminatory and xenophobic images of Haitians as disease-infected aliens. Danticat refers back to the previous section in a relational manner to raise questions about "how we label ourselves and who labels us."[90] She then transitions to the third section, "Creole and Memory," to show that the labels, whether self-imposed or imposed by others, do not cover the myriad identities and multiplicity of people of the African diaspora in general and that of the Caribbean in particular. In the last section, "Diaspora," Danticat defines and embraces the term *diaspora* as a more apt label of inclusiveness and expansiveness to comprehend not only Haitian and Caribbean communities in New York but also the complexity and unbounded contours of her individual identity and place of belonging as part of a collective. Danticat states, "Haiti has nine geographical departments that are actual physical sites. The tenth department is the diaspora of Haiti all over the world. It is not concrete land. It is not a specific state or place, but an idea and an ideal to which we can belong, where we can still be outside and still be a part of the country. When you think about it that is an enormous form of 'inclusiveness' for those of us who live outside of Haiti, in whatever country of the world we are now in."[91] Expanding her definition, Danticat insists on the role of the imagination in the individual and collective perception of, and identification with, the Haitian diaspora and its spatial, communitarian, and spiritual dynamics. She shares stories of her encounters with family members, neighbors, and strangers, describing the various ways Haitians in the diaspora maintain a sense of being Haitian while redefining their identities and understanding of home in the United States.

Certainly, the growth of the diaspora in the 1990s and the political circumstances and obstacles in Haiti presented new sets of concerns and perspectives that pointed to the social and political implications, transformations, and force of Haitians living abroad. While Henry Namphy's administration saw the diaspora as an external foreign force in the late 1980s, Jean-Bertrand Aristide's administration saw the diaspora as an extension of Haiti's nation-state territory in the 1990s. Recognizing their importance to the development of the Haitian nation, Aristide first referred to Haitians living abroad as the "dixième département" (tenth department), an extension of the Haitian nation's nine departments at the time, during a campaign planning session in 1990.[92] He later christened Haitians in the diaspora as the "tenth department" under his presidency.[93] Aristide's public recognition of the diaspora encouraged the development of hometown associations in Haiti and renewed investment in Haiti.[94] But just a few months into his presidency, in September 1991, Aristide was ousted by a military coup. An entire government was sent into exile in Washington, DC, where Aristide mobilized Haitians in the diaspora in ways that turned the Haitian diaspora into a sociopolitical force.

With the support of the Haitian diaspora, African Americans and human rights activists placing pressure on the US government under the presidency of Bill Clinton to intervene and convince Lieutenant General Raoul Cédras to relinquish power, Aristide returned to Haiti in October 1994 to complete his term. Aristide's return coincided with Danticat's first return to Haiti, at the age of twenty-five, and the release of her first book, *Breath, Eyes, Memory.*[95] In 1995, MHAVE, Ministère des Haïtiens vivant à l'étranger (Ministry of Haitians Living Abroad), was created to facilitate exchange and reintegrate Haitians in the development of the

Haitian nation. Under Aristide's administration the ministry "sought to welcome Haitian immigrants who travel as tourists, as investors in Haitian economy, or as aspirant settlers or retirees in Haiti."[96] While Aristide made the diaspora an integral part of the Haitian nation-state and its planning for economic and political development, he was unfortunately unable to pass proposed legislation to officially incorporate the diaspora into the political process. When Aristide's term ended in 1996, his prime minister, René Préval, was elected to serve as president from February 7, 1996, to 2001. He became the second democratically elected president in Haiti and, in 2001, the first president to leave office as a result of regular expiration of his term. When Préval was elected president in 1996, the ministry was retained but transformed. Paul Dejean, who became Préval's MHAVE minister, embraced the term *diaspora* to demarcate institutional, organizational, and policy differences between the tenth department and the ministry and, consequently, differences between Aristide's presidency and Préval's government.[97] These differences tend to both reiterate and blur the insider/outsider paradigm between Haitians living in Haiti and those living abroad. The complexities behind these differences have a lot to do with the emergence of the "tenth department" as a term turned into political rhetoric connected to a particular movement now present in the collective social consciousness of the diaspora. Nonetheless, efforts of both the tenth department and the Ministry of Haitians Living Abroad to incorporate Haitians abroad into the national and political development of Haiti put into question the political rhetoric that defined the diaspora as enemies and traitors under Duvalier. Here diaspora is seen as more politically viable than exile. It is this political redefinition of the collective identity of Haitians living abroad that has made the concept of diaspora a popular and recognizable term to Haitians living in Haiti and abroad.

During this period, and as a result of the stalemate in Haitian politics, the Haitian diaspora also developed a new political consciousness that would be immersed in American politics and centered on the needs of the diaspora in the United States.[98] Responding to these transformations, Danticat returns to the meaning of "dyaspora" in 2001 with the publication of *The Butterfly's Way: Voices from the Haiti Dyaspora in the United States.* Edited by Danticat, this anthology is a compilation of thirty-three contributions, including essays, poetry, stories, and letters written by Haitian Americans of different generations and backgrounds who "travel between many worlds." In her introduction to the anthology, Danticat reflects on the "multilayered meaning of the word" while paying homage to Haitian journalist Jean Dominique, who was assassinated on

April 3, 2000.[99] Maintaining the idea of "inclusiveness," Danticat redefines diaspora as "a floating homeland, an ideological one, which joined all Haitians living in the diaspora."[100]

Haitian Diaspora in the Twenty-First Century

The election of George W. Bush in 2000 was seen as a turning point in US immigration policy as the United States seemed poised for reform. But the September 2001 terrorist attacks derailed the promises and efforts made by the Clinton and George W. Bush administrations to loosen restrictive provisions of the 1996 Illegal Immigration Reform and Immigration Responsibility Act. Danticat's political consciousness would also evolve during this period along with her activism, which includes speaking out in favor of immigrant rights as a board member of the National Coalition of Haitian Rights and protesting the deportation of Haitians demonstrating against New York police brutality.[101]

The 9/11 events, along with the decline of the US economy, led to public and policy conflation of terrorism and immigration and subsequently to a resurgence of xenophobia, particularly toward the Muslim immigrant community.[102] As Danticat asserts, Haitians, like most immigrants, have become part of a post-9/11 suspect community: "We are indeed, all of us, suspects. However, as immigrants, we live the double threat of being both possible victims and suspects, often with deadly consequences."[103] It is within this new post-9/11 context that Danticat published *The Dew Breaker*. Breaking the binary between victim and perpetrator, Danticat's eponymous dew breaker is both victim and perpetrator. A number of articles by Danticat about both documented and undocumented immigrants would follow, among them the 2006 piece "Out of the Shadows," wherein Danticat tells the story of her cousin Laris, who she says had been "too poor and too frightened to seek medical care for because he'd come to Miami by boat and was undocumented."[104]

The publication of *The Dew Breaker* coincided with the continued implosion of political and economic instability in Haiti. Democracy was once again thwarted in Haiti when the country was faced with another successful coup against Aristide on February 29, 2004. The coup was the justification for the establishment of the United Nations Stabilization Mission in Haiti (MINUSTAH), the UN peacekeeping operation led by Brazilian soldiers. But Haitians in Haiti and the diaspora viewed the creation of MINUSTAH as a second US occupation. MINUSTAH showed its force when it raided Cité Soleil, a slum located near Port-au-Prince, in 2005, and again in 2007 for gang activity; the raid resulted in numerous civilian casualties. The United Nations has declared the area the most dangerous place in the world, and it has been incorporated into cinematic images of global slums. In an op-ed piece published in 2004 entitled "A Very Haitian Story," Danticat pointed to these gang activities in Haiti's slums as the impetus for Haitians leaving the country. In the op-ed, she argued that Haitians should be granted temporary protection status while "Haiti tries to recover from the political plagues and environmental disasters suffocating it."[105] These political plagues of the time are examined in Danticat's memoir, *Brother, I'm Dying,* wherein she recounts the story of her uncle's escape from gang members in Bel Air by boarding a plane to Miami on a valid multiple entry visa only to be arrested and taken to Krome Detention Center to die five days later from maltreatment at age eighty-one. In the fifteenth chapter of the memoir, "Beating the Darkness," Danticat, with painstaking effort, recalls the violent encounter between UN soldiers and gang members that put her uncle's family in danger and turned his church into a bullet-ridden compound and, subsequently, a place for gangs to set up residence. Just three months before this unfortunate event, Danticat's father was diagnosed with terminal pulmonary fibrosis, and four months after her uncle's death Danticat gave birth to her firstborn, a daughter whom she named Mira, after her father. In an interview, Danticat stated, "Everything I had ever written was so I could learn to tell this story. This is the most important story of my life."[106] Danticat merges these important events in her life to critique discriminatory immigration policies, a critique that will become more forceful under the Trump administration.

Global Reverberations

Once known as the Pearl of the Antilles and the first black republic in the world, Haiti is now perhaps environmentally the most vulnerable country in the world. Haiti's centuries-old pattern of environmental devastation has taken a turn for the worse. With frequent storms, hurricanes, and numerous fault lines, the country is prone to environmental stresses. In 2008, within thirty days, Haitians faced four hurricanes (Fay, Gustav, Hanna, and Ike) that took many lives, destroyed or damaged homes, and wiped out crops. Because of a lack of forest cover, the country is often pummeled during the rainy season. Deforestation and soil erosion, a consequence of tree cutting for firewood and charcoal, have negatively affected agricultural productivity. As a result, Haitians rioted over food prices in 2008, along with other nations such as Egypt, Bangladesh, and

Burkina Faso suffering similar struggles. The public protests of escalating cost of living and high unemployment led to the resignation of President Préval's prime minister, Jacques-Édouard Alexis. The 7.0 magnitude earthquake that ravaged the city Port-au-Prince on January 12, 2010, marked a new chapter in the history of Haiti's environmental struggles and vulnerability. Since the earthquake, Haitian organizations in the diaspora have shifted focus to rebuilding, infrastructure, and relief. No doubt the earthquake has driven remittances up. In 2011, Jean-Claude Duvalier shocked the world with the announcement of his return to Haiti after a twenty-five-year exile. That same year, Aristide returned after seven years in exile. Haiti also made history that year with the inauguration of Michel Martelly, who was sworn in on May 14, marking the first peaceful transfer of power from an incumbent president to a member of the opposition. In 2012 remittances from the US to Haiti totaled $1.1 billion, 20.6 percent of the country's $7.9 billion GDP. In a post-earthquake Haiti, migrants are now seen more than ever as agents of development in the homeland.[107] Dependency on remittances is not unique to Haiti, as other developing countries rely on financial support from their diaspora. Dual citizenship in Haiti was finally legalized in June 2012 when the 1987 constitution was amended to allow Haitians living outside of the country to own land and run for low-level office. Political instability and environmental disaster continue to thwart development. In October 2014, Hurricane Matthew, a category 4 hurricane, ravaged Haiti, killing many and causing massive damage in the south of the country. The death of President René Préval on March 3, 2017, at age seventy-four was a shock to many. These events have affected not only Haitians in the country but also Haitians in the diaspora. The diasporic political engagement of Haitians within what Laguerre describes as the Haitian diasporic public sphere has been transformed in the twenty-first century. It refigures relations between homeland and host countries and encourages transnational networks and exchanges in ways that put into question traditional notions of nationalism, citizenship, and civic engagement. These realities expose, as Danticat asserts, the "long umbilical cord" the Haitian diaspora has with the homeland.[108]

Global Structures of the Haitian Diaspora

Danticat's imaginative appropriation of specific historical events is a heuristic method of reconfiguring the Haitian nation beyond geopolitical boundaries and organizing the Haitian diaspora through a shared history of global migration and displacement. Danticat's telling and recalling of the history of displacement through the lens of individual voices is about uncovering silenced narratives. Inducing an echo effect, these histories generate narratives that become the creation myths of Danticat's Haitian diaspora and her diasporic subjects; the reinscription of these historical silences is Danticat's defiance against an ahistorical, oversimplified representation of Haitian people. Danticat transmits and translates these silenced and marginalized histories as social and collective memory to a global community of readers with, more likely than not, little to no knowledge of such histories. In particular, the histories of atrocities are excavated and renarrated diasporically to rescale Haitian history so that it is not only made legible but also expands beyond geographical boundaries and nationalist constraints and agendas. Danticat's imaginative remapping and recalling of Haitian history from a diasporic lens is a self-reflexive and relational approach to nation and diaspora that decodes and decenters the traditionally nationally organized Haitian community and its history. Danticat's decoding and decentering of Haitian national history through the diasporic subject, however, calls not for a disembedding from specific places and histories but for a rescaling and expansion of them in ways that compel socioterritorial reconfiguration of local and national spaces and histories in global contexts.[109] In this manner, nation and diaspora cannot be presented as disparate spaces, but can only be seen as dialogically linked and intertwined elements of a totality marked by multifaceted global histories of migration and displacement.

2 Echo Chamber
in *Create Dangerously*

Maybe I'm just an echo-chamber. It isn't out of modesty that I say
this; I really believe it.

—Marguerite Duras, *Woman to Woman*

Unlike the ideologically driven narratives of political commitment,
Danticat's fictions are not about speaking on behalf of the masses,
but attempt to establish a space where the voices of the disempowered
victims and their persecutors are allowed to speak.

—Michael Dash, "Danticat and Her Haitian Precursors"

I would like us to move beyond these tropes of speaking to or for, and
of being only between two worlds. We are at the same time speaking
to no one and everyone.

—Edwidge Danticat, interview with Garnet Cadogan

THE ECHO chamber, as it is more generally understood in our
contemporary Western imagination, emerges as assent, affirmation, con-
firmation, and concert of shared convictions. Media discourse currently
uses the metaphor of echo chamber to signal an enclosed univocal system
that magnifies the voices and repeated ideas of like-minded people and
insulates them from alternative perspectives.[1] In *Create Dangerously: The
Immigrant Artist at Work*, Edwidge Danticat, I argue, offers a different
definition of echo chamber, one that is not about an enclosed homogenous
system but about an open-ended system and network of relations for the
diasporic subject, wherein the diaspora is imagined as a heterogeneous
community of voices that is simultaneously whole and fragmented. Danticat evokes the echo chamber metaphor to show the dynamic relation
among nation, diaspora, displaced subjects, and the immigrant writer.
This relation manifests itself in the intimate engagement between the
reader and the writer. Danticat presents diaspora as the collective dialogic
space where the silenced voices of the nation's individual marginalized,

displaced, and disavowed subjects, and their particular histories magnify and reverberate as repeated echoes. The immigrant writer, as echo chamber, has the gift of hearing and listening to these voices, a desire to gather and connect these fragmented voices through intertextual word play, and a responsibility to transcribe and inscribe them for the reader through the practice of recall. In *Create Dangerously*, which includes twelve essays written between roughly 1999 and 2010, Danticat affirms a conscious commitment to magnifying the dispersed, multiple, and diverse voices that make up the Haitian diaspora as compensation for multiple forms of physical, psychic, and literary separations and fragmentations. *Create Dangerously* is a nuanced reflection of silence and censorship in the reading and writing process, one that homes in on not only the impact of being forcibly separated from the oeuvres of writers and artists but also the creative production that emerges from these imposed silences in order to memorialize lives.

Edwidge Danticat published *Create Dangerously* in 2010, the year a 7.0 magnitude earthquake hit Haiti, killing approximately 300,000 people and wreaking havoc in the capital city of Port-au-Prince and surrounding areas. A thoughtful reflection on the relationships among art, exile, the immigrant writer, and the process of reading and writing, *Create Dangerously* begins with an updated version of a Toni Morrison lecture Danticat delivered in 2008, the second in the lecture series commenced in 2006 at Princeton University. Danticat's lecture and its revised published version in *Create Dangerously* are inspired by Albert Camus's 1957 address, the title of which, "Create Dangerously," Danticat borrows. In the address, Camus explains, "To create today is to create dangerously. Any publication is an act, and that act exposes one to the passions of an age that forgives nothing. Hence the question is not to find out if this is or is not prejudicial to art. The question, for all those who cannot live without art and what it signifies, is merely to find out how, among the police forces of so many ideologies (how many churches, what solitude!), the strange liberty of creation is possible."[2] Danticat builds on Camus's reflection on the relationship between art and political engagement in the opening essay by examining artist persecution and censorship under the Duvalier regime in the 1960s. In doing so, she echoes Camus's assertion that art and artists can no longer be divorced from history and social reality. This history of silence and censorship in Haiti is pertinent to understanding Danticat's preoccupation with collecting and connecting various and sometimes seemingly disparate source materials to reconstruct her own life and the lives of others.

The first essay of *Create Dangerously* recalls the story of the execution of Marcel Numa and Louis Drouin on November 12, 1964. Numa and Drouin were two of the thirteen Haitian members of Jeune Haiti, a group of thirteen young Haitians who had returned to Haiti in August of that year to fight in a guerrilla war in hopes of toppling the Duvalier dictatorship. Danticat presents this historical event to set the stage for the narration of her own childhood experiences, the migratory experiences of her parents, and the experiences of a generation of artists. Danticat explains:

> I have always been curious about these young men, Marcel Numa and Louis Drouin, who had left Haiti and were living in Queens and decided to return to Haiti to fight the dictatorship and ended up dead in the last openly state-sponsored public execution in Haiti. For me, and a lot of people I talked to, their deaths signaled a more brutal dictatorship and created a new reality that drove a lot of Haitians away from their homeland. That connection between this very brutal act and the further migrations it inspired has always intrigued me. Even though it happened five years before I was born, I have always felt that it is, in part, why I am here, why my parents and so many other people have left Haiti. That's why it's not only a very tragic story but a type of creation myth for me, in which a whole new generation of Haitian immigration emerged from that act. After the executions, people also tried to react with art, by reading and producing plays or reinterpreting Greek plays. I feel as though a new generation of artists also came out of that and I wanted to highlight some of that in the book.[3]

Danticat uses this particular story of Numa and Drouin as an anchor to reflect on a historical period in Haiti when writers and political activists faced the constant fear of state-condoned execution and its citizens lived under the constant threat of censorship. Danticat links the story to the experience of migration and the creative writing process, both of which are inseparable from the Duvalier dictatorship in Danticat's inscription of Haiti. But Danticat had to reconstruct and retell this story through the assemblage of various sources (photographs, newspaper and magazine articles, films, and books). She rewrites this story as "creation myth" from a diasporic lens to explain significant moments that mark the beginnings of the Haitian diaspora and account for the creative production of Haitians within the country during this period despite the threat of exile and execution to enforce censorship. In Danticat's diasporic imaginary, this particular historical moment is the link that directly or indirectly binds the subjects of Danticat's narrative and grounds Haiti as both the echo that gets silenced and the raw material source of the echo. Danticat constantly engages in symbolic returns to the source in her writing through the practice of recall.

In her review of *Create Dangerously,* Colin Dayan describes the collection as an act of commemoration that "stakes out a place of remembrance."[4] Danticat's "labor" as a writer, Colin argues, is to "remember the dead and bring it back from oblivion."[5] Danticat, Dayan writes, "dares readers to know the unspeakable," the "unwanted and ignored."[6] Indeed, the essays that follow the opening essay continue with stories that honor the lives of individuals, living and dead, who occupy Danticat's diasporic imaginary and shape her consciousness. Danticat offers the stories of family members, such as her aunt Ilyana, a seventy-five-year-old illiterate woman who passed away having never left her ancestral village of Beausejour, and two cousins, one of whom died of AIDS, and another during the earthquake. She also pays homage to important well-known political figures, visual artists, and activists such as Jean Dominque, an agronomist and journalist who was assassinated in 2000; Jean-Michel Basquiat, an American artist of Haitian and Puerto Rican descent who died of a heroin overdose in New York during the 1980s; Hector Hyppolite, a Haitian painter and third-generation vodou priest whose talent as an artist was recognized in the 1940s; Daniel Morel, a contemporary photojournalist who has been documenting Haiti for over twenty years and became famous for his photographs of the earthquake in 2010; and Alèrte Belance, a young woman brutally assaulted by Haitian paramilitary forces who staged a successful coup against President Aristide in 1991 and used violence to silence his supporters thereafter. Danticat's collection is also consumed by references to Haitian writers and their literary texts, among them, Jacques Roumain and his novel *Gouverneurs de la rosée* (*Masters of the Dew*), Felix Morisseau Leroy and his poem "Tourist," Marie Chauvet and her trilogy *Amour, colère et folie* (*Love, Anger, Madness*), and Jan J. Dominique and her memoir, *Mémoire d'une amnésique.* Other intertextual references are also made to non-Haitian writers, such as Cuban author Alejo Carpentier and his work *Kingdom of This World,* African American writer Toni Morrison and her novel *Song of Solomon,* and French author Jean Genet and his play *Les nègres.* These references evoke multiple historical periods in Haiti's history and literary crossings. Later chapters expand Danticat's historical framing of Haiti beyond the Duvalier period to ground these literary crossings not only in space but in time. One chapter offers an overview of Haiti's two-hundred-year history as an independent nation and its fraught relationship with the United States, while another chapter presents Haiti as the double of the United States in an astute reflection on the plight of immigrants and disenfranchised communities in the United States that can only be read as "the other America" in the wake of Hurricane Katrina. Danticat's *Create Dangerously,* in its dialogic structure, is itself an echo of Camus's rejection of monologic art. In her collection, Danticat shows that the art of writing involves the gathering of fragments or components of various previous texts that come into dialogue to form new diasporic narratives.

The collection further exposes Danticat's conscious and self-reflexive awareness of her own need to inscribe and reinscribe the stories she hears through conversations, interactions, and exchanges with individuals who make up the Haitian community in Haiti and in the diaspora. The individuals and their stories collectively become the muse that molds Danticat's diasporic imaginary and informs her diasporic consciousness. I argue that if Danticat, as both immigrant and writer, offers herself as an echo chamber, then the voices she gathers are Echo-like subjects who represent myriad and diverse diasporic stories of displacement that are also reverberations of not only the nation's silenced and suppressed individual stories and collective histories but its history of censorship. The Haitian immigrant writer finds creative acts of resistance and narratives strategies to counter the threat of silence and proliferate voices to form a powerful chorus.

The Echo Chamber of Duras and Barthes

The collection ends with a final chapter entitled "Our Guernica," a response to the January 12 earthquake, wherein Danticat also shares the individual life and death of her cousin Maxius (along with his son Nozial) and attempts to narrate the collective loss of thousands who died that day. In the essay, after describing Haiti as both slippery and sacred ground, Danticat writes, "Maybe that was my purpose, then, as an immigrant and a writer—to be an echo chamber, gathering and then replaying voices from both the distant and the local devastation" (159). Certainly, Danticat is not the first writer to use the imagery of echo chamber to describe the writing process and the responsibility to speak on behalf of others. In her fifth interview with Xavière Gauthier in 1973, Marguerite Duras ends the conversation by describing the process of writing and making film as one that involves hearing a community of voices. As shown in the epigraph to the present chapter, Duras describes this consciousness of voices as an echo chamber, the space of hearing and listening that takes place on the stage and on the screen. Much earlier in the interview she presents the idea of the antechamber as clear consciousness, where no sound exists.[7] This for Duras is the dark room, the other space of reading and writing that takes place offstage, offscreen. A French novelist, playwright, and experimental filmmaker whose French parents emigrated to Vietnam, where the writer was born, Duras is well known for her experimental use of the voice-over technique in film and her inscription of the feminine voice.[8] Born Marguerite Donnadieu, Duras was interested in both the metaphoricity and the materiality of voice. As Mary Noonan asserts, she created "theatre that put voiced words in the spotlight."[9] But the theater also represented the empty space of nonrepresentation, the space consumed by silence and nonverbal sounds. Writing, for Duras, also involves the process of listening to the silence as the sound of primary loss and the transmuting of sounds into texts.

The allusion to Duras in Danticat's collection of essays is evoked at the beginning of the essay "Create Dangerously." Describing the execution of Numa and Drouin, Danticat writes, "Time is slightly compressed on the copy of the film I have and in some places the images skip. There is no sound" (3). The link is also made in Danticat's discussion of plays that were read and staged in Haiti during the dictatorship (98). Thus, very early on in the collection, Danticat, as echo chamber, becomes the disembodied voice and narrator who inscribes images and sounds that are not only representable and locatable but also unknowable and silent. Danticat is describing to the reader the cinematic scene, a scene that inspires Danticat to fill in the gaps and give sound to the silences. If Danticat's text interpolates Duras here, it was not done intentionally by the author. When I asked about this intertextual reference to Duras in my interview with her, Danticat responded, in part, "Duras's writing is extremely evocative. She is a kind of distant model."

Danticat's work, much like that of Duras, explores the omnipresence of voice. But Danticat's own voice-over narrative technique is not an authoritative loud "voice of god" but a small voice that nonetheless offers spiritual guidance and wisdom. In an interview with Garnet Cadogan, Danticat explained,

> Again, not to sound too mysterious, but there is so much happening when I am writing that I don't quite understand. In many ways this is linked to the fact that your subconscious is doing most of the work when you're in the middle of any creative act. Yet sometimes, on good days when the writing is going well, you feel like there is someone on your shoulder whispering things in your ear that you are just transcribing. You're a vessel. You don't even notice time going by. The words just flow. On those days, some people say that the muse has been

by. I like to say that my ancestors have been by, sharing with me some of what they have learned over several lifetimes, because there is no way I can individually know what everyone in my bloodline has known together, collectively.[10]

Like Duras, Danticat communicates with voices that mysteriously come to her. The text creates ties of affiliation with Duras by recalling and reworking the echo chamber metaphor to specify the particular challenges and responsibilities of the immigrant writer in the twenty-first century. In doing so she centralizes the power of both the speaking subject and the listening subject in the writing process. At the same time she stresses the reading of and listening to silence as part of the immigrant writer's practice of writing.

The recall and appropriation of the echo chamber metaphor evokes not only the practice of listening but also the practice of intertextuality. *Create Dangerously*, in its intertextual mapping of literary influences, also suggests the work of French literary critique Roland Barthes and his definition of the literary text as echo chamber. Barthes writes, "In relation to the systems which surround him, what is he? Say an echo chamber: he reproduces the thoughts badly, he follows the words; he pays his visits, i.e., his respects, to vocabularies, he invokes notions, he rehearses them under a name; he makes use of this name as of an emblem (thereby practicing a kind of philosophical ideography) and this emblem dispenses him from following to its conclusion the system of which it is the signifier (which simply makes him a sign)."[11] For Barthes, whom Danticat evokes and quotes in her discussion of Dany Laferrière's definition of a writer, the echo chamber, as a product of the totality of language and its relations, gives sound to silences within a text through intertextuality. The text for Barthes is "woven entirely with citations, references, echoes, cultural languages, antecedents or contemporary, which cut across it through and through in a vast stereophony."[12] Echo chamber, as stereophony, involves the pleasure and practice of "writing out loud," producing "vocal writing"[13] and the "grain of voice."[14] In *The Pleasure of the Text*, Barthes explains, "Text means tissue; but whereas hitherto we have always taken this tissue as a product, a ready-made veil, behind which lies more or less hidden meaning (truth), we are now emphasizing, in the tissue, the generative idea that text is made, is worked out in a perpetual interweaving; lost in this tissue—this texture—the subject unmakes himself, like a spider dissolving in the constructive secretions of its web."[15] Interestingly, this notion of interweaving echoes Danticat's description of writing as an activity much like "braiding hair" in "Women like Us," the epilogue to her collection of short stories, *Krik, Krak?*, a collection that relies on the pattern of storytelling and conjures African folkloric figures like the trickster spider Anansi. The quote from Barthes that Danticat uses, "A text's unity lies not in its origin, but its destination" is also significant, as it points to the very dialogical and polyphonic nature of *Create Dangerously*, Danticat's insistence on the role of readers in the writing process and her reconfiguration of the question of origin as "creation myth." In his seminal 1967 essay, "The Death of the Author," Barthes writes,

> Thus is revealed the total existence of writing: a text is made of multiple writings, drawn from many cultures and entering into mutual relations of dialogue, parody, contestation, but there is one place where this multiplicity is focused and that place is the reader, not as was hitherto said, the author. The reader is the space on which all the quotations that make up a writing are inscribed without any of them being lost; a text's unity lies not in its origin, but its destination. Yet this destination cannot any longer be personal: The reader is without history, biography, psychology; he is simply that someone who holds together in a single field all the traces by which the written text is constituted.[16]

But Barthes's call for the death of the author in order to privilege the reader is not one that Danticat affirms. It is not echoed in *Create Dangerously*. For Danticat, it is the relation between the reader and the writer in historically specific contexts that gives weight to the echo chamber metaphor. Authors are readers, and readers become authors. And this exchange forms the network that creates the plurality of texts and leads to an "explosion" and "dissemination."[17] This plurality includes the recognition and visibility of the author, not as original creator but as a principle actor in the writing process. In this manner Danticat's sense of the author is more like the "author function" defined by Michel Foucault in his 1969 essay "What Is an Author?" Danticat is not shy in naming all the authors that influence her work. She provides her readers with not only the general reference but also the historical, personal, and ideological and discursive contexts that centralize the writing subject. Danticat even engages with and cites her own work in *Create Dangerously*, as evident in her insertion and discussion of the letter that became the afterword to *Breath, Eyes, Memory* in her essay "Walk Straight." But she does so in a way that demystifies the image of the author away from the traditional notion of author as original creator and genius of the text. For Danticat, there is no anxiety of influence.[18] Rather, influence is embraced and becomes a necessary part of the act of creation and re-creation.

Creation Myths

In *Create Dangerously,* Danticat offers a relational approach to exile literature and diaspora literature that necessitates constant literary returns,
revisions, and intertextual exchanges. Danticat is mindful of the cross-
generational bond of writers of the twentieth century. What all writers
share in common is the desire to tell a story in spite of, and perhaps as a
result of, separation and displacement. What distinguish these writers are
generational circumstances and material conditions of displacement. Danticat writes, "We the storytellers of the world, ought to be more grateful
than most that banishment, rather than execution, was chosen for Adam
and Eve, for had they been executed, there would never have been another
story told, no stories to pass on" (6). Danticat is fascinated by the creative
responses of Haitian writers to the executions during this period and the
many stories that, nonetheless, have been lost as a result. Her writing is
always an attempt to retrieve a lost story and pass it on to her readers.
The book itself becomes a part of this continuum of stories that need to
be excavated and revived so that they too may be passed down to new
generations of Haitians living in the diaspora who are further separated
from these stories by the experience of migration and must reclaim and
revise them to understand the emergence of new subjectivities. This is
pertinent to understanding the productive contradictions of continuity
and discontinuity, rupture and connection, wholeness and fragmentation
that form Danticat's diasporic consciousness.

Danticat admits that the execution of Numa and Drouin is one of
what she defines as the "creation myths" that haunts her own writing.
It is a creation myth that allows Danticat to understand the world of
diaspora as the experience of violence, alienation, separation, mortal-
ity, and human fallibility. Although the 1964 execution occurred five
years before Danticat was born, the event, she says, "feels present, even
urgent" (7). The threat of death is not physical but psychological and
has serious implications. She therefore presents the story of the execution
to the reader, describing the video of the execution to new generations.
Danticat's readers are pulled into Danticat's experience while at the same
time recognizing the privileges they have as members of the diaspora and
as readers.

Danticat explains that not reading and writing under the Duvalier dictatorship was not about lack of creative expressions but about survival.
Danticat writes, "I used to fear their reading my books, worried about
disappointing them. My stories do not hold a candle to having lived under

dictatorship for most of your adult life, to having our neighbors disappear and not being able to acknowledge it, to being forced to act as though these neighbors had never existed at all. Reading and perhaps ultimately writing, is nothing like living in a place and time where two very young men are killed in a way that is treated like entertainment" (12). She states that while no one in the family witnessed the execution, they talked about it incessantly: "When I first started returning as a public person, as an 'author,' to Haiti, a place where people trace your failures and successes along family lines, I was often asked if there were any writers in my family. If there were, I do not know. But another thing that has always haunted and obsessed me is trying to write the things that have always haunted and obsessed those who came before me" (13). Writers are not the only ones haunted and threatened by these stories. Everyday individuals were affected, including individuals of Danticat's generation. In Danticat's diasporic consciousness this results in a sense of responsibility. Thus Danticat rewrites the threat of silence and offers a new reading of literary "work" for immigrant writers of her generation. The dangerous nature of the "work," albeit under different historical circumstances, and the very awareness of these circumstances allow for a natural alliance between immigrants, artists, and readers:

> The immigrant artist shares with all other artists the desire to interpret and possibly remake his or her own world. So though we may not be creating as dangerously as our forebears—though we are not risking torture, beatings, execution, though exile does not threaten us into perpetual silence—still, while we are at work bodies are littering the streets somewhere. People are buried under rubble somewhere. Mass graves are being dug somewhere. Survivors are living in makeshift tent cities and refugee camps somewhere, shielding their heads from rain, closing their eyes, covering their ears, to shut out the sounds of military "aid" helicopters. And still, many are reading, writing, quietly, quietly. (18)

The work is redefined to account for different historical circumstances and new threats to artistic freedom in the twenty-first century. In *Create Dangerously,* Danticat explains the urgent task of memorializing individual lives, asserting, "In the face of both external and internal destruction, we are still trying to create as dangerously as they, as though each piece of art were a stand-in for a life, a soul, a future" (20). All emigrant writers compensate for experience of separation and loss through creative defiance to a directive. All emigrant writings are acts of survival under "dangerous" circumstances that threaten the writers' lives, and the lives of those who came before them, into silence.

Pan's Echo and Alèrte's Dismemberment

Though Danticat is not the first writer to use the metaphor of the echo chamber, she may very well be the first writer to conjure it to pronounce a nuanced and dynamic relationship between the nation and its diaspora in the era of globalization and to figure diasporic subjects and their relationship to homeland and questions of silence and fragmentation in ways that induce the echo trope in the diasporic imaginary. It is now quite common for writers and scholars to use the disembodied voice of Echo and her encounter with Narcissus in the Ovidian story of Echo and Narcissus in *Metamorphoses*[19] to elaborate on the relationship between voice and agency, the idea of linguistic captivity and sense of double displacement in women's lives. Ovid tells the story of Echo, the nymph of woods and mountains who is described as having the gift to weave tales and capture the attention of others with her oratory abilities. In the story, the goddess Juno punishes Echo for using this gift to distract the goddess from noticing the adulterous activities of her husband, Jupiter. As punishment, Echo is deprived of initiating speech; she can only repeat the last words she hears.[20] When Echo meets the beautiful Narcissus while roaming the countryside, she falls in love. But Narcissus, in refusing the love of others, becomes enamored by his own reflection. Narcissus dies of grief, his body disappears, and a flower (narcissus) grows in its place. Suffering from unrequited love, Echo, on the other hand, withers away to bones and turns into stone. All that is left is her voice: "Now only voice / is left of her, on wooded mountainsides, / unseen by any, although heard by all; / for only the sound that lived in her lives on."[21] Feminists use this story to examine woman's place under the system of patriarchy. Echo embodies the feminine voice, its loss of creative powers, and its fragmentation. She also represents the marginalized female with no origin, no parents, no place of belonging.[22] A tangential character who signifies the repetition of others' ideas, Echo also becomes "the paradigm of women's dependency."[23] She has a tragic relationship with voice: her words are initiated by a man's voice; her own voice is powerless, her speech devoid of meaning. In postcolonial discourse, Echo represents the absence of third world women's individual voices. Gayatri Chakravorty Spivak, for example, asserts that Echo is the subaltern female, a historically muted subject who cannot be heard or read and is dependent on another's discourse. The figuration of Echo, in its "questioning of European universalist superego," is important to "the world wide collectivity of conscientized feminists of color from bourgeois origins or in passive capitalist social relations."[24] This reading is critical to scrutinizing narcissistic individuality and cultural homogeneity in European masculinist and imperialistic discourses and agendas.

There is, however, a less well-known and more violent story of Echo that also highlights the centrality and survival of voice under the system of patriarchal domination. But this is a story of feminized resistance, defiance, and perseverance. It also offers a gendered reading of the story of diaspora as experience of dispersal and displacement that is so fundamental to Danticat's work. This story of Echo is not associated with Narcissus but with the god Pan and can be found in the pastoral poem account of Daphnis and Chloe by the Greek author Longus. Set on the Greek island of Lesbos, this second-century romantic tale of the courtship between young lovers who were both abandoned by their birth parents as babies and raised by shepherds explores the theme of innocence and young love. Pan is one the gods of the countryside and dwells among mountain caves. Any myth that involves the life and circumstances of people in the countryside meshes well with Danticat's works, as they allude to the lived experiences of peasants. But the central figure most important to Danticat here is not the god Pan but Echo. In book 3 of this story by Longus, Daphnis tells Chloe the story of Echo to explain the phenomenon of Echo, of which Chloe appears to be ignorant. Echo's gift is her ability to play every instrument and sing every kind of song (thus the acoustic phenomenon of echo). Pan is both captivated by and jealous of Echo's voice. In this story it is not Narcissus but Pan who desires and seeks Echo's love. Rejected by Echo, Pan, the god of nature and mountain wilds, uses his powers to drive shepherds and goatherds mad; they in turn brutally tear apart Echo's limbs, which are scattered all over the world.[25] Her punishment is literal dismemberment. But Pan does not succeed in silencing Echo. Though physically fragmented, her voice retains the ability to produce music; it is the scattering of her limbs that makes it possible for her voice to be heard everywhere. It is my contention that this version of Echo offers some critical insight into Danticat's evocation of the echo chamber metaphor to explore the relationships among voice, women's lived experiences of resistance and their silenced histories, and Danticat's preoccupation with mutilated limbs. Danticat's *Create Dangerously* is an homage to the power, survival, and persistence of individual voice and its relationship to a collective history of state-sanctioned violence. Nowhere is this more evident than in Alèrte Belance's story, the only story in the collection that begins and ends with the subject's spoken voice.

In the chapter "I Speak Out" Danticat focuses on the story of Alèrte, who was abducted on October 16, 1993, from her home in Haiti and taken

to the killing fields of Titanyen by members of the Front pour l'avancement et le progrès Haïtien.[26] The thirty-three-year-old wife and mother of
three children was left for dead.[27] In "I Speak Out," Danticat recalls an
interview conducted at Alèrte's home in a housing project in Newark, New
Jersey, for a documentary entitled *Courage and Pain* produced by Haitian
American filmmaker and screenwriter Patricia Benoit. The documentary
tells the story of a dozen Haitian torture survivors who were nearly executed. The narrative of "I Speak Out" does not begin with Danticat's own
voice but with a quote from the interview, much like a voice-over inserted
into the text. The quote ends with Alèrte talking directly into the text to
a reader/audience: "Hear my story, what I have experienced" (73). It then
shifts to a narrative that acknowledges collective voices, multiple sources
(oral, textual, visual) and different points of view from multiple characters
with different languages who contribute to the telling of the story. They
include Alèrte's husband, her children, the camera, the nonspeaking Creole
producers, and the director. As Alèrte talks, the voices of her girls playing
nearby, an image of innocence that counters the striking violence of Alèrte's
story, are heard. When Alèrte stops talking, her husband picks up the
narrative and tells parts of the story that involve him as the initial target
of FRAPH. Alèrte's son, who is described as a shy little boy, also speaks
of seeing his mother in the hospital for the first time. Relying not just on
Alèrte's memory but also the memory of others, Danticat presents the recall
of the horrific event dialogically. This multivocal, multilingual, multiframe
perspective in the text parallels the structure of the documentary that is
being created. As Danticat asserts, in the undistributed documentary, "All
tell different versions of the same story, of being beaten, macheted, shot,
and tortured, and of nearly dying in a country they loved but where they
could no longer live" (84). Alèrte represents a broader collective story of
bodily violation and dismemberment that Danticat uses as source material
to tell a diasporic story of dispersal, symbolic fragmentation, and loss of
wholeness. But in the dialogic and diasporic recall of Alèrte's story, Danticat creates a textual site of what Toni Morrison calls "re-memory," the
repeated recall of a collective forgotten or repressed memory that bears on
the present moment.[28]

   Danticat's refiguration of the dismemberment of Haitian citizens' bodies in the diasporic imaginary through the individual story of Alèrte both
echoes and displaces the traditional narrative of the violated whole (male)
body as primal site of violence and trauma in the national imaginary.
Certainly the most prominent and haunting figure of dismemberment in
Haiti's national imaginary is Jean-Jacques Dessalines, founding father of

Haiti whose assassination and desecration of whose corpse through dismemberment on October 17, 1806, represent a site of traumatic wound in the history of Haiti's formation into nationhood. Danticat does not mention Dessalines in the telling of Alèrte's story, but the similarity in dates of dismemberment of Alèrte (October 16) and Dessalines (October 17) is uncanny. More convincingly, the comparison of Alèrte's body to "chopped meat they sell at the market" by Alèrte's husband is a textual allusion to Dessalines. Interestingly, Alèrte's son later echoes parts of his father's words. The phrase and its repetition are textual moments of re-memory. The phrase is also an instance of historical double recall: it simultaneously evokes Dessalines and the less well-known revolutionary historical figure of Dédée Bazile, known as Défilée-La-Folle, the "madwoman" who is believed to have gathered and reassembled Dessalines's body parts for a proper burial after the massacre at Pont Rouge.

Scholars such as Joan Dayan and Jana Evans Braziel point to the coupling of Dessalines and Défilée in the Haitian imaginary. Citing the important work of Dayan, Braziel explains, "As a couple, Défilée and Dessalines manifest an interlocking, corporeal mythos of the founding of the Haitian Republic."[29] Danticat's focus on the mutilated female body through Alèrte's story here offers the reader an opportunity to recalibrate an understanding of the wounded citizen body within the body politic of the nation-state broadly and Haiti's male-centered revolutionary history specifically. Danticat also reveals how these histories are echoed in diasporic and transnational spaces and reconfigured in diasporic imaginaries explicitly and implicitly. As Braziel asserts, "Défilée persists across national borders, moves within new transnational sites, and lives on in diasporic imaginaries."[30] Focusing on Danticat's story collection *Krik? Krak!*, Braziel contends, "Danticat relies on the legendary and revolutionary figure of Défilée as an ancestral and maternal forebear for Haitian women, both those in Haiti and in diaspora."[31] Making a clever connection between the process of "re-membering" and the act of dismemberment, Braziel asserts, "By re-membering Défilée, Danticat stitches together—across the spaces of diasporic distance and the times of historical past to a reembodied presence—an ancestral line for femmes d'Ayiti beginning with Dédée Bazile and extending lòt bò dlo (the other side of the waters) to her diasporic daughters. Restoring broken genealogical lines requires an act of embodied memory and willed creation."[32] Certainly, Danticat symbolically re-members fragments of Haiti's history through historical re-visioning of its heroic maternal figures. But more than re-visioning, Danticat's echoing of women's silenced history through the act of gathering, collecting, reassembling, and retelling in *Create Dangerously* requires a particular attention to the relationship between the Echo trope and figures of dismemberment, one that points simultaneously to women's embodiment and disembodiment in androcentric histories.

In Danticat's diasporic imaginary, Alèrte is a modern Echo, a story of dismemberment and survival, of the power of voice. What I am suggesting is that in Danticat's diasporic imaginary, diaspora encompasses echo subjects who imagine and narrate the nation's silenced histories differently. Alèrte, as echo subject, also represents the silencing of Haitian women and the suppression of their gift as storytellers by the nation-state in its privileging of male paradigms and narratives of subjectivity and authority. Like Défilée-La-Folle, Danticat symbolically gathers the different parts of Alèrte (as individual, mother, daughter, and wife) and reassembles the totality of not only her voice but her being. From Danticat's diasporic lens, the citizen who leaves the nation space after having been severed in parts and disfigured like a wounded soldier is also a powerful metaphor of diasporic fragmentation and loss of wholeness. But the figure of the dismembered and displaced woman who tells her own story in her own voice turns both the national and diasporic narrative of fragmentation on its head, highlighting the feminized space of dispersion and the significant role of the (female) body and its voice in the process of recalling and re-membering unspeakable acts of state-sanctioned violence condoned in the name of the nation. In both instances, severed and missing limbs trigger re-memory.

When Alèrte speaks of her experience, she describes the mutilation of not only her body but also her tongue: "They sliced me into pieces with machete strokes. They cut my tongue and my mouth: my gums, plates, tooth and jaw on my right side. They cut my face open, my temple and cheek totally open. They cut my eye open. They cut my ear open. They cut my body, my whole shoulder and neck and back slashed with machete blows. They cut off my right arm. They slashed my left arm totally and cut off the ends of all the fingers of my left hand. Also, they slashed my whole head up with machete blows" (75–76). Alèrte's ability to tell her story in a clear manner, despite her tongue being cut in two, astonishes everyone. Recognizing Alèrte's spirited defiance (84), Danticat describes her act of telling as "courageous" (78). Danticat writes, "She not only suffered, however, but against all odds she also survived and thrived. And her testimony was a great gift to many others who were still trying to stay alive, and to the more than eight thousand others who died under the junta's rule" (85). It is clear that Danticat recalls Alèrte's own voice to retell this story as testimony of survival, resistance, and defiance against all odds. But there is another reason for the recall: Alèrte's voice was silenced by the spectacle of her mutilated body in the name of ideology or nationalist idealization. For example, when Danticat brings up Alèrte's presence on *The Phil Donahue Show,* where Danticat herself was a member of the audience, she notes, "Her story was told more visually than in her own voice" (83). Danticat relies on Alèrte's own voice and supplements her voice with testimonies from her own family to offer a more holistic picture of Alèrte, one that moves beyond her suffering and victimhood to expose her individuality, humanity, and dignity. For Danticat, it is important that Alèrte's body isn't reduced to a site of national trauma and absence for narratives of the nation. In the assemblage of Alèrte's story of survival, Danticat offers an alternative narrative of healing and regeneration that cannot neatly be co-opted.

Female Metaphors, Female Voices, and the Feminine Text

In an interview published in 2003, Danticat states:

> When I was growing up, most of the writers I read were male. I don't think I read a single female writer until I came to the United States. So writing almost felt like it was a forbidden activity. Being poor and being female, it was unheard of to write books. It was a double transgression. Using those [female] metaphors, for me, wasn't a way of saying writing was natural for a female, but almost to impose these "female" metaphors and female-linked activities on what is often taken as male territory. It's saying, as Paule Marshall did in an essay about "kitchen poetry," that yes, there is a poetry in women's daily lives and activities. And that there are parallels between cooking a meal and writing, or quilting and writing, or braiding hair and writing. You don't have to go on a hunt or go to war to be a writer.[33]

Here Danticat paraphrases the words of Paule Marshall, who has been a major inspiration in her writings, particularly *Breath, Eyes, Memory,* and to whom Danticat was drawn during the 1980s at a moment when she was discovering women writers for the first time. Danticat juxtaposes the very personal space of writing for the woman writer at home with the objective voice of the hero writer who constantly leaves the home space, evoking the literature of combat in Haiti. This literary tradition glorifies the heroes of the revolution to promote a rhetoric of national solidarity in ways that exclude women and the significant roles they played in the revolution and the construction of the Haitian nation.

Indeed, the prototypical migratory subject in much Haitian literature during the twentieth century has been male, and inscriptions of migration have been informed through the alienation and marginalization of Haitian women's experiences and voices. Women in traditional Haitian literature exist as peripheral characters. Nineteenth-century Haitian literature, as Régine Latortue makes clear in her dissertation, "The Woman in the Haitian Novel," was profoundly patriotic and nationalistic in content. Latortue points out that the only well-known women writers in nineteenth-century Haitian literature were poets Virginie Sanpeur, the wife of the famous poet Oswald Durand, and Ida Faubert, the daughter of President Salomon.[34] Haitian women's individual and particular identities are undermined by problematic representations of women constructed to uphold a very male-centered understanding of Haitian national identity. Haitian women are represented in Haiti's literary tradition as symbols of oppression and as sexual objects. Danticat's novel *Breath, Eyes, Memory* centers on female characters and the matrilineal family structure to counter such representations and the silencing of Haitian women's voices and stories. In her work, Danticat consciously attempts to evoke and revise Haitian folktales and history from a feminized lens to recognize the very central presence of women and women-centered stories and histories.

However, Haiti's male-centered literary tradition does not mean that Haitian women have not been contributors to this tradition since its birth following Haitian independence in 1804. In fact, as Latortue notes, the only writer who is remembered before 1804 is Anacaona, the Indian queen who was killed in 1597. Although women writers were not visibly present in the nineteenth century, by the mid-twentieth century, they were publishing novels and contributing to what is now recognized as a rich literary tradition. Haitian women writers such as Virgile Valcin, Nadine Magloire, Marie-Thérèse Colimon-Hall, and most famously Marie Vieux Chauvet transformed the contours of Haitian literature during the twentieth century and influenced the novels of more recent Haitian women writers in Haiti and the Haitian diaspora. Virgile Valcin's *Cruelle destinée*, the first novel by a Haitian woman was not published until 1929, during the last few years of the American occupation. Indeed, *Cruelle destinée* deals with the complexities of race, gender, and class during the occupation by developing alienated and victimized Haitian female characters. Another novel, Annie Desroy's *Le joug* (1934) also takes the tragedy of the American occupation as subject to engage the politics of racial, sexual, and national identity. These novels constitute a corpus of what Nadève Ménard defines as the "occupied novel," wherein a major thematic concern is the romantic and sexual relationships between Haitians and foreigners.[35] These early Haitian women novelists began to expose in their fiction the interconnections between the political space of the Haitian nation and the private space of women's bodies and sexuality.

During the Duvalier regime, a period that haunts Danticat's texts, Haitian women writers tackled issues of history, nationality, gender, and class from a female point of view to critique Haiti's political and social circumstances and expose the ways in which Haitian women have been oppressed and rendered invisible. Haitian women writers of this period include Liliane Devieux-Dehoux (*L'amour, oui, la mort, non,* 1976); Nadine Magloire (*Le mal de vivre,* 1968); and Marie Chauvet, whose novels *Fille d'Haiti* (1954), *La danse sur le volcan* (1957), *Fonds des nègres* (1961), *Amour, colère, folie* (1969), and *Les rapaces* (written in the 1970s but published posthumously in 1986 under her maiden name, Marie Vieux) span three decades. *Amour, colère, folie* was infamously banned by Chauvet's family: her husband bought all the copies for fear of the danger it posed to the family. It is recognized as one of the first literary works that dares to criticize openly François Duvalier's regime and the Haitian bourgeoisie. Other works of this period include Marie-Thérèse Colimon-Hall's *Fils des misère* (1974). Colimon-Hall's collection of short stories, *Le chants des sirènes* (1979), explores more succinctly the theme of exile and emigration as consequences of the Duvalier regime. Danticat taps into this literary history as a reservoir of source texts to magnify the voices to Haitian women.

Intertextual Voices and Literary Ancestors

In her essay on Haitian women writers, Marie Denise Sheldon asserts, "The woman writer in Haiti . . . appears a solitary figure, isolated, deprived of literary history per se and a community to sustain her project."[36] In *Create Dangerously,* Danticat explains the difficulty in tracing what she calls the "literary ancestors" that came before her. In their absence, she tries to understand the challenges her "blood ancestors" faced: "Perhaps, just as Alice Walker writes of her own forebears in her essay "In Search of Our Mothers' Gardens," "my blood ancestors—unlike my literary ancestors—were so weather-beaten, terror-stricken, and maimed that they were stifled. As a result, those who somehow managed to create became, in my view, martyrs and saints" (14).

Recognizing the overwhelming economic, political, and social challenges her blood ancestors faced, Danticat considers herself an "accident of literacy": "We think we are people who might not have been able to go to school at all, who might never have learned to read and write. We think we are the children of people who have lived in the shadows for too long. We sometimes even think we are like the ancient Egyptians, whose gods of death demanded documentation of worthiness and acceptance before allowing them entry into the next world" (20). Here, Haitians double as Africans to allude to the primal separation from Africa as motherland. African diasporic subjects found creative ways to survive against the harsh dehumanizing conditions and systems of oppression that aimed at stifling their voices and obliterating their existence. They endured the psychic consequences of the primal separation from Africa and the multiple separations that followed. Danticat finds creative ways to communicate.

In the essay "Walk Straight," Danticat creates a direct intertextual link between *Breath, Eyes, Memory* and *Create Dangerously* to articulate the relationships among ancestry, oral tradition, women-centered spaces, and writing. The title of the essay is a direct intertext to Tante Ilyana's voice in *Breath, Eyes, Memory.* When Sophie visits a "tree-lined ceremony" at the top of the hill in the novel, her aunt Atie observes, "Walk Straight, you are in the presence of family" (149). The essay in *Create Dangerously* describes Danticat's first return to Beausejour, a rural area of Léogâne, where her great-grandparents are buried and where her seventy-five-year-old aunt Ilyana still resides. This is a story of return to the mountains, to the people who have been ignored, the "people without electricity, telephone, doctors, morgues" (23). Danticat shares with her readers the genesis of the afterword in *Breath, Eyes, Memory.* While the readers who are familiar with the afterword know that she wrote it while sitting on her great-grandmother's grave (mentioned in the first line of the acknowledgments), the reader learns that the afterword was inspired by a book of essays titled *Afterwords: Novelists on Their Novels* that Danticat actually had with her on this visit. Danticat's positionality (physical, literary, and literal) is significant here. It allows her not only to blur the divide between fiction and reality but also to bridge the distance between Léogâne and New York, between generations, and between silence and censorship. The movement of the afterword from the addendum to the body of the text in this essay also reveals the significance of the afterword exercise in her development as a writer. She affirms her identity as a novelist at the site of her great-grandmother's grave, the location of ancestors who were illiterate and whose own words were transmitted orally. Having a book with her in Haiti, Danticat represents the generation that transcribes her ancestors' stories so that their deaths will be memorialized not only in stone but in a book. Linking her writing to her grandmother, Danticat also claims the authenticity of her voice, one that emerges from a history of marginalized women who had to tell their stories in creative ways.

In chapter 4, "Daughters of Memory," Danticat offers an honest reflection of the literary influences that marked her own beginnings as both serious reader and writer. She describes the experience of discovering two new shelves of books labeled "Livres Haïtiens" that appeared, sometime after the Duvalier regime had ended, at the main branch of the Brooklyn Public Library she frequented weekly. A significant part of Danticat's search for home is also a search for her literary ancestors to bridge the relationship between reader and writer severed by Duvalier. Consequently, it only makes sense that such a search begins in a public library, a democratic space whose purpose is to preserve archives, disseminate history and cultural memory, and bring readers and writers of all backgrounds and from all over the world together without attention to differences of race, class, and gender. One of the books she checked out is Jacques Roumain's *Gouverneurs de la rosée*. It is through Roumain that Danticat learns the social significance of a work of fiction and its connection to real lives. In "Edwidge Danticat's Top Ten List," where Danticat lists her top ten books, she states:

> I read this book when I was ten years old; it was the first novel in which I recognized people I knew living in circumstances similar to my life and my world. It was also the first time that I realized books could not only help us escape but hold a mirror to our lives, to help us examine a problem and ponder—along with the characters—a possible solution. It was my first engagée or socially engaged novel, one that showed me that the novel could have many roles, that fiction could be used for different purposes without losing its artistic merit. It made me want to write the types of books that could inform and entertain as well as help others live, through a powerful narrative, a heartbreaking, painful, and even redemptive experience.[37]

Danticat confesses that she maintains a silent conversation with Jacques Roumain that publicly manifested itself in *The Dew Breaker* and emerged out of a longing to converse with him face to face. The recognition of the absence of this parental male literary figure is critical to Danticat's writing process. But it is interesting that Danticat chooses to keep this intertextual relationship implicit, as if to assert her departure from the ideologically nationalist intent behind Roumain's work and those of his generation. Roumain's text is not dominant in this intertextual play.

The other book Danticat checked out from among what remained was Jan J. Dominique's *Mémoire d'une amnésique* (*Memoir of an Amnesiac*), a nonlinear account of a young girl growing up under the Duvalier dictatorship and becoming an activist in Montreal. Blending fiction, reality, and memory, Dominique explores the relationships among exile, loss, and memory by focusing on a daughter's separation from her father, whose absence is a result of the oppressive regime. It is in reading Dominique's memoir that Danticat becomes fascinated with the question of memory and the complex psychological impact of the dictatorship on familial relationships, the fine line between love and lovelessness, and the silences that prevent us from being real with our failures and forces us to, as Danticat asserts, cultivate communal and historical amnesia. Danticat also creates a lineage that traces her own writing to Dominique's intertextual relationship with Roumain as a literary parent. It is in feeling the absence of Roumain that Dominique becomes what she herself describes as a "literary orphan" and writes her first novel. Likewise, Dominique's separation from her biological father, the agronomist and journalist Jean Dominique, assassinated at age sixty-nine, led her to write her second novel. Focusing on this idea of the literary orphan, Danticat plays with the dialogue between the biological father and the literal father, using it to complicate once again the definition of kinship and ancestry. Having written about Jean Dominique in a previous chapter in ways that link back directly and implicitly to Roumain, Danticat also reasserts her position as a writer who takes the liberty of blurring the lines between fiction and reality, between history and mythmaking.

In the chapter "Daughters of Memory," Danticat spends quite a bit of time discussing another influence, Marie Vieux Chauvet. A novelist, playwright, poet, and daughter of an exiled senator, Chauvet became a high-profile writer in exile after the publication of her book *Amour, colère, folie* in 1968. Chauvet's second husband, Pierre, a light-skinned Haitian, later convinced the prestigious Parisian publisher Gallimard to cancel distribution of the book for fear of retaliation from the Duvalier regime. He also bought the rights to the novel and stored copies in a warehouse in Port-au-Prince.[38] She was forced into exile in New York, where she married her third husband, a white American. Chauvet died of a cerebral hemorrhage on June 19, 1973, at the age of fifty-seven. The trilogy remained in warehouses for twelve years. Set in 1939, the triptych is recognized as a cornerstone of Haitian literature. Danticat discloses that her own attempts to write short stories that rely on myths and folklore come from her reading of *Amour, colère, folie*. Danticat finds herself in this trilogy, exclaiming, "This is me," (68) while both reading the book and attempting to write her own stories. For example, the daffodils she offers her readers in *Breath, Eyes, Memory* stem from a real story that actually become an invented myth in the novel, what she describes as a fake-lore, only after reading Chauvet's meticulous descriptions of butterflies and owls pregnant with meaning (68). In Chauvet's absence, Danticat's work engages an intertextual conversation with the writer. But Chauvet's death and the acknowledgment of her absence make Danticat recognize herself as a literary orphan. She explains, "Inasmuch as our stories are the bastard children of everything that we have ever experienced and read, my desire to tell some of my stories in a collaged manner, to merge my own narratives with the oral and written narratives of others, begins with my reading of the two books I eagerly checked out from the Livres Haitiens section of the Brooklyn Public Library that day, books that could have been written only by literary orphans to offer to other literary orphans" (62). As Jan J. Dominique did with Roumain, Danticat maintains a conversation with Chauvet, wondering how she would perceive the world today, how she would transcribe, for example, Haiti's catastrophic earthquake. Danticat's self-representation as a literary orphan also reveals her own fear of abandonment and desire to reinvent herself in ways that work through the trauma of separation from family members as a result of migration as well as through the separation from a canon of Haitian women writers as a result of silencing and censorship. She talks about her writing as a collage because, for Danticat, her writing begins with the search for other voices, literary and oral, recognizable and unrecognizable, that came before her. This is Danticat's creative way of coming to subjectivity and expanding our notion of kinship in ways that move beyond biological scripts.

Against Silence: Echo Chamber as Chorus

It is an understatement to say that voices of loss, mourning, and separation have magnified since the earthquake. Danticat generously lends her own voice to raise awareness about Haiti's circumstances. But Danticat has never felt at ease with being "the voice" of a community. She explains, "No one elected me to speak on their behalf either in Haiti or the United States. I'm certainly not going to assign myself that role because it would be presumptuous and arrogant and just plain too much. To express an opinion, I would have to take a survey first. I can add my voice to someone else's. I can help raise other voices. But I can't take on this massive undertaking that you're suggesting. I would fail miserably. I don't have the personality for it or the stamina."[39] As evident in Danticat's collection, the Haitian diaspora encompasses many voices of individuals, a chorus, and Danticat's imagined reading audience. This chorus, in its diversity and critique, is not always supportive: "I can hear now as I write this cries of protest from other Haitians my age (and younger and older, too) shouting from the space above my shoulders, the bleachers above every writer's shoulders where readers cheer or hiss and boo in advance. They are hissing now, that chorus, or a portion of it, decrying this as both a contradiction and a lie. 'I read Haitian writers when I was twelve,' they say, but I must stop and turn to them now and say, I am speaking only for myself" (60). As an immigrant writer and "public author" Danticat must navigate between her individual voice and the collective voices of the Haitian diaspora. Recognizing her role as author also makes her a "public person" (13). Danticat uses her own voice after the earthquake to amplify the community of voices that make up the Haitian diaspora: "I tried to say some of this whenever I went on the radio or television, whenever I wrote my articles of fifteen hundred words or less. They were therapeutic for me, these media outings, and helpful, I hoped, in adding one more voice to a chorus of bereavement and helping to explain what so many of us were feeling, which was deep and paralyzing sense of loss" (158). Danticat calls writers to fill up this space of lack. Undeniably for Danticat, this polyphonic community after the earthquake becomes a "chorus of bereavement" (162).

For Danticat, the world is polyphonic, and the proliferation and convergence of voices is the story of diaspora. This community of voices is not a uniform one, nor is it a utopian collectivity but, rather, a productive way of being with and in relation to other voices in Haiti and in the diaspora and a process of writing in displaced contexts in relation to other texts. Danticat shows that, like the relationship between text and reader, the relationship between Haiti and its diaspora is dialogic: they inform and constitute each other. In *Create Dangerously*, Danticat brings together these voices, living and dead, separated by time, space, and gender, creating links that both frame her individual identity and make her part of a collective community. It is the collective and individual voices that create a chorus of bereavement that Danticat calls an echo chamber. But as we shall see in the following chapter, when the voices of women in particular magnify in this chorus, the echo chamber exposes the creative strategies of survival that counter the patriarchal ordering of Haitian society and the systematic silencing of women's lives and their narratives of displacement.

3 Haitian Echoes

Tradition and Nation in *Breath, Eyes, Memory*

> Listening to the song, I realized that it was neither my mother nor Tante Atie who had given all the mother-and-daughter motifs to all the stories they hold and all the songs they sang. It was something that was essentially Haitian. Somehow, early on, our song makers and tale weavers had decided that we were all daughters of this land.
> —Sophie Caco, *Breath, Eyes, Memory*

> My being Haitian has a great deal to do with my writing. First of all it's the lens through which I look at the world, one of the lenses, including being a woman and being part of the larger African Diaspora. It gives me a place to start.
> —Edwidge Danticat, interview with Zita Allen

AFRICAN DIASPORIC scholar Chinosole coined the term "matrilineal diaspora" to name the women-centered spaces of diaspora in black women's literature that disrupt male-dominated and hegemonic master narratives of the black diaspora. Matrilineal diaspora, Chinosole writes, represents the "cultural and historical genealogy of Black women autobiographers in the United States with implications for other women of African descent" and "allows for a gender-sensitive discourse which is distinctly womanist."[1] Framing the concept through an examination of Audre Lorde's politics and poetics in *Zami: A New Spelling of My Name*, Chinosole perceives matrilineal diaspora as the poetic expression of women's "capacity to survive and aspire, to be contrary and self-affirming across continents and generations"; it enables black women worldwide "to experience distinct but related cultures while retaining a special sense of home as locus of self-definition and power."[2] The principle mode of this empowered affirmation and recognition of cultural difference is what Chinosole calls "nonpolarized duality," or "creative irreconcilability."[3] This principle of nonthreatening difference informs three modes of consciousness present in Lorde's biomythology and in the concept of matrilineal diaspora: "collective memory rendered through myth and legend that recaptures the past; the memory or personal experience that records the personal narrative; and a mythical fantasy dream state that projects into the future through desire."[4] Thus matrilineal diaspora is a way of imagining diasporic collectivity, global connectivity, and redefining kinship; it privileges a mythic consciousness that relies on legendary connections, memory, and historical recovery; it necessitates creative strategies and practices of survival and cultural adaption critical to women's self-definition, self-awareness, and self-preservation; and it calls for a revision and creative improvisation of the Du Boisian notion of double consciousness to position the "irreconcilable differences" that are characteristic of black diasporic subjectivity as empowering, not debilitating.

In this chapter, I argue that this principle of nonpolarized duality or creative irreconcilability that grounds Chinosole's matrilineal diaspora also informs Danticat's diasporic imaginary and consciousness and her commitment to articulating a productive and empowering dialogically linked relationship between the Haitian nation and its diaspora. I analyze Danticat's debut novel, *Breath, Eyes, Memory,* to make the argument that Danticat deconstructs, revises, and subverts Western myths of displacement and their reinterpretations in male-dominated narratives of subjectivity that frame duality and "irreconcilable differences" as pathology. In doing so, Danticat centers African and African diasporic mythology that offers alternatives to Eurocentric notions of duality in the formation of (self-)identity and in master narratives of the experience of displacement. But she also calls for their revaluation to account for New World experiences of displacement and the formation of new diasporic subjectivities to move beyond the bind of Western notions of black subjectivity that ground the Du Boisian formulation of double consciousness. Furthermore, in *Breath, Eyes, Memory,* Danticat both refines and subverts this foundational idea of double consciousness by presenting alternative figurations of the double and staging three different but related practices of doubling: the psychological process that attends to a splintered psyche resulting from the trauma of separation, the spiritual process that articulates the desire to return to primordial wholeness, and the creative process that entails revisionary practices that involve creative weaving of history, memory, myth, and personal accounts in narratives of diaspora to account for a multiplicity of voices and plural subjectivities.

Danticat reworks Du Bois's theory of double consciousness and shifts the notion from its African American milieu to its non-Western settings by introducing the figure of the Marassa, the principle of divine twins that is deeply rooted in African and Haitian cosmologies, as the central figure of the double and twoness in *Breath, Eyes, Memory*. Though related to the Marassa, the Haitian vodou practice of doubling, as Danticat's novel reveals, is a distinct spiritual process that works through and disrupts the dualistic view of the world in terms of opposites and in terms of good and evil. For Danticat, doubling is also a New World coping mechanism of survival that involves a psychic process of dissociation between the material and the spiritual body as a result of traumatic experiences. Lastly, Danticat presents doubling as both a creative process that embraces the multiplicity of identities and the creation of new identities formed out of the experience of movement and displacement. Danticat's early articulation of bicultural identity and critique of binaries[5] emerge out of these various processes of doubling and figuration of the double that are invoked, inscribed, and textualized in her writings and define her own evolving double consciousness and movement toward a diasporic consciousness of multiplicity and expansiveness. For Danticat the Haitian diasporic experience of displacement, seen through these three stages of doubling, is a key site that situates the racialized experience of black communities beyond its American context, in a broader African diasporic framework, but it also speaks to the historical, cultural, and literary specificities of Haiti. This double consciousness and articulation of biculturality are, for Danticat, early stages in the formation of diasporic consciousness that deconstruct the myriad dichotomies grounded in Western mythology implied in the concept of double consciousness.

However, as I will discuss, Danticat's novel offers alternative readings of duality, figurations of the double, and strategic acts of doubling that account not only for cultural differences and alternative mythologies and cosmologies but also for gendered differences and nonpatriarchal modes of being. *Breath, Eyes, Memory* exposes the ways in which myths order and encode patriarchal norms and masculine desires that structure the lives of women, silence their voices, and define their roles as mothers of the nation while at the same time they exclude them from the narratives of the nation. Using the mother-daughter motif, Danticat looks at the ways in which women encode and decode these norms in women-centered spaces of creativity and intimacy. Such matrilineal spaces impart female knowledge and strategies of survival to cope with the experience of displacement. In *Breath, Eyes, Memory,* Danticat asserts the need to reclaim oral tradition and the practice of storytelling to tap into this reservoir of feminine knowledge and wisdom. I suggest that Danticat pulls from the myth of Persephone, Demeter, and Hades to both recenter and reclaim

Haitian women's voices and matrilineal knowledge silenced by state-sanctioned violence. To unsilence and magnify Haitian women's voices, Danticat relies on a diasporic imaginary and consciousness that privilege oral tradition, memory, and mythic fantasies. She also reworks the experience of displacement from the perspective of a Haitian girl forming identity in diaspora while maintaining ties to home. But the novel is not only about the affirmation of diasporic subjectivity and reclamation of women's voices; it reveals a nuanced meditation of the relation between the oral and the written, one that foregrounds the significance of both the individual and collective voices of women in the process of narrating a story. This is most evident, I argue, through Danticat's tropic formation and permutations of Ovid's figuration of Echo as storyteller in *Metamorphoses,* and this can only be surmised through a relational reading of both the Homeric and Ovidian versions of the myth of Demeter, Persephone, and Hades. The title of this chapter, "Haitian Echoes: Tradition and Nation in *Breath, Eyes Memory,*" implies a double meaning that alludes to the echo trope: "Haitian echoes" are both the Haitian heroines in Danticat's *Breath, Eyes, Memory,* Echo-like subjects who face the threat of silence and absence, and the very tropes particular to Haitian culture and oral tradition that Danticat uses to appropriate, disrupt, and rewrite Western notions of the double and doubling.

Double Consciousness and the Double Bind

In *The Souls of Black Folk,* which examines the plight of African Americans at the dawn of the twentieth century, W. E. B. Du Bois writes:

> The Negro is a sort of seventh son, born with a veil, and gifted with second-sight in this American world, —a world which yields him no true self-consciousness, but only lets him see himself through the revelation of the other world. It is a peculiar sensation, this double-consciousness, this sense of always looking at one's self through the eyes of others, of measuring one's soul by the tape of a world that looks on in amused contempt and pity. One ever feels his twoness, —an American, a Negro; two souls, two thoughts, two unreconciled strivings; two warring ideals in one dark body, whose dogged strength alone keeps it from being torn asunder.[6]

Du Bois's double consciousness stresses the struggle between two points of view existing simultaneously, and the Hegelian structure of identity/identification is fundamentally tied to an other outside of the self. This structure allows for the definition of the nation's citizens and fuels the mechanism of inclusion/exclusion. Du Bois's understanding of the Afri-can American experience within this binary framing also elucidates the tensions and contradictions of African diasporic identity formation in the United States. Du Bois is a key figure in black internationalist politics and consciousness of the twentieth century. Calling for more transnational articulations that account for the gendered contours of twentieth-century black subjectivity, VèVè Clark proposes the term "marasa consciousness" to revise definitions and theoretical framings of diaspora and black iden-tity within African American scholarship and masculinist notions that figure the black male subject as ideal citizen of a radically new vision of the modern nation-state. Clark defines "marasa consciousness" as a "mythical theory of textual relations based on the Haitian vodou sign for the divine twins, the marasa," and a third stage in diasporic development, with the first two representing the new letters movement and Caribbean anticolonial writing.[7] Clark continues, "Marasa consciousness invites us to imagine beyond the binary. The ability to do so largely depends on our capacities to read the sign as a cyclical, spiral relationship. On the surface "marasa" seems to be binary. My research on Haitian peasant lore and rit-ual observances has revealed that the tension between oppositions leads to another norm of creativity—to interaction or deconstruction, as it were."[8]

Possessing the skill to read a sign like the Marassa necessitates what Clark calls "Diaspora Literacy," the narrator's and the reader's ability to comprehend the multicultural, multilingual literature of Africa, Afro-America, and the Caribbean from an informed indigenous perspective. Such skill "demands a knowledge of historical, social, cultural, and politi-cal development generated by lived and textual experience."[9] Clark's term echoes Gloria Anzaldúa's notion of "Mestiza consciousness" as a third element and new mythos that embraces ambiguity, contradiction, and the plurality of identities. For Anzaldúa, "Mestiza consciousness" is a survival strategy used to overcome physical and conceptual borders and to "break down" and transcend the "subject object duality"; it is a way of stretching the psyche "toward a more whole perspective, one that includes rather than excludes."[10]

Primal Displacement and the Mother-Daughter Motif

Breath, Eyes, Memory is a loosely autobiographical bildungsroman Dan-ticat submitted as her master's thesis at Brown University.[11] The novel is set against a background of the Duvalier regime in Haiti during the 1980s. It chronicles the psychological trauma of multiple forms of sexual oppression and political terror imposed on the lives of Haitian women by the Tonton Macoutes. It unveils the life of Sophie Caco, a young Haitian girl who is forced to leave her home and her Aunt Atie in the small rural impoverished village of Croix-des-Rosets, Haiti, at the age of twelve to be with her young mother, Martine, in Brooklyn, New York. In this new urban, noisy, and cramped environment, Sophie struggles to hold on to memories of home in Haiti as she attempts to acculturate into her new life and deal with an overbearing mother traumatized by the rape experience that caused her to flee Haiti. When Sophie, a child of rape, turns eighteen, she is further devastated by her mother's constant testing of her virginity. This physical act of inserting a finger into the vagina not only humiliates her but also results in trauma, self-mutilation, and bulimia. Although she escapes her mother's testing by causing self-inflicted bodily harm, gets married, and has a child, Sophie must confront the psychological impact of such an experience and the nightmares her mother passed on to her. Unable to enjoy the sexual act, Sophie temporarily leaves her African American husband, Joseph, and makes a trip to Haiti with her six-month-old daughter, Brigitte, to understand her own struggles and those of her mother. Grandmè Ifé, the old matriarch in Dame Marie, the village where Sophie's ancestors are buried, uses her gift of storytelling to impart female knowledge, wisdom, strength, and family history to her granddaughter Sophie. Tante Atie also participates in Sophie's needed initiation into womanhood and motherhood. Sophie returns to the United States and begins the process through therapy. She attempts to reconnect with her mother, who now wants to be her friend. But the news of Martine's pregnancy makes it impossible to repair and renew the mother-daughter relationship. The pregnancy sends Martine into a frenzy: she commits suicide by stabbing her unborn child seventeen times. Shortly thereafter, Sophie makes another trip to Haiti, this time with Martine's boyfriend, Marc, to bury her mother. The novel ends with Sophie returning to the site of her mother's rape in Dame Marie right after the funeral. Attacking the cane field and beating a cane stalk, Sophie liberates herself by releasing her rage, pain, and grief.

Danticat's novel explores a daughter's alienation from her mother and the consequence of generational bond and conflict, which are compounded by the experience of migration and sexual trauma. The mother-daughter relationship is a significant motif in *Breath, Eyes, Memory*. Danticat relies on this motif to make sense of the migration experience that is transforming a young woman in diaspora caught between Haitian culture and American culture. It is the experience of migration that, for Danticat, defines familial memory, ruptures relationships with loved ones, and in the process, transforms Haitian identity and creates new Haitian diasporic spaces and subjectivities. In a 1996 interview with Renée Shae, Danticat stated that it is not so much the relationship between the mother and daughter as it is the circumstances of migration that shaped the fabric of the relationship that fascinates her.[12] In a later interview, Danticat explains,

> Migration changes many things for us. One of the most visible effects of migration is how it changes family dynamics, how we lose familial connections—sometimes with extended family members, sometimes with immediate family members when we migrate. When a family moves to a new country, sometimes the children gain all the power, and the parents lose their authority. For example, the children become fluent in a language and become the ones who speak for the family. Yet they still have to be children at home and obey their parents. I am interested in how families adjust to that, how they adjust to these little traumas and big ones as well, as when you lose a family member in a boat crossing. How do you define yourself when you're removed from your family? What becomes of you? What becomes of them? It's not unusual for a grandchild to go back to Haiti and not be able to speak to his or her grandparents because of a language barrier. A language barrier within a family? That to me is interesting. I like to explore all the ways that families are changed by migration.[13]

Migration and acculturation are critical themes in *Breath, Eyes, Memory*. This is not surprising, as Sophie loosely reflects Danticat's own migration story and process of acculturation in the United States. Moreover, Danticat wrote the novel during the 1990s, a period wherein, as I have already discussed in detail in chapter 1, Haitian society and Haiti's people, culture, and consequently its literature were undergoing some major transformations resulting from the impact and increased flow of emigration to the United States.

Breath, Eyes, Memory was also published at a moment when the corpus of Haitian women's literature in Haiti was experiencing significant growth. The novel emerged at a moment when Caribbean women immigrant writers in particular were obtaining recognition and speaking to the specificities of their experiences of displacement and migration as distinct from their black male and African American counterparts. Critical anthologies of Caribbean women writers, such as *Her True-True Name: An Anthology of Women's Writing from the Caribbean* (1989), and about Caribbean identity, such as and *Out of the Kumbla: Caribbean Women and Literature* (1994), are among the early works that have broadened the discourse of black feminist criticism to incorporate non–African American black women writers and the cross-cultural exchanges between black women.[14] Such anthologies are the product of developing global networks of exchange and solidarity among women writers of the African diaspora. *Breath, Eyes, Memory* explores these connections and global female-centered diasporic spaces by exploring the impact of migration on familial relationships between women, particularly the relationship between a mother and her daughter.

Rewriting the Myth of Demeter and Persephone

The myth of Demeter, Persephone, and Hades is the myth most frequently adopted by black women writers to explore complex mother-daughter relationships. The Homeric *Hymn to Demeter,* which was written 650 BCE, is the earliest known written account taken from an oral tradition created to honor gods and goddesses of the Greek pantheon.[15] The other well-known version comes from book 6 of Ovid's *Metamorphoses,* which was written five hundred years after Homer. In *African American Literature and the Classicist Tradition,* Tracey Walters asserts that African American women writers in particular invoke the myth to explore fraught relations between mothers and daughters.[16] Sophie's relationship with her absent mother, Martine, is certainly uneasy. A few scholars have already noted the rewriting of the myth of Demeter, Persephone, and Hades in Danticat's *Breath, Eyes, Memory.* David Cowart argues that Danticat invokes the myth not only to explore the mother-daughter relationship but to render a double identity that is characteristic of an immigrant consciousness. He describes Sophie as "Persephone never fully reconciled to life in the underworld."[17] Analyzing the story of the lark and the girl in the novel, Cowart in fact asserts that all the heroines in *Breath, Eyes, Memory* are "Persephone doubled" and live with some version of double consciousness.[18] However, as Susana Morris asserts, the story of the lark and the pomegranate is not only a direct reference to the Western myth of Demeter, Persephone, and Hades[19] but is also evidence of new mythologies of survival in the African diasporic imagination. Other literary scholars point to the Homeric *Hymn to Demeter* to examine Danticat's diasporic rewriting of the trope of the daffodil, a flower of the genus narcissus, as symbol of transplantation and representation of diasporic subjectivity. Jana Braziel, for example, describes Danticat's daffodils as "flowers of diaspora" and diasporic "flowers of adoption" that affirm sites of resistance, postcolonial survival, and adaptation.[20] Cowart views references to daffodils as "emblems of immigrant hope for rooting and flourishing in diasporic soils" and symbols that articulate the "complex play on transplantation, rootedness, and postcolonial sensibility."[21] Later in the chapter, I present the daffodil as a symbol of patriarchal intrusion and suppression of matrilineal spaces of intimacy and creativity. But I want to suggest here that we reread the Homeric *Hymn to Demeter* and the Ovidian renditions, "Echo and Narcissus" and "The Rape of Proserpina" in *Metamorphoses,* relationally to explore what I perceive as the allusion and tropic permutations of Ovid's echo in Danticat's novel. Reading the myths relationally offers critical insights not only into the symbol of the daffodil but also into the place of Echo as trope in Danticat's diasporic imaginary and Danticat's preoccupation with voice, secrets, storytelling, and the threat of perpetual silence in *Breath, Eyes, Memory.*

Undoubtedly, both versions of the myth tell the story of separation and reconnection between mother and daughter. They both highlight the main plot of the story: the abduction of an innocent child by the god of the underworld, the grieving wandering mother in search of her lost daughter, the daughter's loss of innocence and transformation as queen of the underworld, and her partial return to her mother. The myth honors the female deity Demeter and her daughter Persephone and celebrates the Eleusinian mysteries of an agrarian sacred cult and its purification rites. These ritual ceremonies were performed in Eleusis, Greece, during an annual one-week festival to worship Demeter, mother earth and goddess of agriculture and fertility.[22] Eleusinian mysteries, the most famous of secret religious rites of ancient Greece, were open to all, men and women initiates who had to temporarily adopt names with feminine endings during the initiation.[23] But the myth is also said to be associated with Thesmophoria, another Greek festival and ancient ceremony that lasted for three days. Contrary to the Eleusinian mysteries, Thesmophoria excluded men from participation. The festival, reserved exclusively for married women, was an occasion for women to discuss private customs, share sorrows of motherhood, express anger against men, and claim their sexuality.[24] Both ceremonies included the sacrifice of a pig. It should be noted here that it is by no happenstance that Danticat's *Breath, Eyes, Memory* includes the story of Louise's pig, which she sold to flee Haiti by boat. The story should not be read as tangential to the narrative but as a representation of Haitian peasant culture, which is critical to Danticat's diasporic consciousness and a central indicator of Danticat's intentional fusion of Western mythology, Haitian mythology, memory, and history in the novel.

Walters further asserts that twentieth-century women writers use the story of Persephone to explore the rite of passage from girlhood to womanhood.[25] Indeed, the myth is told to prepare women for their gendered roles as women and mothers, to explain the balance of opposites, and to describe their place in a patriarchal society. But the myth is also appropriated by women and feminists to articulate the suppression of goddess freedom, the significance of the primordial mother and the mother-daughter bond, the paternal violation of matristic and matrilineal spaces,[26] and the radical imagining and of a postpatriarchal world.[27] Aside from the mother-daughter motif, contemporary writers focus on Persephone's victimization to explore the theme of sexual violation.[28] African American women writers in particular reenvision the story of abduction and rape to give Persephone a voice to speak out against patriarchal violence. In Danticat's diasporic coming-of-age narrative, she develops the story of Martine's experience of rape by the Tonton Macoutes (who are always representative of the terror and violence of the Duvalier regime) to critique the gendered rhetoric of nation and the discourse of nationalism grounded in heteronormative structures of patriarchy, Victorian norms of femininity, colonialist notions of culture, and homogenizing formulations of identity. As mentioned earlier, the allusion to the myth is directly made through the story of the lark and the pomegranate in the novel. But besides the rape, the myth's potent themes of separation, alienation, loss, journey, transformation, reunification, and reintegration are central to Danticat's novel. Indeed, diaspora narratives also appropriate the story of Persephone to articulate not only the extreme loss that results from displacement but also the rewards of such a scattering. In separating from her mother, Persephone, in the Homeric *Hymn*, gains not only self-awareness but also access to two worlds concurrently, she becomes a divine messenger and "vehicle that links the two realms of over-world and underworld,"[29] the living and the dead. As Tmara Agha-Jaffar asserts, "It was the seductive power of the narcissus that makes all of these very important connections, transformations, and border crossing possible."[30] Indeed, Sophie's diasporic journey results in immediate transformation and double consciousness: On her first night in New York, Sophie looks in the mirror and sees a new person: "I looked at my red eyes in the mirror while splashing cold water over my face. New eyes seemed to be looking back at me. A new face all-together. Someone who had aged in one day, as though she had been through a time machine, rather than an airplane. Accept your new life. I greeted the challenge, like one greets a new day. As my mother's daughter and Tante Atie's child." [31] Over time, the journey allows her to gain greater awareness of herself and her native culture; she also now has access to multiple worlds, multiple cultures, and multiple identities and experiences. This is evident, for example, in her marriage to Joseph, an African American Creole from Louisiana, and in the birth of her daughter, Brigitte, who represents a new hyphenated identity. This access also plays out in her relationship with the other two members of the sexual phobia group: Buki, the Ethiopian college student, and Davina, the middle-aged woman.

Like her heroine Sophie in *Breath, Eyes, Memory,* Danticat embodies the border-crossing qualities of Persephone. As an immigrant writer of diaspora, and as the literary voice of Haiti who translates and transcribes the country's history, culture, and circumstances to not only an American audience but a global audience, Danticat too is Persephone doubled.

Narcissus, Daffodil, and Patriarchal Captivity

But it is the notable differences between the two versions of the myth that reveal, I suggest, subtle tropic permutations of the myth of Echo and Narcissus in Ovid's "The Rape of Proserpina" that are pertinent to under-standing Danticat's complex appropriation, fusion, deconstruction, and subversion of both myths to meditate on the experience of displacement in diaspora and the formation of diasporic subjectivity. In the *Hymn* the flower narcissus is introduced early on as a trap planted by a maiden in cahoots with Zeus to enchant the young girl, Persephone, who is engaged in the act of "plucking" the narcissus and is only named toward the end of the *Hymn*. Indeed, in the Homeric *Hymn,* the flower narcissus is central to the drama. It is a symbol of patriarchal control and loss of innocence and is thus necessary for self-awareness.[32] In Ovid's version, Proserpina, who is immediately named, is not picking narcissus but an assortment of lilies and violets. In fact in Ovid's rendition, Narcissus is nonexistent.

The first subtle allusion to Danticat's permutation of the myth of Persephone, Demeter, and Hades appears through the symbol of the daffodil. The daffodil is a common name for any flower of the genus narcissus. But as symbol in Danticat's novel, it also reveals intertextual references to postcolonial Anglophone Caribbean women's literature and their subversion of the daffodil to disrupt the European poetic imaginary. A Wordsworthian trope of Englishness more broadly and the romanti-cized landscape of England's countryside more specifically,[33] the daffodil is demythologized and redefined as a metaphor of colonial oppression and imposition, of colonial education, and of the literary authority of male speakers in novels by Caribbean women writers such as Jean Rhys, Jamaica Kincaid, and Michelle Cliff.[34] They rework the daffodil trope to articulate the colonial past, anxiety of separation, early childhood conflict, and admiration of absent figures (mothers, fathers, and homeland).

Scholars of Haitian literature point to the daffodil metaphor to explore Haitian strategies of survival and transformation. In a special issue of the *Journal of Haitian Studies* on the work of Danticat published in fall 2001, Helen Pyne-Timothy and Marc Christophe examine the daffodil metaphor in Danticat's work. Pyne-Timothy writes in her article that Danticat's Haitian daffodil is "iron strong" like the Haitian people,[35] while Christophe asserts in his article that the "acclimated European daffodil" is a "symbol of resilience and purity."[36] Other scholars would later explore the metaphor to articulate the diasporic experience. In her comparative analysis of Danticat and Kincaid, Jana Braziel states that while Kincaid's loathing of daffodils in her novella *Lucy* reveals the oppressive nature of British colonial education, Danticat's appreciation of the flower in *Breath, Eyes, Memory* speaks to the complexities of transplantation, adaptation, and adoption that constitute the diasporic identity.[37] Similarly, Simone A. James Alexander describes the daffodils in *Breath, Eyes, Memory* as a representation of "one of the multifaceted notions of diaspora, in this case, an imperial diaspora."[38] Carine Mardorossian in her discussion of the same novel argues that the European yellow daffodil "signifies the flower's successful adaptation to its topical surroundings."[39] Indeed, Danticat develops the trope of the daffodil to unsettle homogenized identities and leave room for plural identities formed out of disruption, displacement, uprooting, and flux.

As I have articulated in my 2003 article on Danticat's *Breath, Eyes, Memory,* the daffodil is representative of unfixed and determined identities. It "signifies the ways in which Haitian identities are hybridized and constantly pulled and pushed from various directions" and exposes the "inability to speak the constricted homogenous language of nation-state within migratory experience."[40] I assert that Danticat "revisits the notion of rootedness and relocates it within the space of migratory movements" to call out the limitations of bordered identities and embrace diasporic and transnational identities and positionings.[41] Elizabeth Walcott-Hackshaw states that the daffodil is one of many botanical metaphors Danticat uses to "discuss cultural identity in order to 'reinforce the complex, transient nature of return.'"[42] More recently, Jennifer J. Nichols, who revisits the trope in *Lucy*, argues that daffodils "function as a symbol of white US feminism (and femininity) that Lucy rejects."[43] Daffodils, for Nichols "call to mind both the gendered work of cooking and sewing and the image of bourgeois women dressing up . . . to have tea."[44] It is a "glaring symbol of interlocking exploitations."[45] In my close reading of the daffodil in this chapter, I am interested in Danticat's use of the daffodil to rewrite what Spivak describes as the world of the narcissistic European superego, the anxiety of patriarchal intrusion into women's spaces to police their lives. I also argue that Danticat reworks the daffodil to put into question myths and traditional nationalist narratives that order patriarchal notions of family and naturalize the relationships among mother, land, and nation.

In *After the Fall: The Demeter-Persephone Myth in Wharton, Cather, and Glasgow*, Josephine Donovan asserts that in late nineteenth- and early twentieth-century literature, the myth "allegorizes the transformation from a matricentric preindustrial culture—Demeter's realm—to a male-dominated capitalist-industrialist ethos, characterized by growing professionalism and bureaucracy: the realm of patriarchal captivity."[46] This realm of patriarchal captivity, I argue, is immediately articulated through the symbol of the daffodil at the very beginning of *Breath, Eyes, Memory*. The novel commences in Croix-des-Rosets, Haiti, with Sophie contemplating the daffodil on the Mother's Day card she has made for her aunt Atie: "A flattened and drying daffodil was dangling off the little card that I had made my aunt Atie for Mother's Day. I pressed my palm over the flower and squashed it against the plain beige cardboard. When I turned the corner near the house, I saw her sitting in an old rocker in the yard, staring at a group of children crushing dried yellow leaves into the ground. The leaves had been left in the sun to dry. They would be burned at night at the konbit potluck dinner" (3). The city of Croix-des-Rosets is not the idealized English countryside that represents Wordsworth's native home; it is a limbo city of workers who "labored in baseball or clothing factories and lived in small cramped houses to support their families back in the provinces" (11). From the perspective of the community members, the ability to leave this landscape is supposed to reap rewards, not a sense of nostalgia, as many succumb to a life of exploitation at home. Moreover, Sophie's interaction with the daffodil is certainly not the Wordsworthian individual and romanticized poetic articulation of being in harmony with the flower; instead we are presented with discord. There is indeed a violent struggle with the flower from multiple perspectives. Sophie is pressing her hand over the flower; the children are collectively crushing it, and when Atie receives the card, she forces the "baby daffodil back in its place" (8). Rejecting the card, Atie says, "It is for a mother, your mother. . . . When its Aunt day you can make me one" (9). Atie rejects Sophie again when she volunteers to read the words on the card to her. This creates another violent interaction between Sophie and the daffodil: she plucks out the flower and drops it under her shoes (9).

In her nightmares, Sophie is being chased by her mother, Martine, through a field of wildflowers. Martine at this stage is the one character who does not appear to be struggling with the flower. In fact Martine, when she is introduced to the reader, is presented as having a strong positive identification with flowers. In the picture of Martine in Tante Atie's room, she has a large flower in her hair (8). We learn later that it is Martine who loves daffodils; we do not fully know if Sophie independently loves daffodils or if she is being socialized to love them, along with the color yellow, as it is Atie who expresses Sophie's love of daffodils. Martine's association with flowers and the daffodil in particular is always in relation to some display of patriarchal dominance and surveillance. Through the picture, the masculine frame is inverted. Martine is the absent parental image who hovers over the lives of Sophie and Atie and watches their every move. She is also a disembodied voice that assumes a controlling, dominant role. The first introduction to Martine's voice comes as a directive from a cassette tape: "I want my daughter" (16). She accepts the normative role as mother but situates it within her own individual desire. Nonetheless, she is only present as an object, and her voice is mediated through another object. Martine also buys into the idea of individual success in America and believes that Sophie's separation from Atie and from Haiti is "the best thing that is ever going to happen" to her (14). The displaced community of Croix-des-Rosets also buys into this capitalist ethos of success.

Even though Martine is an absent figure, she has control over Sophie in her dreams: "My mother's face was in my dreams all night long. She was wrapped in yellow sheets and had daffodils in her hair. She opened her arms like two long hooks and kept shouting out my name. Catching me by the hem of my dress, she wrestled me to the floor. I called for Tante Atie as loud as I could. Tante Atie was leaning over us, but she could not see me. I was lost in the yellow of my mother's sheets" (28). I read the daffodil here as a specific moment of patriarchal intrusion, captivity, and narcissistic individuality. The reenactment of patriarchal captivity is inverted here through the figure of the absent dominating mother, which affirms individual desire. There is no recognition of collectivity and the desire of the other. The encoding of patriarchy through the mother exposes not only the intrusion of patriarchy in matrilineal domestic private spaces but also the role women play in sustaining and reproducing the norms of patriarchy. Interestingly, when she finally meets her mother face to face, Sophie sees a weak figure: "She did not look like the picture Tante Atie had on her night table. Her face was long and hollow. Her hair had a blunt cut and she had long springly legs. She had dark circles under her eyes and, as she smiled, lines of wrinkles tightened her expression. Her fingers were scarred and sunburned. It was as though she had never stopped working in the cane fields after all" (42). Though Martine adheres to the individualism of the American dream and its vision of success, her lived experiences disrupt this illusion. In this American metropolis, Martine works hard not only to take care of herself but also to send money back to Haiti. And when Martine herself is unable to achieve the American dream, she projects all her hopes and desires onto her daughter.

But the loosening of the daffodil can also mean the loss of a matristic world. The power and poetic uses of the daffodil as symbol of fertility and feminine creativity and speech are displaced. Instead, the flower is flattening and drying and, ultimately, completely disappears (21). Thus the daffodil can also be read as the intrusion of masculinist literary authority in feminine narrative spaces. Interestingly, the Mother's Day card becomes a palimpsest, wherein the poetic voice of Sophie in written form is no longer legible. This text only exposes the imprisonment of a master narrative of the idealized strong mother that adheres to the representation of women in literary narratives of the nation: "My mother is a daffodil / Limber and strong as one. / My mother is a daffodil, / But in the wind, iron strong" (29). But Sophie's mastery of the idealized script of the biological mother must also been made illegible so that the card can allow room for new voices, new texts, and new understandings and inscriptions of motherhood and womanhood.[47] Later in the book, when Sophie returns to Haiti, the reader learns that Tante Atie memorized the words in the card and eventually writes them down in a composition notebook. She only gains the courage to learn to read and write after she leaves Croix-des-Rosets and returns to her mother's home, the place of her birth, in Dame Marie. Atie, as a progressive character, inscribes her poetic voice to offer alternative female-centered narratives. But while Sophie views Atie's ability to read as freedom (119), the Mother's Day card as palimpsest is also a sign of resistance to the privileging of the written text over oral traditions. It is not a matter of one or the other but the necessary fusion of the two for preservation. Though the card became very wrinkled "and the penciled words were beginning to fade" (29), Atie's memorialization allowed for the preservation of Sophie's poem. She says, "I have never forgotten those words. I have written them down" (108). Here Danticat calls for the fusion of the oral with the written to recover and textualize oral narratives but also to engender new narratives of motherhood and womanhood. As Sharron Eve Sarthou writes, "Danticat's work formalizes the oral tradition and the unspoken histories by translating them into the written word."[48] Certainly, Danticat's insertion of the Negro spiritual song "Sometimes I Feel like a Motherless Child" at the end of the novel (215) is an indication of this embrace of orality in text to account for diverse New World experiences and perspectives of displacement. But it also exposes African diasporic mythologies and creative articulations of displacement that link loss of home and nation to primordial loss of the mother. It is also a recognition of the need for more inclusive and expansive narratives of motherhood and kinship ties.

The trope of the daffodil is developed around three figures: the absent mother figure; the surrogate, adopted, spiritual mother Atie; and the confused, displaced child, who later becomes a mother. To reclaim the daffodil, the card must make room for more complex images and narratives of girlhood, motherhood, and womanhood. The relationship between the daffodil and the celebration of Mother's Day brings up the question of adoption and expansion of kinship ties that disrupt biologically assigned roles. How does adoption simultaneously disrupt and affirm the fixity of identities and the nurturing roles of women specifically, as well as the discourses that surround notions of *terre natale* in general? Atie's adoption of Sophie disturbs the portrayal of the blood or biological mother as the most nurturing maternal figure in the same way as the daffodil disturbs the notion of the native land as pure and untainted ground that nurtures her "blood" children and rejects all others. Although Sophie knows that her mother is elsewhere, she nonetheless recognizes Atie as the maternal figure, naming her symbolically when she presents the card to her. Thus Atie, the adopted mother, is viewed as the true mother, while Martine is presented at the periphery of the relationship between Atie and Sophie. Yet because Martine is on the outside of her native land and Atie remains inside her native land, the relationship between Atie and Sophie references a narrative of national belonging. Danticat, however, subsumes and marginalizes the language of nation by confronting the question of adaptation and adoption while linking the two terms semantically. Martine's migration results in Sophie's adoption by Aunt Atie; Sophie's migration leads to adaptation within a new environment. Both adoption and adaptation are critical for Sophie's survival. The daffodils, Atie tells Sophie, are European flowers brought to Croix-des-Rosets by a French woman. The transplanted flowers adapt and flourish in Haiti, so much so that they become Haitian, a part of the Haitian landscape (21). They are natural-ized. In New York, Sophie herself becomes a flower of adoption that also transforms and takes on a new identity that represents both the culture of her native land and that of her new home. In putting into question traditional notions of roots and blood ties, Danticat forces the reader to acknowledge how migration and separation complicate familial relation-ships, not just national identities. She also shows how national identities and the political rhetoric of nation are dependent on the structures of the family in personal home spaces. To dismantle fixed national identi-ties, Danticat leaves room to embrace a new fluid understanding of kin-ship and family ties that develop out of the migratory experience. While migration has ruptured families and created a large population of people living away from their homeland, the diaspora provides an opportunity to strengthen relations with home and family members and expand the Haitian community.

Women as Storytellers, Sophie as Echo-Like Subject

The Mother's Day card as palimpsest is one of the early moments of Dan-ticat's preoccupation with the linked relationships among speech, oral tra-dition, and the written text in the novel. Certainly Danticat pulls from the myth and Caribbean women's revisioning of the narcissus to foreground this link. But I want to argue here that Danticat is not only rewriting the trope of Narcissus but also recalling the Ovidian figure of Echo as story-teller. Danticat rewrites the myth of Echo to foreground the significance of Haitian women's art of storytelling. There are other differences between the *Hymn* and the Ovidian version that must be noted here. In the *Hymn,* when Hades grabs her away in his golden chariot, Persephone calls upon her father, Zeus, but it is her mother, Demeter, who hears her "immortal voice" and attempts to come to her rescue. In Ovid's version, when Dis (a name for Pluto) abducts Proserpina, she does not call to her father but to her mother, Ceres, and her friends. In the *Hymn,* Persephone is tricked and forced to eat pomegranate seeds, while in Ovid's version Proserpina innocently picks the pomegranate and eats seven seeds from the fruit. In the Homeric version, the mother, Demeter, is the central character, and all other characters in the story are introduced through Demeter's viewpoint and experiences. In the Ovidian story, the mother, Ceres, is one of many complex and individualized characters who tell the complete story of Persephone's rape. In the Homeric version, Persephone, who appears to have a knack for telling stories, finally describes her own experience of the rape and experience in the underworld in a poetic voice. In the Ovidian version, a lot more attention is paid to a collectivity of voices that tell the story of Proserpina's rape, journey, and transformation from different angles. And the women are bonding through the act of telling stories or listening to them. These elements of the Ovidian story that privilege the feminine voice of the storyteller fit well with my earlier claim that Danticat's characters are Echo-like subjects.

It is Ovid's distinctive characterization of virgin muses and goddesses as Echo-like subjects who have the gift of storytelling that interests me here. Like the nymph Echo in the myth of Narcissus and Echo, they are faced with the threat of silence and nonexistence but find creative ways to communicate. They experience or bear witness to trauma. They undergo serious transformations, dissolving into water, streams, pools, or fountains. For example, Cyane witnesses the abduction and rape of Proserpina and speaks out against it, but she is silenced by Dis (Pluto). Heavily affected by the rape, she dissolves in a pool of tears. Like the nymph Echo, Cyane's limbs melt away, and her bones lose firmness until nothing remains. As a result, Cyane is unable to verbally tell Ceres the story. Ovid writes, "Cyane, who would have told her the story / had she not herself been changed; but though willing in spirit; / her mouth, tongue, and vocal apparatus were absent".[49] But she still found a way to communicate and testify to Ceres despite the loss of voice by offering physical proof of the abduction. Arethusa is another nymph and witness who turns into liquid. Unlike Cyane, however, Arethusa is a stranger in Sicily, a guest, a visitor who is displaced from her homeland because of the threat of sexual assault and violation by another character, Alpheus, a river God. She adds her voice to the story by testifying to seeing Proserpina and her transformation. She is the one who tells Ceres that the separation and the incident have transformed her into "Queen." She also later tells Ceres her own story of displacement and transformation into a spring to escape the intrusion of Alpheus.

The daughters of Achelois, the nymphs who were Proserpina's companions and with her during the time of the abduction, are also Echo-like subjects whose virgin divine voices and gift of storytelling need to be protected and preserved: Ovid writes, "And so that your tunefulness which the ear finds so pleasing / should not be lost, nor your gifts of vocal expression / your maidenly faces remain, along with your voices" (730–38). Interestingly, in Ovid's story the custodian of the underworld, Acalaphus, who exposes Proserpina's secret act of eating the pomegranate, is punished for having a "tattling tongue" and testifying to the misdeed.[50] It was his disclosure of the secret that kept Proserpina from returning (716). Proserpina, now queen of the underworld, turns him into an owl, a bird of ill omen, "a slothful portent of evil to mortals" (725). But the owl in Greek mythology is not only a messenger of bad news but a sacred creature that has the power to both mask deception and speak the whole truth.

I suggest that Sophie displays all the qualities of Ovid's muses and goddesses in "The Rape of Proserpina," who are tropic permutations of the nymph Echo in the myth of Echo and Narcissus. The word for echo in rabbinic literature is *bat kol*. It literally means "daughter of a voice." Bat kol is described as a message without a sender, an anonymous source, bearing inside information but lacking authority. The characteristic attribute of the bat kol is the "invisibility of the speaker and a certain remarkable quality in the sound, regardless of its strength or weakness."[51] Sophie reclaims her grandmother's legacy as a storyteller and Haiti's oral tradition to magnify the voices of Haitian women silenced by state-sanctioned violence and patriarchal oppression. To do so, Sophie must acknowledge an African past and embrace the diasporic consciousness of her grandmother Ifé and her ancestors. (Ifé, the name of an ancient Yoruba city, represents Yoruba creation mythology.) Sophie, whose name means wisdom in Greek, doubles as her grandmother's folk voice in new diasporic to encode and decode Haiti's history, cultural traditions, African roots, and "secrets" in writing. In doing so, she not only imparts local knowledge that accounts for Haiti's cultural specificities and traditions; she also creates a link between the individual and collective voices of Haiti with those of the diaspora. She makes space for new narratives and myths that account for the African diasporic experiences of displacement more broadly and New World experiences of Haitian Americans more specifically.

In her essay "Rewriting Folklore: Traditional Beliefs and Popular Culture in Edwidge Danticat's *Breath, Eyes, Memory* and *Krik? Krak!*," Marie-José N'Zengou-Tayo explains, "Haitian popular culture is constantly transforming itself due to the changes that occurred in the lives of the peasants, due to forced migration towards the cities and foreign countries. In these new environments, traditions are reshaped and acquire new meanings in order to help the migrant to adjust to his new environment. Danticat's tales illustrate this restructuring of Haitian culture as she creates new myths for new spaces and new ways of living and for a new breed of Haitian-Americans."[52] Danticat relies on the fusion of Western and non-Western myths to articulate the diasporic experience and alternative notions of duality and twoness. The new myths Danticat creates for Haitian diasporic subjects derive from a distinctive Haitian tradition and the awareness of a struggle of being between two cultures. In the novel, Danticat introduces the reader to the Marassa figure, ancient divine twins in the vodou religion who represent duality and doubleness, and the figure of Erzulie, which fixes women's identities between two extremes (the virgin mother image and the hot-blooded sexual figure). Both figures disturb the very polarity they establish and move beyond their dual framework. They offer an alternative understanding of duality, doubleness, and double consciousness.

Marassa, the Double, and Splitting of the Diasporic Traumatic Body

Martine tests Sophie when she begins to express an interest in the opposite sex. After coming home late from a date with Joseph, a musician who is much older than her, Sophie finds her mother waiting for her with a belt. As Sophie is being tested by her mother, Martine, she tells the story of the Marassas:

> The Marassas were two inseparable lovers. They were the same person duplicated in two. They looked the same, talked the same, walked the same. When they laughed, they even laughed the same, and when they cried, their tears were identical. When one went to the stream, the other rushed under the water to get a better look. When one looked in the mirror, the other walked behind the glass to mimic her. What vain lovers they were, those Marassas. Admiring one another for being so much alike, for being copies. When you love someone, you want him to be closer to you than your Marassa. Closer than your shadow. You want him to be your soul. The more you are alike, the easier it becomes. When you look in a stream, if you saw that man's face, wouldn't you scream? Wouldn't you think he was hiding under a sheet of water or behind a pane of glass to kill you? The love between a mother and a daughter is deeper than the sea. You would leave me for an old man who you didn't know the year before. You and I we could be like Marassas. You are giving up a lifetime with me. Do you understand? (84–85)

In her exploration of the Marassa concept in three short stories from Danticat's edited collection *Haiti Noir,* Toni Pressley-Sanon argues, "It is only through the marasa concept that a complete . . . picture of the processes at work in diaspora consciousness can be discerned."[53] Examining the use of the trope in *Breath, Eyes, Memory,* Christophe states that the figure "encapsulates the novel's dark themes of rape, incest and sexual phantasm."[54] Christophe also connects the vodou symbol with the myth of Narcissus because of its doubling effect of water as mirror that also functions as an act of projection.[55] As Mardorossian asserts in her analysis *of Breath, Eyes, Memory*, Martine "shares Narcissus' yearning for a reflection of identity that will restore her sense of wholeness."[56] As her daughter is transforming into a woman, Martine's desire to return to psychic oneness and primordial wholeness is heightened. Indeed, Martine attempts to preserve the mother-daughter bond through narcissistic identification with Sophie. Martine projects and imposes aspects of herself onto Sophie to curtail Sophie's necessary independence, which involves recognition of difference. Martine wants Sophie to be united with her like "inseparable loves"; she achieves this union through the act of placing her finger in her daughter's vagina. At the moment of testing, Sophie becomes Martine's double, since she now experiences what Martine experienced as a young woman. Moreover, Martine's double sexual repression, experienced within both a collective gendered space and the private relationship between mother and daughter, is redoubled in Sophie, who must also deal with this dual oppression. Thus Martine tests Sophie not just under obligation but also to create a bond that links her forever to a shared suffering and a collective abused body. In placing her daughter within the frame of her own lived experience of sexual oppression, Sophie becomes Martine's Marassa.

The testing here is posited at the exact moment of union, doubling, and splitting of identities. Sophie's own doubling also occurs at the moment of testing. She creates a twofold image of herself, restricted to the violence imposed on the body on the one hand and escaping the body through the imagination on the other: "I had learned to double while being tested. I would close my eyes and imagine all the pleasant things I had known" (155). Once she is able to separate the collective space of her body from the individual space of herself, she is able to prevent an imposed homogenized identity. Although Martine takes control of her daughter's body, she does not succeed in fully conforming Sophie's identity with her own. This doubling creates a splitting, which ultimately ends in rupture and further bodily injury.

In an interview, Danticat explains her use of the Marassa figure. She asserts, "I wanted to use all the connotations of twins in the story. Going back to the mother-daughter relationship, the idea that two people are one, but not quite, they might look alike and talk alike, but are, in essence, different people."[57] In *Breath, Eyes, Memory*, this experience with the double in itself can be paralyzing, not transgressive, if it cannot account for difference. But doubling in the vodou context is related to but different from the principle of the Marassa. Danticat further explains, "The idea is that someone is double a person but really one person—as opposed to twins who are really two people."[58] She further observes, "Doubling acknowledges that people make separations within themselves to allow very painful experiences but also the separation allows space to do very great things."[59] When Sophie is being tested by her mother, she begins to double by trying to relive in her mind "pleasant memories" and "special moments" (84). But this act of splitting the body in two allows Sophie to inflict violence on her own body to prevent future tests. Sophie's use of the pestle to inflict bodily self-harm is also an act of freedom: "My flesh ripped apart as I pressed the pestle into it. I could see the blood slowly dripping into the bed sheet. I took the pestle and the bloody sheet and stuffed them into a bag. It was gone, the veil that always held my mother's finger back every time she tested me" (88). The removal of the "veil" by the pestle as phallic symbol is what is needed for Sophie to become a woman and embark on a journey of self-discovery. But this will be unattainable without the feminine principle. In West African tradition, the mortar and pestle together are symbols of the masculine and feminine principles. Danticat's use of the pestle evokes Audre Lorde's appropriation of the metaphor to explore female-to-female erotic power and freedom.[60] But the image of the pestle, the male principle, without the mortar, the female principle, symbolizes destruction. Thus Sophie's self-mutilation, like Martine's rape, exemplifies the violence and violation of the female body by the destructive influence of patriarchal epistemology.

For Sophie and Martine, physical violence on the body ends the testing they endure in their youth. In Martine's case, physical violence, that is, the rape, also removes the "veil" and stops the testing. Martine tells Sophie, "I realize standing here that the two greatest pains of my life are very much related. The one good thing about my being raped was that it made the testing stop. The testing and the rape. I live both every day" (170). Sophie, too, perceives her self-mutilation with the pestle as a way of "breaking manacles" and names it as an act of freedom. Nonetheless, Sophie does not gain full control of her body, and her journey is not complete. Although she leaves her mother's house and marries Joseph, she becomes bulimic and has no sexual desire for her husband. In fact, she sees a therapist and joins a sexual phobia group to overcome her disgust with sex and her body. In the sexual act with her husband, she learns to double. Revealing the psychological effects of the testing, she observes, "It [the testing] is the most horrible thing that ever happened to me. When my husband is with me now it gives me such nightmares that I have to bite my tongue to do it again" (156). Sophie later reveals, "After I got married, all through the first year I had suicidal thoughts. Some nights I woke up in a cold sweat wondering if my mother's anxiety was somehow hereditary or if it was something that I had 'caught' from living with her. Her nightmares had somehow become my own, so much so that I would wake up some mornings wondering if we hadn't both spent the night dreaming about the same thing: a man with no face, pounding a life into a helpless young girl" (182). Sophie becomes her mother's double, suffering from insomnia and dreaming the same nightmares of male authoritarian control and terror. The double figure, and the doubling that splits the mind and the body as opposites, only creates pathology for both of them. She and her mother become true Marassas, divine spiritual twins (200) only after they are both in Haiti together in the female-centered space of Dame Marie and with Grandmè Ifé, the matriarch of the family.

Erzulie and Mythical Connections in Transnational Spaces

Sophie tries to cope with the complexities of her sexuality through her imagination. However, she is constantly being pushed and pulled back into reality by it. The function of the imagination, then, is twofold. It allows the women to escape the reality of their lived experiences; simultaneously, it vividly exposes them to the degradation of their lives. Danticat articulates this through the figure of Erzulie, whose dual identity asserts the ideal representation of the female at the same time as it destroys and exploits the ideal. In "Erzulie: A Women's History of Haiti," Joan Dayan describes Erzulie as a figure that expresses an ideal at the same time as it exposes the real and oppressive lived experiences of Haitian women: "Erzulie, the goddess or loa of love in Vodoun, tells a history of women's lives that has not been told. Born on the soil of Haiti, this goddess has no precedent in Yoruba or Dahomey. In her varying incarnations, she bears the extremes of colonial history. Whether the pale and elegant Erzulie-Freda or the cold-hearted, savage Erzulie je rouj, she dramatizes a specific historiography of women's experiences in Haiti and throughout the Caribbean."[61]

Erzulie and her particularities specifically deal with Haitian history, politics, and women's concerns. Paradoxically, the figure of Erzulie is often represented in traditional literature to constitute nationalist narratives and masculine rhetoric. Danticat reformulates the figure of Erzulie as a "nonpolarized duality," which is used effectively to reiterate nationalists' discourses and to question and subvert the very discourses it reiterates.

Specifically, the travels of the Erzulie figure in the novel signify a reformulation of Haitian women's particularities within a transnational space. After Sophie returns from Haiti with the Erzulie statue her grandmother gave her, she presents it to her therapy group during one of her sessions: "Davina had a whole room in her house set aside for our meetings. When we came in, we changed into long white dresses that Buki had sewn for us. We wrapped our hair in white scarves that I had brought. As we changed in the front room, I showed them the statue of Erzulie next to our other keepsakes, the pine cones and seashells we collected on our solitary journeys" (201–2). Erzulie's movement into a transnational space raises the question of translation. How is Erzulie translated when she is removed from Haitian soil? At stake in Erzulie's translation, as Dayan asserts, are her particularities: "If we try to understand Erzulie's attributes by looking to Africa or to Europe, to Oshun, to Yemanja, to Oya, to the Virgin Mary or Venus, or as the Haitian Louis Maximilien has argued, to Helen, or as Emanuel Paul adds, to 'Ishtar of ancient Babylon' (venerated as 'she who gives herself to everyone'), we cannot account for her particularities."[62] The narrative suggests that while Erzulie's distinctiveness must be recognized, such acknowledgment does not necessitate fixity. Although Erzulie is situated with other artifacts, she still maintains a private and autonomous relationship with Sophie. This is asserted when Sophie leaves the group with Erzulie for a secluded place. Erzulie is presented as a complicated icon and artifact that signifies the resistance to sexual oppression and repression of Haitian women and is translated within a cross-cultural struggle to overcome them.

The novel's articulation of the complexities of Haitian sexuality and duality also moves beyond a specific Haitian space into a transnational space. The sexual phobia group of three women signifies the sexual oppression that traverses multiple boundaries. Aside from Sophie, who must deal with the trauma of her mother's testing, there is Buki, the Ethiopian college student who must come to terms with the mutilation of her sexual organs when she was a little girl, and Davina, a middle-aged Chicana who, raped by her grandfather for ten years, is still trying to heal from the devastating experience. The group speaks of their pains and sufferings to a black woman therapist who is also a Santería priestess. These women are able to speak of their specific experiences cross-nationally and cross-culturally: although they are separated by national and cultural identities, they are connected by traumatic experiences that make them uncomfortable with their gender and sexuality. This group is representative of a matriarchal diaspora that speaks specifically to the historical injuries of the black female body, injuries that become memory performed in the body. This collective memory is triggered and becomes flesh on the individual black female body that experiences the bodily injury. Such trauma and injuries necessitate the embrace of non-Western practices of healing and transformation of consciousness that move beyond the polarized duality.

In *Breath, Eyes, Memory,* Danticat uses the personal narrative form and the voice of a female protagonist to expose the gendered and historical specificities of Haitian women within the myriad issues Haitians face as a whole. Writing at a moment when Haitians are claiming, more emphatically, multiple home spaces, Danticat explores the complexities of Haiti's current diasporic and transnational space by presenting female characters who must come to terms with the complex consequences of gendered oppression and sexual violence that cause women to feel a sense of exile from their bodies and that silence their voices. Danticat's novel explores the way women of the African diaspora find creative ways to reclaim and reinscribe their own stories of displacement to combat the threat of perpetual silence, to speak out against patriarchal intrusion and violation, and to feel at home with their contradictions and multiplicity.

4 *The Dew Breaker* as Écho-Monde

> We know ourselves as part and as crowd, in an unknown that does
> not terrify. We cry our cry of poetry. Our boats are open, and we sail
> them for everyone.
>
> —Édouard Glissant, *Poetics of Relation*

> Intertextuality could be regarded as a deepening by superimposition
> or overlay, or as a means of injecting the vibration of diversity into the
> text. But it could also be envisaged as a form of memorialization—
> creating or consolidating, that is, a sense of textual tradition.
>
> —Mary Gallagher, *Soundings in French Caribbean*
> *Writing since 1950*

WHEN DANTICAT defined her understanding of diaspora in her
1995 lecture, "Haiti: A Bicultural Experience," she referenced *Éloge de
la Créolité* by Martinican writers Jean Bernabé, Patrick Chamoiseau, and
Raphaël Confiant, as well as the work of Saint Lucien poet and playwright
Derek Walcott to articulate the multiplicity of her own identity as a result
of the primal forced displacement and, subsequently, double displacement that engender the African diaspora and the Caribbean diaspora
respectively.[1] In her lecture, Danticat explains, "The truth is I am all these
things: Haitian, Haitian American, a citizen of the Americas, of the Caribbean. Afro-Caribbean. Afro-American."[2] In her closing remarks, Danticat
evokes the café au lait metaphor to convey the blending of these identities
in diaspora. She explains, "We all define our diaspora, our nostalgia in
a personal way. It is not one or two places, uni or bi-culturalism, but the
mix, the café-au-lait, which we make of it."[3] A decade later, in one of the
first interviews following the publication of *The Dew Breaker* in 2004,
Terry Hong asked Danticat about the transformation of her own identity
as a settled immigrant in the United States: "Now that you've been in this
country for many years, do you feel American? As an immigrant, have you
found a sense of peace with both your Haitian and American identities?"
Danticat answered,

> I have always been comfortable with being both Haitian and American. It's easier these days for immigrants to go back home. Haiti's a 90-minute flight from Miami, and I find myself going back there all the time now. I don't have to trade Haitianness for Americanness like a lot of older immigrants did. I have spent more time in the United States now than I have in Haiti, so I feel very American, but I also feel very Haitian. That's what's exciting about America these days. We don't necessarily have to melt and disappear into some kind of ideological stew. We can be who we are, contribute what we can to American culture, and still retain our ties to our native countries.[4]

Here, Danticat eschews the metaphor of the melting pot, dismissing it as an old framing of American identity that no longer holds in the twenty-first century because of the ability of immigrants to easily travel "back home" and retain ties to their "native countries." The harmonious and utopian vision of cultural mixing in Danticat's earlier discussion of diaspora is disrupted by her more recent acknowledgment that the melting of people, nationalities, and cultures into an "ideological stew" not only promotes a homogenous mixture, what Édouard Glissant describes as the "uniform blend,"[5] but also leads to the erasure or misrecognition of existing cultures and identities. Notice that in specifying the mixing as "ideological," Danticat separates the historical cultural mixing of the Caribbean from ideologies that promote utopian hybridities. In her answer to Hong's question, Danticat also maintains two distinct but relational selves that evoke the transnational contours of the Haitian diaspora in the United States today. The complex reality of Haitians in the diaspora, for Danticat, serves as a model that not only destabilizes the old melting pot vision of America and its notion of immigration integration but also engenders a dialogic vision of multiplicity and expansion, one that embraces interrelational ties as well as multiple forms of crossings and returns (real, imagined, spiritual, political, cultural) between the homeland and its diaspora. Danticat's answer also suggests that America as a nation of immigrants in the era of globalization and transnational exchange offers the possibility of a pluralistic vision of identity and culture, one that reconciles the values of individuality and self-formation as markers of modernity with those of community and the collective "we" as markers of tradition without eliding the contradictions, tensions, and ambiguities that drive this dialectic. In her diasporic imaginary, Danticat exposes and destabilizes Hegelian dialectic and Cartesian dualism that serve as primary models of subjectivity and citizen formation to interpolate the subject as the totality of fragmented parts and distinct identities not coming into a synthesis but engaging in relation. This destabilization opens the space for a new understanding of processes of integration and disintegration as well as new articulations of the dynamics between wholeness and fragmentation formations of a diasporic consciousness. Such radical articulations move beyond what Alison Landsberg describes as the melting pot fantasy of imagining the American body and psyche as single, national, and whole.[6]

In this chapter, I argue that Danticat's *The Dew Breaker* explores the evolving transnational and pluralistic contours of Danticat's diasporic subjects in ways that foreground a poetics of relation, in Glissant's sense, and its instance of écho-monde, wherein the art of echoing is presented as a polyphonic narrative weaving and confluence of identifiable and unidentifiable parts, intertexts, voices, ideologies, thematic repetitions, repetition of phrases, temporal moments, and spatial orientations. In my analysis of *The Dew Breaker*, the echo trope manifests as repetition and revision of texts that produce a relational double, a strategy of working through and transgressing the psychic anxiety of fragmentation and separation that produces alienation. This relational double is presented in the way Danticat, I argue, articulates the dialogic between the nation and the diaspora in *The Dew Breaker* as a matter of a shared obsession with genealogy, preservation, and desire for wholeness. I propose that we read *The Dew Breaker* as a textual genealogy of the Haitian diaspora that disorders, redefines, and expands our very understanding of genealogy itself beyond and against the linear national masculinist frame and heteropatriarchal norms of filiation that stress an ideal unitary self and the construction of identity as a natural phenomenon. In Danticat's diasporic imaginary, the relational double is used as a way for the writer to both master and transgress the binaries that maintain a monological and monistic ordering of the national imaginary and its corollary narratives of origin, family and ancestry, history, wholeness, unity, and community. But the process of transgression in the diasporic imaginary for Danticat is not a disavowal of traditional narratives of the nation but rather a self-reflexive rewriting that necessitates mastery, deformation, and reformation of these narratives in a relational and dialogic manner. Such rewriting exposes and unsettles not only the monological world embodied in the figure of paternal authority as master signifier but also the inherent dialogue involved in the process of reading and rewriting the text of literary "forefathers" to foreground the figure of the mother and the female/feminine voice. Danticat recalls, recovers, and unveils literary predecessors to engage in a dialogue and magnify the multiplicity of the intertextual field that grounds the relationship between the reader and the writer. She does so by working through the structural complexities of fragmentation, displacement, and dismemberment in texts. In expanding the intertextual field to incorporate oral narratives, Danticat also highlights the primacy of coexisting voices and the relationship between the listener and the speaker. Through a complex intertextual play among different voices, words, phrases, themes, and texts, Danticat, in *The Dew Breaker,* I argue, retains ideas of origin, wholeness, unity, family, ancestry, history, and community to reenact them as "the stuff" of both nation and diaspora but also to disentangle them from fixed narrative structures, ideological frames, authoritarian law of forefathers, and totalitarian absolutes that suppress women's voices/narratives and hinder heterogeneous, pluralistic, and liberatory possibilities of imagining the world, our place in it, and our relationships to each other.

The Paternal Order and the Universe of Fragments

Read as either a novel or a collection of nine linked short stories, *The Dew Breaker* explores the interconnected world and transnational lives of Haitians in Haiti and the United States, all of whom are explicitly or implicitly traumatized by the brutal twenty-nine-year regime of François Duvalier and his son, Jean-Claude Duvalier. *The Dew Breaker* begins with "The Book of the Dead," a short story that was published in the *New Yorker* in 1999, as were a number of the stories in this collection. In fact seven of the nine stories were previously published.[7] Danticat introduces, in this first story, told in the first-person voice of Ka Bienamé, a young sculptor and substitute art teacher who makes a trip from Brooklyn to Tampa, Florida, to deliver a sculpture, a three-foot mahogany figure of her father, to Gabrielle Fonteneau, a young Haitian American star of a popular television series and an art collector. The sculpture is Ka's representation of how she imagines her father in prison. But Ka's sixty-five-year-old father, who has joined his daughter on this trip, has disappeared with the sculpture after spending one night with his daughter at a hotel in Lakeland, Florida. Finding her father gone the following morning, Ka must confront the actress, who is anxiously waiting for the artwork. Remaining without a first name throughout the book, Ka's father, M. Bienamé, eventually returns without the sculpture, as he has thrown it in a man-made lake. Upon his return to the hotel, he takes his daughter to a seating area near the lake, where he reveals to her both the fate of the statue and the family secret, that he was not the prisoner she always believed him to be but instead a prison guard who tortured prisoners. In his attempt to explain to his daughter why he does not deserve being immortalized, he tells Ka, "I don't deserve a statue . . . , not a whole one at least. You see, Ka, your father was the hunter, he was not the prey."[8] The vivid scar on his face is not a reminder of violence imposed on him but evidence of his crime of murder and a past he constantly tries to conceal.

Exposure of the scar functions as a metaphor for the process of unveiling an already dismembered and disremembered past. Ka says, "I am so used to his hands covering it up that this new purposeful motion toward it seems dramatic and extreme, almost like raising a veil" (22). This unveiling creates anxiety for the young artist, whose imagination of a "prisoner father" she "loved as well as pitied" (31) has turned into "the single subject" (4) of her creativity. M. Bienamé's destruction of the statue and disclosure of the family secret, an outcome of his own anxieties and fear of being recognized, result in the loss of Ka's subject. Bu the loss of the visual object as imaginary paternal subject, I argue, initiates and engenders the possibility of rearticulation and renarration, one that makes room for the maternal subject, which appears in the story as background and afterthought. The faint emergence and recognition of the maternal subject in Ka's imaginary necessitates, firstly, mastery of the symbolic order and law of the father and, secondly, its displacement. The displacement of the symbolic father allows for the erosion of the singular author/subject/voice and a reading and recognition of fragmented narratives that foreground the absent but ever-present maternal figure and, consequently, the multiplicity of different authors/subjects/voices coexisting dialogically. What begins as a search for the father's story turns into re-memory of the mother and, by the end of *The Dew Breaker*, Ka's initiation into her mother's story.

In "Danticat's *The Dew Breaker*, Haiti, and Symbolic Migration," Jennifer E. Henton takes up the question of subjectivity and loss by reading *The Dew Breaker* with Lacanian psychoanalytic concepts of jouissance and nom du père/name of the father.[9] Henton begins by asserting, "Set in another scene . . . Danticat's Haiti engenders the psychoanalytic subject differently because Haiti castrated the colonial father early on and this castration is immutable. Still, the 'third world' subject already resides at the site of psychoanalytic inquiry."[10] This third world "subject of the oppressed" works from multiple spaces of loss and is represented by Ka, whose subjectivity, Henton argues, emerges when Ka suffers her father's loss.[11] For Henton, Haiti as "secondary backdrop of the novel" stages a scene for the father's loss, a loss that is not only marked by absence or silence in the imaginary but provokes "jouissance" in the Lacanian sense.[12]

Henton observes, "Ka has no access to Haiti's other scene, its place holder status for loss of the paternal order of the father: colonialism." Henton rightly argues that when the statue is destroyed, Ka experiences a break in "her imaginary connection to her father."[13] Consequently, Henton continues, "Ka's scene involves loss: her victim father is missing, her status of him is missing, her heritage is missing. This complex traversal of dream, image, symbol, hallucination all return Ka to Haiti."[14] The Haiti that Ka returns to is not the historic Haiti but the Haiti of Duvalier that she attempts to reconstruct in her imaginary. Henton then makes another major move in her analysis by introducing a second Lacanian concept, *le nom du père,* or the name of the father, to link historic Haiti to the Duvalier regime and the larger paternal order of symbolic law. In Henton's description of Duvalier's colonialist interpretation of the name of the father, which functions in Danticat's text as delusion, not desire, a polarized duality is created:

> The symbiosis of the personal and public father breaks down in *The Dew Breaker* because of Duvalier's colonial/Haitian demands. Whereas the public and private father (or some restricting figure) usually work in unison to uphold the law, here the public father largely cancels out the private father. The private father initiates the symbolic order by barring the child from the mother—the familial, roughly speaking. Here, the options are eradication or enjoyment of Duvalier. Duvalier insisted that the private father go missing or function as a metonymical substitute for himself, hence the Dew Breaker.[15]

Henton's analysis concentrates on a displacement of the father and his reduction to symbol and metonym of Duvalier, who, Henton argues, "usurped the familial" and the private father.[16] Thus, for Henton, the dew breaker's namelessness in the novel functions "as a return to the father's house, not the father's power."[17] Even when Henton discusses the emergence of the mother at the end of her analysis, the maternal figure remains part of the paternal function of the symbolic order.[18] Henton writes, "The presence of the mother initiates a move from delusion about the father to dream of the father."[19] But the displacement of the paternal object of desire, and faint presence of the mother, I argue, initiates a return to the primal scene of fragmentation, to the unspeakable, the space outside and beyond language. In order for Danticat to transgress language, she must master it.

I continue the Lacanian reading of "The Book of the Dead," but I offer a different interpretation of the first story, which is centered on the emergence of the mother as transgression of the symbolic order and its representations of the patriarchal nuclear family. Naming is significant here, and Henton is right to conjure the name of the father concept, but what Henton unfortunately misses in her analysis, and what I will develop later in this chapter, is the significance of the dew breaker's family name, Bienamé, as a constructed public knowable and fictional identity, a name that creates a textual genealogical bridge to the Bienamé family in Jacques Roumain's *Gouverneurs de la rosée* (*Masters of the Dew*), which offers a classic ideal representation of the patriarchal nuclear family. In my analysis, the name Bienamé functions as a signifier linked to the master signifier of the father, one not limited to the particular context of Duvalier but one that expands into the law of filiation and kinship names as well as the intertextual play between texts bounded by a network of signifiers grounded in the name of the father. In my analysis, I argue that Danticat dismembers texts to break apart the paternal signifier and its archetypal/prototypical images that attempt to define identity as a unified indivisible whole. Displacement and fragmentation of texts not only expose the fantasy of wholeness but also offer entry into the imaginary space of the mother and possible entry into the maternal text. I thus point to another Lacanian concept: the *corps morcelé*, the body in pieces or the fragmented body, to, on the one hand, understand Ka's relationship with not only her father but also her mother and, on the other hand, explore Danticat's understanding of wholeness and fragmentation in the diasporic imaginary.

In *Écrits*, Lacan defines the role of the fragmented body in the mirror stage:

> The mirror stage is a drama whose internal pressure pushes precipitously from insufficiency to anticipation—and, for the subject caught up in the lure of spatial identification, turns out fantasies that proceed from a fragmented image of the body to what I will call an "orthopedic" form of its totality—and to the finally donned armor of an alienating identity, that will mark his entire mental development with its rigid structure.
>
> This fragmented body . . . is regularly manifested in dreams when the movement of an analysis reaches a certain level of aggressive disintegration of the individual. It then appears in the form of disconnected limbs or of organs exoscopically represented, growing wings and taking up arms for internal persecutions that the visionary Hieronymus Bosch fixed for all time in painting. . . . But this form turns out to be tangible even at the organic level, in the lines of "fragilization" that define the hysteric's fantasmatic anatomy, which is manifested in schizoid and spasmodic symptoms.[20]

Lacan discusses the mirror apparatus in the unification of the ideal "I" with the statue as object projection and the appearance of doubles as heterogeneous nature of psychic realities. This heterogeneity is expressed in what he calls the "imagos of the fragmented body." For Lacan, the imagos of the body in pieces are "images of castration, emasculation, mutilation, dismemberment, dislocation, evisceration, devouring, and 'bursting open of the body.'"[21] These images, as metaphors of fragmentation, speak to a primordial discord the infant experiences with the body. They are at odds with the mirror image of the unified body. The end of the mirror stage as part of the imaginary order for Lacan initiates the dialectic of the "I" to the social situation articulated by the Freudian Oedipal complex.[22] This marks the beginning of the symbolic order, wherein the imago of the father displaces the imago of the mother (in the preoedipal imaginary) to sustain both paternal authority and the illusion of wholeness. It is my contention that in *The Dew Breaker,* which rewrites the Oedipal narrative, characters and texts must be taken apart and put back together differently. The textual fragmentation, what I am calling the text in pieces, like Lacan's body in pieces, points to both the individual's anxiety of fragmentation and desire for wholeness that all characters in the text experience at some level. In "The Book of the Dead," this tension between the fragmented body and the whole body is articulated through the presentation of, and anxiety about, the carved wooden sculpture that represents the imago of the father.

Valery Kaussen, in her analysis of *The Dew Breaker,* looks at the significance of the Egyptian sculptures in relation to Ka's sculpture. She writes, "The Egyptian sculptures at the Brooklyn museum and those that the daughter creates of her father, then, are complex images that both deceive and reveal, comfort and trouble, depending on the knowledge of the spectator."[23] Regal and humble in its representation, the completed sculpture of the father is Ka's unique and creative attempt at embracing the fantasy world of her own imagination. From Ka's perspective, the statue represents a desired wholeness that is already threatened by fragmentation. She says,

> I checked on the sculpture, just felt it a little bit through the bubble padding and carton wrapping to make sure it was still whole. I'd used a piece of mahogany that was naturally flawed, with a few superficial cracks along what was now the back. I'd thought these cracks beautiful and had made no effort to sand or polish them away, as they seemed like the wood's own scars, like the one my father had on his face. But I was also a little bit worried about the

cracks. Would they seem amateurish and unintentional, like a mistake? Could the wood come apart with simple movements or with age? Would the client be satisfied? (6–7)

Ka's ideal representation of her father is not an image of perfection, an ideal I image; rather, it is an image that attempts to offer a more real and natural representation, one that does not attempt to hide any flaws and that inevitably exposes the idea of wholeness as fleeting. At the same time, the sculpture makes tangible the fictional story that maintains the single-subject narrative and illusion of wholeness, which Ka's father views as a kind of jouissance, a pleasure only fully experienced and achieved in the afterlife. But the pleasure principle is the very reason Ka creates sculptures: she makes statues to "amaze" her father (19). Perhaps because she has achieved this goal, the statue initiates the death drive and move toward self-destruction. M. Bienamé tells his daughter, "When I first saw your statue, I wanted to be buried with it, to take it with me into the other world" (17). He also recognizes himself in the statue. He admits to Ka, "I am one of those statues" (19). But this self is not the ideal "I" that M. Bienamé needs to maintain for self-preservation. As such, Ka both recognizes and misrecognizes her father in the statue. Ironically, while Ka aims to satisfy her father's desire for wholeness through her imaginary, M. Bienamé maintains the illusion of wholeness by reinscribing Ka into the laws of the symbolic order. He performs the paternal function through symbolic death of the imaginary image by throwing the sculpture in the lake, asserting his authority in both the construction of his image and in the telling of his story. The father's story, a story of fragmentation, therefore must constantly be juxtaposed to an eschatological narrative of the soul, which insists on wholeness as jouissance, an experience only achieved after death.

Indeed, the sculpture gets co-opted into the "universal world of fathers" (12); this was never Ka's conscious intention. Deprived of control over her own consciousness, Ka is immediately pulled into the world of her father's past. This is not unusual for Ka, as she is used to her father's influence on her life. Sitting in front of the man-made lake where M. Bienamé has thrown the sculpture, Ka observes, "Again, I'm there simply because he wants me to be" (15). There are other instances that expose M. Bienamé's authoritative and narcissistic tendencies. At one point M. Bienamé tells his daughter, "Ka, no matter what, I'm still your father, still your mother's husband" (24). Ka's own desires have been sublimated for her father's pleasure. When Ka's father recalls reading passages from *The Book of the*

Dead to her daughter while sitting by the lake, Ka does not express joy in this childhood memory:

> But this recollection is hard for me to embrace. I had been terribly bored by *The Book of the Dead*. . . . It had seemed too selfish of him not to ask me what I wanted to listen to before going to bed, what I wanted to read and have read to me. But since he'd recovered from the measles and hadn't died as we'd both feared, I'd vowed to myself to always tolerate, even indulge him, letting him take me places I didn't enjoy and read me things I cared nothing about, simply to witness the joy they gave him, the kind of bliss that might keep a dying person alive. (18)

Toleration also includes maintaining the heteronormative order and patriarchal fantasy world of wholeness, wherein M. Bienamé transmits his own desires to his daughter, who has learned to mimic her father's desires in order to develop a relationship with him.

The father thus maintains authorial power and mastery of his own representation by telling his story to his daughter: she does not have the right to author his text, or her own for that matter. But the destruction of the sculpture elides the linear progression and dualistic structure of the very story he attempts to tell, one that begins with him symbolically birthing his daughter into being by naming her: "When you were born, I look at your face, I think, here is my ka, my good angel" (17). Ka's father constantly repeats this story to his daughter, so often that Ka can complete his sentences. Ka has mastered this Egyptian narrative about the reunion of body and soul in the afterlife. Ka's father reinstates the paternal function of the name of the father as signifier by constantly returning to his own desires and lost object, which can only be articulated and made recognizable through a dualistic frame. The appearance of the double through the image of Ka points to the father's desire for wholeness and reunion with the homeland as a past already marked by fragmentation, a past that one can only return to after death.

The father's confession, however, initiates a process of discovery for Ka, one that prompts both the narrator and the reader into the mystery of her parents' past, their birthplace in Haiti, identities, and enigmatic silence. This process of discovery involves a reconsideration of wholeness and a return to the primal experience of fragmentation, separation, and loss that defines what Lacan describes as the imaginary realm. When Ka discloses to his daughter that he has thrown the sculpture in the lake, she reimagines her lost object in terms of dispersion, missing pieces, and dismembered parts. Ka speculates, "The cracks have probably taken in so much water that the wood has split into several chunks and plunged to the bottom. All I can think of saying is something glib, something I'm not even sure my father will understand" (15–16). For Ka, the imagined splitting of the sculpture directs her to a space outside of the father's narrative, a space outside of the symbolic realm and beyond language. This way of imagining objects as fragmented is not new for Ka. M. Bienamé recalls, "When I took you to the Brooklyn Museum, I would stand there for hours admiring them. But all you noticed was how there were pieces missing from them, eyes, noses, legs, sometimes even heads. You always noticed more what was not there than what was" (19). Destruction of the sculpture pulls Ka back into a universe of fragments and opens the space for interrogating what is missing and absent as well as acknowledging multiple and differing perspectives. Thus the opening line of the story, "My father is gone," elicits both the anxiety of separation and the first stage of individuation. While Henton posits that this line works from a space of loss, I argue that it is a space of recovery, one that initiates the possibility beyond the symbolic order of the father and toward the imaginary space of the mother. Entry into the absent maternal text creates opportunity for rewriting and the articulation of new language, new forms of expression that mark the diasporic imaginary and its insistence on plurality and multiplicity as consequence of the primal experience of fragmentation.

The journey Ka embarks on with the destruction of her artwork also allows for the possible entrance into the world of the mother's past and maternal genealogy to rediscover the fragmented text differently. When the father makes his definitive statement, "Your father was the hunter, he was not the prey" (20), Ka is confused and wonders,

> Is he going to explain why he and my mother have no close friends, why they've never had anyone over to the house, why they never speak of any relatives in Haiti or anywhere else, or have never returned there, or, even after I learned Creole from them, have never taught me anything else about the country beyond what I could find out on my own, on the television, in newspapers, in books? Is he about to tell me why Manman is so pious? Why she goes to daily Mass? I am not sure I want to know anything more than the little they've chosen to share with me all these years, but it is clear to me that he needs to tell me, has been trying to for a long time. (21)

But this path to the mother's story is constantly deferred. As Ka explains,

> There is no space in my brain to allow for whatever my mother might have to confess. Was she huntress or prey? A Thirty-year-plus disciple of my father's

coercive persuasion? She'd kept to herself even more than he had, like someone who was nurturing a great pain that she could never speak about. Yet she had done her best to be a good mother to me, taking charge of feeding and clothing me and making sure my hair was always combed, leaving only what she must have considered my intellectual development to my father. (22)

And yet images of her mother as a young woman fill her head, and the questions she has for her mother are many (23). But Ka's mother, who only emerges in the story through muffled and disrupted telephone conversations, appears as a passive subject also caught up in the authoritarian universe of the father. When she speaks, she articulates her husband's desires. Interestingly, Ka evokes the trope of ventriloquism through her dialogue with her mother: "As my mother is speaking, this feeling comes over me that I sometimes have when I'm carving, this sensation that my hands don't belong to me at all, that something else besides my brain and muscles is moving my fingers, something bigger and stronger than myself, an invisible puppetmaster over whom I have no control" (25). In her reading of *The Dew Breaker,* Elena Machado Sáez observes, "The puppetmaster description evokes the figure of the untouchable dictator whose power and control appears to infiltrate all aspects of her life."[24] In my reading, the "puppetmaster" description signals what Lacan describes as the primary stage of bodily fragmentation and discord in the imaginary space of the mother. In the symbolic realm dominated by the figure of the father, the mother's voice cannot fully be heard. In her exchange with her mother, Ka subtly expresses both the primacy of the father and his voice and the displacement of the female maternal subject and her voice. Between the father's transmission of monologic speech and the mother's disrupted speech, Ka "is the keeper of both speech and silence" (32). To get to the mother's story, and the complexities of fragmentation, she must make a number of narrative detours and moves away from the Oedipus narrative as master text that sustains the imago of the father and displaces the imago of the mother. For Danticat, these narrative detours leave traces that manifest as intertextual echoes, which are fundamental in the strategy of writing and rewriting the displaced subject through dialogic relation.

Poetics of Reverberation

Danticat's conscious and intentional weaving of diasporic subjectivities and their predicaments in transnational spaces reveal what Édouard Glissant defines as a "poetics of relation" that is a constitutive element of the African diaspora more broadly and manifest most visibly in the Caribbean. In his seminal work, *Poetics of Relation,* originally published in French as *Poétique de la relation* in 1990, Édouard Glissant articulates this poetics of relation as a dynamic of interconnectedness wherein the notion of identity is defined by relation: "Each and every identity is extended through a relationship with the other," Glissant writes.[25] Grounding his poetics in the principle of Deleuzian rhizomatic thought and its reframing of the root system,[26] Glissant begins with the assertion that the monolingual root is no longer important.[27] For Glissant the image of the rhizome prompts "the knowledge that identity is no longer completely within the root, but in relation."[28] Glissant thereafter introduces the notion of errantry as a concept that opposes the "totalitarian drive of a single unique root"[29] and instead privileges movement and relation: "Because the thought of errantry is also the thought of what is relative, the thing relayed as the thing related. The thought of errantry is a poetics, which always infers that at some moment it is told. The tale of errantry is the tale of relation."[30] In terms of language, relation is spoken multilingually;[31] in terms of ideology and politics, relation rightfully opposes the totalitarianism of any monolingual intent.[32] As ontology, relation is a way of being and entails parts that cannot be split into original elements.[33] Glissant writes, "Each of its parts patterns activity implicated in the activity of every other. The history of peoples has led to this dynamic; they need not stop running in their own momentum to join in this movement, since they are inscribed in it already. They cannot, however, 'give on and with' until they reach the point at which they go beyond assenting to their linear drive alone and consent to a global dynamics-practicing a self-break and a reconnection."[34] In relation, elements join one another without conjoining or merging in expanse of relation,[35] in the circularity of a complex whole that makes up what Glissant calls the "interactive totality."[36] These elements become interdependent unities that function not as models but a "revealing échos-monde."[37] In Glissant's imaginary construct of relation "thought makes music."[38] Thus échos-monde are the creative ways communities express confluences. They lend themselves not to generalizations but to diversity and ambiguity, what Glissant calls the "force of opacity."[39] Glissant writes, "*Echos-monde* are not exacerbations that result directly from the convulsive conditions of relation. They are at work in the matter of the world; they prophesy or illuminate it, divert it or conversely gain strength within it."[40] Stressing the polyphonic aspect of relation and écho-monde, Glissant continues:

In order to cope with or express confluences, every individual, every community, forms its *échos-monde,* imagined from power of vainglory, from sufferance or impatience. Each individual makes this sort of music and each community as well. As does the totality composed of individuals and communities.

Echos-monde thus allow us to sense and cite the cultures of peoples in the turbulent confluences whose globality organizes or *chaos-monde.* They pattern its constituent elements and its expansions.[41]

Representing a plurality of perspectives, Danticat's diasporic subjects in *The Dew Breaker* navigate through an opaque diasporic space of relation and confluence. Their stories move nonlinearly between the past and the present, between homeland and diaspora, first-person and third-person narrative voices, localizable and nonlocalizable geographical spaces. Nothing is clear, fixed, and straightforward. Everything is fragmented, with parts that can only be made legible through association, doubling, and repetition. In its patterns of intertextual echoing as repetition, revision, and double, in its insistence on plurality and ambiguity and in its dialogic movement between the homeland and the nation, Danticat's *The Dew Breaker* is a masterful instance of écho-monde.

Indeed, a number of scholars have analyzed Danticat's work, not just *The Dew Breaker,* to highlight this Glissantian poetics of relation. Rocio Davis, in "Oral Narratives as Short Story Cycle: Forging Community in Edwidge Danticat's *Krik? Krak!*" argues that in Danticat's first short story collection, the "connective patterns on all levels draw these [elements] together into a totality strengthened by varying types of internal cohesion: a title, the development of a central character, the delineation of a community, or an explicit theme."[42] Building on Davis in "'My Mouth Is the Keeper of Both Speech and Silence . . . ,' or the Vocalisation of Silence in Caribbean Short Stories by Edwidge Danticat," Judith Misrahi-Barak examines the relationships among speech, silence, writing, orality, and literacy through a comparative analysis of *Krik? Krak!* and *The Dew Breaker* as short story cycles to argue that silence is used as both theme and technique to uncover the very silences in the text.[43] She further shows the ways in which "intertextual echoes" also function as narrative technique. She explains, "In fact both collections bring the stories together in a network of characters passing from one story to another, echoes, reminiscences, and intertextual allusions that have to be deciphered by the reader himself."[44] These echoes within the text will indeed bring out a "new resonance" and "new voice and consciousness"[45] that include readers as active participants in the narration.[46] Indeed, references to other texts play an important role in Danticat's work. As Kyle Minor asserts in a review of *The Dew Breaker,* "The stories are compelling on their own merits, but it is their small details—passing references to other stories—that are telling."[47] And yet, as I argue, it is the way Danticat imbeds these references in the text to strengthen loose relations between these complex diverse everyday characters (men and women) who are implicated and intertwined in a shared transnational space and history of trauma that is most revealing.

Mary Gallagher takes up the relationship between narrative structure and silence in her essay "Concealment, Displacement, and Disconnection." Gallagher states that the narrative structure of Danticat's "*The Dew Breaker* is a hybrid form and that an essential part of its meaning derives from its subversion of the boundary between the two genres."[48] The book's structure, she argues, reflects Danticat's thematic focus on moral issues of silence, concealment guilt, complicity, witness, redemption displacement, and disconnection. The structure also complements the diversity of the text: "The plurality of perspectives both enriches and complicates the reader's interpretation of the various stories and also reflexively points toward the difficulty of establishing a univocal meaning for any particular character, situation or text."[49] But the impact of *The Dew Breaker,* Gallagher astutely argues, "derives in great part from Danticat's aesthetic of reverberation. This operates most overtly at a thematic and more broadly intertextual level between the different stories."[50] Judith Misrahi-Barak, who builds on the work of trauma studies, examines Danticat's play of intertextuality as an aspect of translation that involves a "working through" of narrative trauma propelled by translation "that can take place through repetition of, and listening to, the *other* text."[51] The very structure of *text* reflects, reverberates, and resignifies the mental process of the *"working through"* propelled by translation and highlights the "tensions of the poly-temporality of trauma" structure of the novel.[52] Focusing on testimonials of trauma, Wilson C. Chen sees *The Dew Breaker* as a collection of diverse testimonies that "simulat[e] the dialogic, polyphonic qualities of a community's response to trauma and displacement."[53] Corinne Duboin points out in "Reprises textuelles dans *The Dew Breaker* d'Edwidge Danticat" that the plurality of the stories, polyphony of voices, and episodic fragmented structure partake in an "alternative approach to creative writing" that engages in a complex intertextual play of repeated phrases and common themes, textual references, and citations that Duboin quite masterfully locates.[54] These various intellectual mappings of silences and echoes of Danticat's *The Dew*

Breaker expose the work itself as, to use a phrase in Danticat's collection, "a fragmented collage with many additions as erasures" (79).

While scholars have pointed out these connected phrases, references, and citations that Danticat divulges in her acknowledgments at the end of *The Dew Breaker,* the intertexts that are not disclosed there are often overlooked. This includes, but is certainly not limited to, Danticat's intertextual play on the names of characters. For example, M. Bienamé, the eponymous dew breaker, creates a genealogical bridge to the Bienamé family in *Masters of the Dew.* Monsieur Christophe and Romain in "Monkey Tails" recall Henri Christophe and Jacques Roumain, founding revolutionary fathers of Haitian history and literature. As Danticat writes in *Create Dangerously,* Haitians evoke names of founding fathers to cite historical connections (103). Similarly, the actress Gabrielle Fonteneau recalls the real life of Haitian American actress Garcelle Beauvais. The character Aline Cajuste in "Bridal Seamstress" is very similar to Alina "Tibebe Cajuste" in *Walking on Fire* by Beverly Bell. It is no coincidence that the story complements the very objective of *Walking on Fire,* which is to foreground Haitian women's stories of survival and resistance. As Danticat states in the foreword to the book, Alina "Tibebe," like Aline in *The Dew Breaker,* has found a way to reclaim her voice. Freda, one of only three first-person narrative voices in *The Dew Breaker,* evokes the goddess Erzulie. This is fitting, as Freda's narrative pulls the reader back into the creative space of the feminine, the space of female diasporic narratives. The names Old Zo and Da in "Night Talkers," as Michael Dash asserts, refer and pay homage to Dany Laferrière and his novel *Pays sans chapeau.*[55] Dash and other scholars point to Danticat's rewriting of the classic narrative of return and its iconic figures.[56] Rhonda Cobham states that the scene of Haitian countryside in the story is reminiscent of Joseph Zobel's 1955 novel *Rue cases nègres.*[57] But the name Old Zo, like Popo in "Night Talkers," a story that captures intimate details of peasant life and customs in Haiti's countryside, also echoes the work of African American writers of the 1930s such as Langston Hughes and Zora Neale Hurston. In the last story of *The Dew Breaker,* the eponymous dew breaker's superior at Casernes Dessaline, Rosalie, is a direct reference to Madame Max Aldolphe, also known as Rosalie Bosquet, the warden of Fort Dimanche, who was also the head of Fillettes Laleau, the female branch of the Tonton Macoutes, François Duvalier's paramilitary force. She was considered Duvalier's right-hand woman.

Besides the naming, the phrases and references that are not easily traced or mentioned in the acknowledgment are also critically important to a close reading of *The Dew Breaker.* Some of these phrases do not have a direct locatable source. For example, in the prison, the preacher's recall of the old saying "Mouritu te salutant, I who am about [to] die salute you" is presented in a satirical manner: "Ave urina. The ridiculous thought entered his mind from some source he couldn't quite recall" (214). A more specific direct reference is to Samuel Beckett and his play *En attendant Godot* (204), which echoes Ka's minimalist artistic style specifically. The mention of nineteen army officers killed under the authorization of Duvalier in the last story, "The Dew Breaker," is actually a historical "nonevent" rarely recalled but that can be traced in *Papa Doc and the Tonton Macoutes* by Bernard Diederich and Al Burt, a book that is mentioned in the acknowledgments.[58] Danticat acknowledges Patrick Lemoine's memoir, *Fort Dimanche, Dungeon of Death,* to echo his sentiments and desire to memorialize silenced moments in history for a new generation of Haitian descendants living in the United States: as Lemoine writes, "While in prison, I witnessed the annihilation of a generation, a silent genocide known only to the few who survived. I solemnly vowed to keep alive the memory of my departed cellmates, and to denounce the terrors of an infernal era in an attempt to prevent this dark chapter in history from repeating itself."[59] These intertextual references expose Danticat as an avid reader who leaves traces in her texts in the hopes that her readers "will go out and find many more books to read about Haiti."[60] But they also reveal Danticat's authorial investment in the meticulous deconstruction of narrative archetypes in *The Dew Breaker,* especially that of the Tonton Macoutes.

Dialogue with Roumain

The first and most obvious intertext of *The Dew Breaker,* Jacques Roumain's *Gouverneurs de la rosée (Masters of the Dew),* is one that is not mentioned in the acknowledgments but nonetheless saturates the book and needs no special recognition. Published posthumously in 1944, *Gouverneurs de la rosée* is set within the historical backdrop of the importation of workers from the Caribbean, particularly Haiti and Jamaica, to Cuba. Known as braceros, these workers provided the cheap labor desired by sugar companies, often American owned, of the early twentieth century. The protagonist in the novel, Manuel Bienamé, develops a proletariat consciousness after spending years cutting cane in Cuba and returns to the village of Fond Rouge fifteen years later to transform the consciousness of the peasants in the village by merging his Marxist ideas with the practice of the *Kombit,* a Haitian tradition of collective labor. Like *The Dew Breaker, Masters of the Dew* raises the question of redemptive death and spiritual reconciliation. But while the drama of redemption and reconciliation plays itself out in *Masters of the Dew* through the plight of a messianic protagonist who singlehandedly raises the consciousness of his family and community, in *The Dew Breaker* there is no one singular voice that consumes the narrative, no authorial ideological intention or linear move toward peaceful reconciliation through sacrifice, no homogenous and harmonious community of Haitian peasants. Instead, the reader finds in Danticat's collection fragmented histories, dispersed individuals, a plethora of ideological perspectives, a diverse community of different class backgrounds. Danticat engages dialogically with *Masters of the Dew* as master text to reconfigure ideas of soul, heritage, origin, wholeness, and community beyond monologic and monistic frames of identity and filiation. The intertextual echo of *Masters of the Dew* in *The Dew Breaker* is an act of recovery and a rewriting and a rereading that moves from traditional filiation to textual and literary affiliation. As Michael Dash asserts, Danticat's novel "that deals with painful reconciliation in the way of the Duvalier dictatorship, *The Dew Breaker,* clearly echoes Roumain's 1944 novel *Gouverneurs de la rosée* in its somber reflection on the metamorphosis of a mobilized peasantry from agents of social transformation into the hired killers of the Duvalier dictatorship."[61]

In *Create Dangerously,* Danticat reveals that she "maintains a silent conversation" with Roumain that "publically manifested itself" in *The Dew Breaker.* Roumain, she writes in *Create Dangerously,* as a journalist, teacher, and citizen, infiltrates her daily life (62). Danticat further states that her awareness of being a "literary orphan" is due to this continuous conversation with Roumain. Thus, as she reveals in *Create Dangerously,* Danticat fashions affiliative ties with her literary predecessors. In describing the movement from filiation to affiliation in the writing process, post-colonial literary critic Edward Said states that critical affiliation puts into question the idea of originality and foregrounds the significance of repetition: "Repetition in a text is useful way of separating history from ideas of 'divine originality.'"[62] For Said, originality involves echoes of texts: "Thus the best way to consider originality is to look not for first instances of a phenomenon, but rather to see duplication, parallelism, symmetry, parody, repetition, echoes of it—the way, for example, literature has made itself a topos of writing. What the modern of contemporary imagination thinks of is less the confining of something to a book, and more the release of something from a book in writing. . . . The writer thinks less of writing originally, and more of rewriting."[63] Said later states that the writer "can be read as an individual whose impulse historically has been always to write through one or another given work, in order finally to achieve the independence . . . of writing that knows no bounds."[64] Rewriting by way of repetition then deconstructs and severs the perceived natural chain of filiation and its link to the quest for originality and origin.

Danticat's rewriting of *Masters of the Dew* is also a rewriting of filiation and community. This is most evident in the story "Monkey Tails." In *Masters of the Dew* Manuel believes that solving the drought issue in Fonds Rouge will unify the community into brotherly communion: "Water would bring them together," Manuel believes.[65] When Manuel finds water, his father expresses one of the clearest moments of traditional filiation: "Yes, hats off to you, Manuel Jean-Joseph! Delira, do you hear? My boy's found water! By himself, with his own hands. I recognize my blood. I recognize my race. That's the way we are in this family—enterprising Negroes—and we don't lack intelligence either!"[66] This mode of identification is reminiscent of the period in which *Masters of the Dew* was originally written and published. Roumain's novel is in conversation with ideas from the Indigenism movement of the 1920s, spearheaded by Jean Price-Mars, who called for psychological and cultural reform of the national soul; the Négritude literary movement of the 1930s and 1940s, which affirmed and celebrated the values of black civilization and culture; and the Africanist Griot movement of the 1930s, which recognized the vodou religion as an important element of Haitian culture. These movements, which have inevitably influenced the eponymous dew breaker's interest in ancient Egyptian culture, relied heavily on a unified vision of self and traditional notions of filiation that Danticat acknowledges in *The Dew Breaker* through Claude's engagement with the community in the countryside upon his return to Haiti: "These people don't even know me, man. They've never seen my face before, not even in pictures. They still took me in, after everything I did, because my mom's told them I was their blood. I look at them and I see nothing of me, man, blank, nada, but they look at me and they say he has so-and-so's nose and his grandmother's forehead, or some shit like that" (102). Ties of filiation persist despite the experience of displacement that ruptures family ties. The structure of *The Dew Breaker* also places emphasis on familial relationships. The three stories that link all the other stories, "Book of the Dead," "Book of Miracles," and "The Dew Breaker," are told from the perspective of the daughter, wife, and father, respectively, modeling the structure of a family nucleus, one that echoes and doubles the Bienamé family in *Masters of the Dew.* The three stories also model the literary conversations Danticat has with Roumain, Alexis, and Marie Chauvet respectively, the trio of writers Danticat defines as the cornerstone of Haitian literature.[67]

In Roumain's novel, filiation through family is coupled with community to present a utopian image of the peasants in the village as one unified single family: "Misery and desolation ravage Fonds Rouge. So let your better judgment have a voice. Yes, blood has been shed, I know, but water will wash the blood away. The new crop will grow out of the past and ripen in forgetfulness. There's only one way to save ourselves—only one, not two. It's for us to make again one good family of peasants, to call together again in the name of brother to brother our union of tillers of the soil, to share our pain and our labor between comrades and comrades."[68] Manuel's death as the symbol of sacrifice for the renewal of community and the development of radical consciousness calls for reconciliation "so that life can begin anew, so the day can break on the dew."[69] However, in Danticat's rendering of community and the struggles of the Haitian workforce disempowered by neocolonial structures of global capital, reconciliation in Roumain's seems highly unlikely. Certainly, the preacher in *The Dew Breaker,* a character whose death the reader experiences intimately, does not offer Roumain's idealism. The preacher's death only reinforces the ambiguity that defines Danticat's writing and her characters: "Maybe his death would . . . move his people to revolt, to demand justice for themselves while requesting it for him. Or maybe his death would have no relevance at all. He would simply join a long list of martyrs and his name would vanish from his countrymen's lips as soon as his body was placed in the ground" (227). Instead of the strengthening of filiation found in Roumain's Manuel and his linear monologic discourse, Danticat, through ambiguous polyvocal displaced characters, explores its breakdown and pitfalls.

In the story "Monkey Tails," Michel, a first-person narrator, records his story to his unborn son, via audio cassette, to pass down memories of his adolescence, around the time of Jean-Claude Duvalier's departure. He is doing so while his pregnant wife is asleep beside him. Like M. Bienamé, Michel projects the primacy of his voice to his unborn son by recording his story, which by the very nature of the act of recording is meant to be passed down and repeated. The story moves between the past events that are being told, dated February 7, 1986, and the present moment, February 7, 2004, the date his son is expected to enter the world. As he prepares for his son's birth, Michel recalls the story of his childhood friend Romain to explain an important moment in Haitian history and transmit a positive memory of manhood and friendship. This echoes the fraternal community embraced by Manuel in *Masters of the Dew*. As in Roumain's novel, water is foregrounded as an important symbol of brotherly community. But Danticat does not choose the symbol to represent the links among man, community, and the natural environment. As opposed to water being a source of community empowerment and environmental abundance, it is presented as a commodity for private enrichment. Monsieur Christophe's water station business, which was sustained under the Duvalier regime, has been dismantled by a crowd seeking retribution against the Tonton Macoutes after Jean-Claude Duvalier and his wife left the country: "A different crowd was emerging now, a crowd of maids, menservants, and indentured children, restaveks, carrying all sort of vessels, including buckets, water jugs, earthen jars, calabashes, and even chamber pots, to gather the precious water" (145). Through the character Michel, Danticat engages and questions the obvious Marxist leanings and assumptions behind Roumain's master text: "Also, there were people with shops in our neighborhood, people like Monsieur Christophe, who had always been and would always be powerful, maintaining authority through control of water or bread or some other important resource, as Romain might say, no matter what was going on politically" (146). Even the Marxist notion of work for the liberation of the peasant community is put into question: 'Strange too how people with means can make the less fortunate feel special by putting them to work" (147–48). In Danticat's intertextual conversation with Roumain, the Marxist model of proletariat struggle is put to the test. And yet the water, beyond ideological intentions, still functions artistically as a literary metonym for cleansing and regeneration: "Maybe the water could be an offering to the god on behalf of all the dead, no matter what their political leanings had been" (146). The symbol of the water in Danticat's texts also portends the liberation theology of democratic leader Father Jean-Bertrand Aristide and his political party, the Lavalas—the flood movement.

The bonds of filiation so fundamental to Roumain's text are severed in Danticat's story and pose a challenge to the father-son relationship so fundamental to the nationalist discourse of the Duvalier regime. The myth of legitimacy behind this discourse is fully exposed in *The Dew Breaker*. Michel's father has always been symbolically dead and turned into a political figure, a sacrifice for the nation, a myth constructed by Michel's mother. In reality, Michel is a "dishonorable secret," the son of Monsieur Christophe, a powerful man in the neighborhood who sells water and does not acknowledge Michel as his son. Through Michel's story, Danticat exploits this reality of absent fathers to examine the paradox between the Duvalier regime's rhetoric of fatherhood in Duvalier's nationalist discourse and the displacement and absence of fathers under a regime that has created "a generation of mostly fatherless boys" (141). Michel tells his story: "I was twelve years old, and, according to my mother, three months before my birth, I had lost my father to something my mother would only vaguely describe as 'political,' making me part of a generation of mostly fatherless boys, though some of our fathers were still living, even if somewhere else—in the provinces, in another country, or across the alley not acknowledging us. A great many of our fathers had also died in the dictatorship's prisons, and others had abandoned us altogether to serve the regime" (141). This juxtaposition of loss of father by death and abandonment is echoed and doubled in Michel's account of Duvalier's departure, who is "father" to the nation, as Michel's mother reminds us. Michel describes this departure as abandonment of his children: "Their departure orphaned a large number of loyal militiamen" (140) who go from being victimizers of the regime to victims overnight. Régulus, who abandons Michel's friend, Roumain, when he is only a month old, is one of those militiamen running for his life. He too becomes part of the narrative of loss, becoming something "political," part of an established myth of the nation.

In *The Dew Breaker,* Danticat highlights and emphasizes the plight of orphaned children, bastard children, and abandoned children through thematic repetition. In doing so, she raises the question of legitimacy, an important component of the chain of filiation. As Glissant asserts, "If legitimacy is ruptured, the chain of filiation is no longer meaningful, and the community wanders the world, no longer able to lay claim to any primordial necessity."[70] In Danticat's world of dispersed diasporic subjects, ideas of family, legitimacy, and origin must be deformed and reconfigured. In fact, the very experience of diaspora reconfigures ideas of family and community. While Danticat pushes for a redefinition, she doesn't call for complete break. These ties of filiation, as she examines them through the figure of Claude, who kills his father, and other characters who lose their fathers through patricide, can be both oppressive and comforting. One must reconsider notions of filiation for new generations of Haitians living in diaspora who are caught between the families they leave behind in Haiti and the families they create in diaspora and who create new myths to understand their current circumstances and individualized experiences.

The Tonton Macoute as Stable Signifier

One immediate instance of Danticat's radical rewriting of *Masters of the Dew* is in the very title of Danticat's book. Roumain's title evokes the empowering but idealized representation of the peasantry and its ties to the land. Manuel, the heroic figure of the novel explains to his mother, "But the earth is a battle day by day without truce, to clear the land, to plant, to weed and water it until the harvest comes. Then one morning you see your ripe fields spread out before you under the dew and you say—whoever you—'Me—I'm master of the dew!' And your heart fills with pride."[71] In a long speech, Manuel avows, "We don't know yet what a force we are, what a single force—all the peasants. All the negroes of plain and hill, all united. Some day, when we get wise to that, we'll rise up from one end of the country to the other. Then we'll call a general assembly of the Masters of the Dew, a great big combite of farmers to clear out poverty and plant new life" (75).[72] But Danticat, in *The Dew Breaker,* is not concerned about the harmonious relation between man and his environment; she is interested in the space of violence that severs relationships. She thus chooses the title *The Dew Breaker,* Danticat's own creative English translation of the Creole term *shoukèt laroze,* a term that refers to the Tonton Macoutes' disrupting the morning dew with their activities of violence and abduction. Danticat found the phrase *dew breaker* appealing because it echoes the America expression *ball breaker,* a tough disciplinarian who is excessively demanding or punishing: "I could have chosen several other ways to translate this, the dew shaker, the dew stomper, for example, but I like the way the words dew breaker echo the American expression ball breaker, which is a more fitting label for these kinds of people."[73] As Rhonda Cobham asserts in a review of *The Dew Breaker,* the possibility of violence in Roumain's translation of *shoukèt laroze* elides that possibility in the Creole context: "Danticat's alternative translation suggests violence as well as mastery. It makes visible the excesses of the nationalist, socialist, and capitalist ideologies that have stunted Haiti's growth during the six decades that separate *The Dew Breaker* from *Masters of the Dew.*"[74]

It is the character Beatrice in "The Bridal Seamstress" who, in giving her testimony to Aline, the journalist intern, introduces and defines the Creole term and exposes some of the violent acts of the Tonton Macoutes: "We called them shoukèt laroze. . . . They'd break into your house. Mostly it was at night. But often they'd also come before dawn as the dew was settling on the leaves, and they'd take you away. He was one of them, the guard" (131). Beatrice discloses to Aline the vicious terror she endured at the hands of a Tonton Macoute: "He tied me to some type of rack in the prison and whipped the bottom of my feet until they bled. Then he made me walk home, barefoot. On tar roads, in the hot sun. At high noon" (132). Other characters in *The Dew Breaker* testify in their own way to the Tonton Macoutes' heinous acts of violence. In the first story, the dew breaker confesses: "I shot and killed him [the preacher], like I killed many people" (22). In "Night Talkers," the reader learns of the fate of Dany's parents at the hands of a Tonton Macoute who made him an orphan when he was only six years old (104–5). In "The Funeral Singer," Rézia is raped by a Tonton Macoute at a young age; Mariselle's father is shot to death leaving a gallery displaying his painting, an unflattering portrait of the president, and Freda's father is arrested and beaten so badly that he risks his own life by taking a boat to "lòt bo dlo."

But these representations of the Tonton Macoutes are counterbalanced by the complex representation of the dew breaker father. This counterbalancing act exposes Danticat's defiance of ahistorical, oversimplified representation of Haitian people in general and the Tonton Macoutes in particular. In a 2005 interview, Danticat explained,

> In a lot of my work, what I try to do is aim at nuance. And I think that sometimes it's the gray of things, the layers, it's fertile for so many grays when you're living between cultures. You know, it's a different kind of shadows. And so, I think it's something that I try to convey in my work; that drawing people away from the general, because when you come from a place that's so often politicized like Haiti, people tend to think about you in terms of generalities, and so I feel like I'm always trying to bring people closer to individual experiences. The wonderful thing about books is that there is a kind of intimacy to them. For a minute, you have the eye of the reader, their attention. So I feel like when I have that, I want to use it to introduce individual lives. It's much harder to dismiss a place or a certain way of life when you've actually met people who come from there. I feel like my writing is a way to introduce people to Haiti in a way that they might not regularly encounter in their lives, and then hopefully inspire them to go further, to learn more outside of the frame of this book.[75]

In offering a more complex representation of the Tonton Macoutes in *The Dew Breaker*, Danticat presents another moment of intertextual echo as rewriting. Danticat recalls the work of Graham Greene as a non-Haitian master text that constructs and disseminates this archetypal image of the Tonton Macoutes and the Duvalier regime that Danticat attempts to deconstruct. She does not hide this intention. In her acknowledgment she discloses the reference to Graham Greene's *The Comedians,* which prompts a critical return to the text. In the last story, "The Dew Breaker," which can be viewed as the master text in the collection, the narrator describes the role of the human rights actors in the narration of this master text: "The human rights people, when they gathered in hotel bars at the end of long days of secretly counting corpses and typing single-spaced reports, would write of the flock's devotion to the preacher, noting, '*Impossible to deepen that night.*' These people don't have far to go to find their devils. Their devils aren't imagined, they're real" (186). Published in 1966, Graham Greene's novel *The Comedians,* about François Duvalier and the Tonton Macoutes, offers a glimpse of political corruption and poverty in the country during this period. In his preface to the book, Greene insists that while the main character, who narrates the book, is an invention, the Haitian characters are real representations of Haitian people. "Poor Haiti itself and the character of Doctor Duvalier's rule are not invented, the latter not even blackened for dramatic effect. Impossible to deepen that night. The Tonton Macoutes are full of men more evil than Concasseur."[76] Danticat's appropriation of the phrase "Impossible to deepen that night" in the context of the human rights group is a rewriting, one that takes Greene to task and attempts to offer a more complex representation, a deepening of the representation that offers more intimacy—thus Danticat's decision to italicize the phrase in the text. As Anthony Bogues asserts, "There is no strange other in Danticat's novel while in Greene's Haiti has become the dark other and the Duvalier regime some mysterious dark force only possible in a land which one writer called 'squalor.'"[77]

Another acknowledged phrase imbedded in *The Dew Breaker* worth mentioning in this discussion of the representation of the Tonton Macoutes: "Tu deviens un véritable gendarme, un bourreau" which, as Danticat reveals, is from the novel *Compère Général Soleil* by Jacques Stephen Alexis, who was captured and tortured at the hands of Tonton Macoutes. Reference to the author is also made within the text; in fact the author is embedded as a minor character in *The Dew Breaker,* a "famous" victim of the eponymous dew breaker: "The way he acted at the inquisitions in his own private cell at Casernes eventually earned him a lofty reputation among his peers. He was the one who came up with the most physically and psychologically taxing trials for the prisoners in his block. He was suffering, he knew it now, from what one of his most famous victims, the novelist Jacques Alexis, had written was the greatest hazard of the job. Tu deviens un véritable gendarme, un bourreau. It was becoming like any other job" (197–98). Conceived in 1949 and published in 1955, Alexis's first novel, *Compère Général Soleil,* revolves around the life of Hilarion Hilarius, an unskilled and uneducated laborer who is also introduced to Marxist ideology. He, however, leaves Haiti with his family for the Dominican Republic because of a crackdown on communism and the economic downturn of the period under President Sténio Vincent. The novel begins in the late 1920s and ends with a strike in the sugarcane fields in 1937, a time marked by the infamous Perejil Massacre, wherein thousands of Haitian migrant workers living near the border between the Dominican Republic and Haiti were killed under the authorization of then president Rafael Trujillo. Like Manuel in *Masters of the Dew,* Hilarion's fated end is death.

The intertextual echo of Alexis's Tonton Macoutes acts as a literary foil to Greene's dehumanized depictions. The phrase in Danticat's novel is not italicized; it blends in with the rest of the text. Beyond the phrase, the whole section is an echo of Alexis's demystifying description of the rural policemen. It is worth repeating here:

> Then it becomes a habit. One day you begin to think it's fun to watch a man scream and pee in his trousers. Some of them pee the minute they see a stick. You burst out laughing, really laughing for the first time. That's when the lieutenant knows that you are ready, and he submits your promotion to corporal. Little by little, you begin finding the job interesting. Beating people becomes a job just like any other. You have become hard and no longer feel anything in particular. A job just like any other. And since they are making you a corporal, well . . .[78]

Danticat uses the work of Alexis as a double to further deconstruct the archetypal image of the Tonton Macoutes and demystify narratives of political violence in Haiti.[79] But in *The Dew Breaker* it is not just representation of the Tonton Macoutes that is at issue. Danticat shows that idealized representations also create distorted images of Haiti and do not do justice to the complexity of Haiti and its people. But foreigners like Graham Greene are not the only ones who participate in creating this irresponsible image. Haitians in the diaspora also create mythic images of Haiti that not only efface complex realities but also become commodified art. For example, in *The Dew Breaker,* Gabrielle Fonteneau as art collector desires idealized representations of Haiti. When M. Bienamé meets the actress, he easily echoes early representations of women in Haitian literature. The father blurts out, "My dear, you are one of the most splendid flowers of Haiti" (29). The image recalls the literature of

Haitian writers like René Depestre, whose *Alléluia pour une femme-jardin* (1973) and *Hadriana dans tous mes rêves* (1988) present a mystifying representation of Haitian women and the idea of Haiti as a lost Eden. Much like his nostalgic representation of his hometown, Jacmel, Mrs. Fonteneau romanticizes their annual trips to Jacmel: "We're fortunate that we have a place to go where we can say the rain is sweeter, the dust is lighter, our beaches prettier" (29). Overlooking the ocean from the mountains of Jacmel, the Fonteneaus enjoy "drinking sweet juice from a coconut fetched from your own tree" (29). Painting a better picture, Mrs. Fonteneau concludes, "There's nothing like sinking your hand in sand from the beach in your own country" (30). All these idealistic images painted by Mrs. Fonteneau are immediately disrupted by Ka's depiction of Haiti in her imaginary, an imaginary that is now altered by the father's disclosure as dew breaker: "I imagine my father's nightmares. Maybe he dreams of dipping his hands in the sand on a beach in his own country and finding what he comes up with is a fistful of blood" (30). Revelation of the family secret exposes her father's dark past and the violence of the Duvalier dictatorship.

Relational Double and Thematic Redoubling

Danticat reimagines both Haiti and the diaspora in the United States as well as their relationship to each other through the coupling of related and seemingly unrelated characters, places, narratives, and texts that can only be understood and coexist in terms of their loose or loosening relations and their link to a particular history of tragedy and national trauma. She dismantles the bipolarizations that divide self and other by developing fragmented characters that shadow each other in the text and become each other's doubles through both their similarities and differences, their filiations and affiliations, their histories and distinct memories. This strategy of the double, structured thematically in *The Dew Breaker* in terms of dual nature, dual soul, dual culture, dual loyalty, dual history, dual trauma, is foregrounded to scrutinize an old framework of subjectivity and self-making that is foundational to the historical narrative of diaspora and to introduce a different relational and dialogic double as a new framework of diasporic subjectivity and self-making that moves beyond dialectical narrative strategies and double-bind thinking in the twenty-first century.

Much as she does in *Breath, Eyes, Memory*, in *The Dew Breaker* Danticat establishes the close link a parent has to a child through the strategy of doubling. This doubling is immediately evoked in Ka's name: Ka is M. Bienamé's spiritual double, one who gives the dew breaker the possibility of transcendence. But the double established to define the identities of both Ka and M. Bienamé and their relation to each other is both a dialectic double bind and a relational double. As Anne, the wife and mother, says, "Between her daughter, who chose not to believe in god, and her husband, who went to the Brooklyn Museum every week, to worship, it seemed to her, at the foot of Ancient Egyptian statues, she felt outnumbered by pagans" (70). Ka's parents in their filial coupling as wife and husband are also doubles of each other: "It has always amazed me how much my mother and father echo each other, in their speech, their actions, even in their business. I wonder how much more alike they could possibly be. But why shouldn't they be alike? Like all parents, they were a society of two, sharing a series of private codes and associations, a past that even if I'd been born in the country of their birth, I still wouldn't have known, couldn't have known, thoroughly. I was a part of them. Some might say I belonged to them. But I wasn't them" (25). Parental figures function as a homogenous duality that threatens the individuality of the child. In the second story, "Seven," this filiation is tested in the relationship of two couples who reunite after being separated for seven years. The silence between them, a by-product of separation and disconnection, prevents serious, productive, fruitful verbal communication. At the end of the collection, Anne, Ka's mother, is doubled as madwoman/healer who dresses the dew breaker's wound, both literally and symbolically. The dew breaker and the prisoner are linked and doubled by association through the experience of migration. M. Bienamé doubles as Emanuel Constant through Anne's anxiety about her husband getting caught. Michel and Freda in the "Funeral Singer" are doubled by the shared experience of losing a father who "disappears" to "something political." In this sixth story of *The Dew Breaker,* Aline Cajuste, a young Haitian American journalist intern writer for the *Haitian American Weekly,* interviews Beatrice Saint Fort, a bridal seamstress who made a wedding dress for the editor in chief and is now retiring. Anne and Beatrice become each other's doubles, as they both are imprisoned by society's heteronormative rules and codes of behavior. Beatrice hides her age and marital status, while Aline hides her sexual identity from her parents.

As Maria Rice Bellamy asserts in her analysis of *The Dew Breaker,* in "Danticat's understanding of the concept of marasa . . . , twinning and doubling creates a framework for understanding Ka's parents' relationship to their traumatic pasts and enables her to imagine a character like Ka's father" (180).[80] Danticat's strategy of doubling is also evident in the similarities of the titles of the two stories: as "The Book of the Dead" speaks to Ka's father's death, "The Book of Miracles" speaks to his rebirth, a transformation that occurs because of Anne's love. Ka's father is the dead resurrected to life; Ka's mother is the miracle. Danticat develops the story of the "The Book of the Dead" within the context of Egyptian funeral rites, to which Ka's father can relate; she structures the story "The Book of Miracles" out of the Christian context of miracles and celebration of Christmas. Danticat also doubles stories thematically: "Seven" and "Water Child" are dual narratives, linked not only by relation between characters (Eric in "Seven" is revealed to be Nadine's ex-lover in "Water Child"). They are also linked as the only two stories that do not have direct relation to the eponymous dew breaker. Yet both stories highlight the indirect impact of the Duvalier regime on intimate heteronormative relationships. The narrative of Michel in "Monkey Tails" and the narrative of the women in "The Funeral Singer" are dual narratives of the "loss of the father" story that marks accounts of the Duvalier regime, while Michel presents his first-person narrative in terms of homosocial bonding between those orphaned and abandoned by the regime to memorialize a male figure (his friend Roumain) and in terms that prepare his unborn son for initiation into manhood. Freda offers a first-person narrative that incorporates collectively the voices of the other characters who form a homosocial network of Haitian women emigrants preparing for a life in diaspora during the 1970s. Through their stories, they honor the memory of their fathers but also rewrite the male-centered story of lost fathers from a feminine, and feminist, lens and diasporic home space where women share their stories of the past and reasons for their migration into the United States over food, drink, and song to heal themselves from their traumatic experiences and cope with their current circumstances.[81]

The Game of Intertextuality as Puzzle

Describing the making and completion of the first story, "The Book of the Dead," in *The Dew Breaker*, Danticat explains,

> When I was done with that story, I became very curious about the father's past and wrote a story to flesh it out, and then everything I wrote after that for a couple of years became part of the father's world. After the father became very clear in my mind, then his wife, the mother, Anne, surfaced, and she intrigued me and I wrote "The Book of Miracles" about her. So these three stories ["The

Book of the Dead," "The Dew Breaker," and "The Book of Miracles"] were linked formlessly but all centered on this person, really, the dew breaker. The book itself became about solving a puzzle, looking at this person—the dew breaker—from all the different angles, so the stories came as I myself was trying to understand these people's connections to one another.[82]

Danticat uses this strategy of the puzzle in ways that push the reader to become actively engaged in the text. The trope of the puzzle appears in Danticat's first novel, *Breath, Eyes, Memory,* to explore the interior life of the character Sophie and her process of identity formation and transformation as a displaced person in the United States. Describing Sophie and her experience, Danticat observes, "Everything is a puzzle. It's almost as if, when she's taken out of where she was and she's in a new place, she has to reform herself, and she has to recreate a self that can survive in this place."[83] This "trope of the puzzle"[84] is strategically evoked in what I call the middle text, the fifth story of *The Dew Breaker,* through the character Claude, who expresses acceptance of his deportation. (Perhaps not coincidently, the fifth stage of grief is acceptance.)

Claude describes his own process of displacement and reformation as a deportee from New York: "It's like a puzzle, a weird-ass puzzle. . . . I'm the puzzle and these people are putting me back together, telling me things about myself and my family that I never knew or gave a fuck about. Man, if I'd run into these people back in Brooklyn, I'd have laughed my ass off at them. I would've called them backward-ass peasants. But here I am" (102). Claude's understanding of restoration as a return to wholeness and remembering of a disremembered past is reminiscent of Sixo's description of the thirty-mile woman in Toni Morrison's *Beloved:* "She gather me, man. The pieces I am, she gather them and give them back to me in all the right order. It's good, you know, when you got a woman who is a friend of your mind."[85] Claude imagines himself as parts of a whole that can be achieved through the act of reclamation. His reintegration into the homeland is an opportunity for redemption and self-recovery. Claude is a "palanit," someone who speaks dreams and nightmares out loud in the night (98), but because he is also able to do so during the day, he is presented as someone who accepts his situation for what it is and is arguably the most redeeming character in *The Dew Breaker.* Claude, as a central figure and in-between character located in the middle text, may very well be the key to the puzzle of identity formation, deformation, and reformation. Certainly, Claude's story echoes the primal crime that grounds the Oedipus complex, patricide. But it is the punishment for this crime, deportation to Haiti, that calls for rearticulation of family and kinship ties and a rereading of displacement. Interestingly, it is the wife of Eric in the story "Seven" who ponders the idea that "the middle is where the truth resides" (48). In both stories, Danticat calls for a reconsideration of truth beyond ethical absolutes of good and evil, right and wrong.

The process of deconstruction and reconstruction of the self is a thematic thread that runs through all the characters, including Ka, who must reconstruct self beyond paternal ties. But Ka's ability to notice "more what was not there than what was" (19) makes Ka only one of the many characters who search for the missing pieces in Danticat's complex play of intertextuality. Like the reader, who is trying to unlock the mystery of the dew breaker and find the missing links, characters attempt to solve riddles. Nadine in "Water Child" tries to "find something else between the lines" of the letter she receives from her parents and carefully preserves. She wonders how "the postal workers in both Port-au-Prince and Brooklyn [had] not lacerated the thin page and envelope" (54). A striking example of the trope of the puzzle is found in Danticat's insertion of a question from the 2003 edition of *Master the GED* in the story "The Funeral Singer."

In the story, three women, Rézia, Mariselle, and Freda regularly meet in a Haitian-owned restaurant located in an Upper West Side neighborhood in Manhattan. The restaurant is owned by Rézia. The three women represent the development and struggles of a diverse Haitian community in the United States. A few scholars have analyzed the story by homing in on its structure. Renée H. Shae, for example, in "Teaching Edwidge Danticat's 'The Funeral Singer'—a Study in Voices," notes that when writing the story, Danticat experimented with form and considered a structure that reflected a song but settled on short divisions. The final structure of fourteen divided sections reflects the high school equivalency class one takes to prepare for the GED exam.[86] Similarly, in *Market Aesthetics*, Machado Sáez states that the narrative mimics an academic calendar and the structure of a syllabus.[87] The very structure of *The Dew Breaker,* which lies between a novel and collection of short stories, is itself an enigma. But here I am interested in the textual placement or displacement of the GED puzzle as an instance of intertextual echo. During week 6, the teacher writes on the board the puzzle that comes from the GED exam: "Two trees, 10 feet apart. Taller tree, 50 feet tall, casts a 20-foot shadow. Shorter tree casts a 15-foot shadow. The sun's shining on each tree from the same angle. How tall is the shorter tree?" (171). Both the structure of the story and the puzzle pushes the reader toward a search for an arithmetical reading of the story. If, as I have been arguing, *The Dew Breaker* is a mastery, displacement, and undoing of the paternal signifier and imago of the father, then the puzzle here is also an echo and rereading of *Oedipus, the King*. The narrative of Sophocles's protagonist Oedipus as a traveler who solves the riddle of the sphinx by providing the correct answer, "Man," and in return gains entry into the city of Thebes is, in *The Dew Breaker,* transposed in order to rediscover the imaginary maternal space and ultimately transgress both the imaginary and the symbolic. The question I raise here is, What happens when the prototypical traveler as a man who represents a single voice that solves the puzzle of human development is replaced by narratives of women on the move? In "The Funeral Singer," three women are trying to gain recognition, rights, and acceptance in New York City by taking the GED language arts class. But they are struggling with "the grammatical rules" and sentences that don't speak to their own lived experiences. They each have a story of displacement that brings them together in diasporic space, and it is outside of the oppressive space of the classroom that they are able to express themselves. Moreover, the forms of expressions are diverse. For example, Freda, the twenty-two-year-old funeral singer and the narrator, wants to introduce herself to her classmates by singing. Ultimately, she grounds her story by calling on the narrative of Brother Timothy, rearticulating it in diasporic space. Furthermore, the image of the father is prominent but not in an oppressive way. Freda's memorialization of her fisherman father lost at sea through the act of singing does not displace the maternal image. In fact, Freda's mother emerges as an important figure in her life. And by the end of the story, Brother Timothy is even imagined as a sister.

Machado Sáez notes that the three women "point to an alternative web of relation for the funeral singer."[88] She continues, "Freda's individual voice as a funeral singer becomes part of a chorus whose collective creativity empowers them to revise the homosocial funeral narrative of a fisherman into one that recognizes the losses of diasporic women."[89] It is Freda who first reacts to the GED riddle: "It sounds like a riddle that could take a lifetime to solve. We have too much on our minds to unravel these types of mysteries. M'bwe pwa" (171). A part of the Haitian storytelling call and response tradition and krik? krak! games, M'bwe pwa indicates that one does not know the answer to a question. The women have not mastered the GED and are having a hard time understanding the riddle. They are still travelers in limbo who need to pass this GED test to gain passage and continue the journey. Danticat's insertion of a GED question underlines the idea that new generations of Haitians in the diaspora must master different kind of texts and narratives to survive in America. But the three women differ from Oedipus: they are not in pursuit of an answer and actually react to the question not with some revelation of an absolute truth but with the recognition that they do not define their lives by absolutes. Rézia says, "We're not God. . . . Who are we to know how tall a tree should be?" (172). They show wisdom in knowing that not all questions are answerable. In Danticat's diasporic imaginary, the GED test, like the riddle in Oedipus, offers passage and access to the new home space, but this comes with a price. Access is expressed not in terms of power, as in the case of Oedipus, but as opportunity embraced with ambivalence, with no fixed destination. Acceptance of unknowable destinies in "The Funeral Singer" is privileged over the desire to solve riddles. The women do not yet know if they have passed the exam. What matters is the creation of female-centered space for mourning losses and their communion as coping strategy to deal with this particular experience of displacement. But in spite of "post-test anxiety" (179), the fourteen-week journey and its completion offers some direction. When the class is finally over, Mariselle says, "I finally unpacked my suitcases" (180). Freda contemplates joining a militia and returning to Haiti. And Rézia holds on to her Haitian restaurant to maintain her sanity. In the process of learning a new language and adapting to a new culture, they all face an unknown future in the diaspora that is influenced by a traumatic past: "And for the rest of the night we raise our glasses, broken and unbroken alike, to the terrible days behind us and the uncertain ones ahead" (181). In the end, the answer to the riddle is not disclosed within the story, but Danticat reveals the answer after the reader has completed *The Dew Breaker*. The GED riddle question later reappears and is answered in acknowledgments of *The Dew Breaker*, in fact on the very last page of the book (244). The appearance of the answer to the riddle as an afterthought implies mastery, displacement, and transgression of the Oedipus narrative. Mastery of language, of the symbolic realm, means mastery of the imago of the father as represented in the Oedipus complex. In this realm, the image of the tree is a genealogical metaphor (tree of life, family tree, for example) that sustains traditional notions of kinship and relation in biological terms. This is not the case in Danticat's "The Funeral Singer," where community and relationships are built by the recognition of shared experiences, shared trauma, and shared desire for healing. Ultimately, in "The Funeral Singer" it is the nonhierarchical plurality of diverse voices (represented by women) in communion that is privileged over the single all-knowing authoritative voice (represented by man) that grounds the logic of the patriarchal family in the Oedipus narrative.

It is no wonder that *The Dew Breaker* ends with a focus on Anne, Ka's mother, who reemerges as an Antigone-like figure caught between two deaths, the death of her two brothers, who were never given a proper burial.[90] The last paragraph of *The Dew Breaker* returns to a phrase from the first story, "The Book of the Dead":

> There was no way to escape this dread anymore, this pendulum between regret and forgiveness, this fright that the most important relationships of her life were always on the verge of being severed or lost, that the people closest to her were always disappearing. The spirits had long since stopped coming through her body via her mysterious spells. . . . These spirits, they'd left her for good the morning that the news was broadcast on the radio that her brother had set his body on fire in the prison yard at dawn, leaving behind no corpse to bury, no trace of himself at all. (242)

If the beginning of *The Dew Breaker* establishes Ka's relationship to both the imaginary and the symbolic realm, then the ending, through Anne's ambivalence, transgresses these orders, and Anne, as mother figure, remains a mystery that must be explored beyond the logic of Oedipus as name of the father. Danticat ends with the reemergence of Anne, whose faint presence is a consequence of her own preoccupation with the image of her brother "walking the earth looking for his grave" (71). This is indeed a fitting ending for a book like *The Dew Breaker,* because Danticat as writer, through the intertextual echo of Antigone, has entered the realm of unwritten laws of the sacred and the dead, the "unspeakable" space beyond language.

As the opening story, "The Book of the Dead," establishes the thread that links all the other eight stories that follow into a fictional unity by the recognition of fragmented parts that form a puzzle. These stories in their fictionally constructed totality give insight into the impact Ka's father, as eponymous dew breaker turned master signifier, has on the intertwined lives of his purported victims. These victims are migratory displaced diasporic Haitian subjects who try to escape the trauma they attempt to leave behind in Haiti but are haunted by the memory of state-sanctioned violence and censorship. They also deal with traumatic experiences and "everyday life problems" they face in the United States.[91] Indeed, victims and perpetrators inhabit crowded, noisy urban transnational spaces in New York and yet are consumed by deafening silence, secrets, responsibilities, and memories that lead to insular, solitary, or secluded lives. Danticat introduces and develops characters whose stories get told between spaces of fear, anxiety of disintegration, self-imposed silence, and uncertainty.

In her analysis of Danticat's first collection of short stories, *Krik? Krak!*, Lisa Ortiz describes Danticat as a weaver of tales who values the voices of deceased ancestors. These ancestral voices, Ortiz writes, are "utterances with autobiographical resonance" conveyed through double-voiced discourse: "The voices from the past resonate in a polyphony of cultural and historical influences upon her own identity as Haitian-American woman."[92] Indeed, in all the stories in *The Dew Breaker*, Danticat implicitly reflects on her identity as Haitian American by offering vivid and current portrayal of Haiti and its diaspora and clearly asserts the interconnectedness between the two. Moving back and forth between New York, Florida, and Haiti, Danticat also offers a grim look at the complex conditions and emotional limbo state of her characters and their relationship to the families and friends they left behind in the homeland. The diverse stories are separated by time (each offers a window to a decade), space (New York, Florida, Haiti), generational differences, and individualized experience; they offer differing narrative voices and points of view (first person, third person omniscient, male voice, female voice, disembodied voice). However, in the book, seemingly unrelated characters and stories cohere because of shared space, shared history, shared pain, and shared language. Together, they present a complex and nuanced look into not only the psychic anxieties of the displaced diasporic subject but also the diversity and heterogeneity of the Haitian diaspora in the United States and its history of migration and displacement. In *The Dew Breaker* this diversity is narrated through an intertextual weaving of immigrant voices that put to the test the melting pot fantasy of wholeness in the American national imaginary. But this novel in stories also asks, How do we dialogue with our dead ancestors in diasporic space? How do we honor those "walking the earth looking for their graves"? To attend to these questions, we must turn to an earlier work, Danticat's historical novel, *The Farming of Bones*, which is the subject of the next chapter.

5 Voices from beyond the (Unmarked) Grave in *The Farming of Bones*

At the still point of the turning world. Neither flesh nor fleshless;
Neither from nor towards; at the still point, there the dance is,
But neither arrest nor movement. And do not call it fixity,
Where past and future are gathered. Neither movement from nor
    towards,
Neither ascent nor decline. Except for the point, the still point,
There would be no dance, and there is only the dance.
I can only say, *there* we have been: but I cannot say where.
And I cannot say, how long, for that is to place it in time.

—T. S. Eliot, *Four Quartets*

How DOES one echo the voices of the dead? How do they return to the space of the living in the present or occupy one's imagination and consciousness? How do they move in material, ideological, and imaginary landscapes marked by massive migration of people? More specifically, how do echoes get translated in the diasporic imaginary of a writer invested in returning to the past to memorialize the individual lives of anonymous and unheard dead subjects displaced by interlocking histories of colonialism, imperialism, and global capitalism? What are the challenges to this act of symbolic return in the imagination, a return that must bypass or disrupt the linearity of official historical recollections and narratives to penetrate intimate subjective spaces of loss, nostalgia, and despair? How does a writer, through this act of literary transgression, this movement beyond time or against the chronological narrative logic of history, face the weight of haunting memories that repeat and torment the living? In what language does one speak or narrate memories that appear as impenetrable silences and profound individual wounds that also represent a collective trauma? Does the echo chamber in such instances transform into a site of collective mourning to resound the chorus of bereavement? Is the echo chamber the material or ideological body through which diverse voices pass and travel from beyond the grave to overcome the violence of voicelessness? How does that departed body translate its continued and haunting presence into ancestral speech, silent address, or testimony? And what do these forms of communication from the outer world reveal about the voices of living displaced subjects who experience multiple forms of traumatic silencing? These are the fundamental questions that emerge when reading Edwidge Danticat's third book, *The Farming of Bones,* a historical novel about the 1937 Haitian massacre that, I argue, affirms that the very act of narrating and translating echoes exposes not only the challenge of expressing language(s) before or beyond speech but also a writer's communion with the invisible world and the voices of ancestors that inhabit it. These voices in Danticat's diasporic imaginary manifest in the form of shadows, revenants, and ghosts who travel to the world of the living to transmit messages or appear in dreams—the inner life of a subject—to activate memory and offer protection against the dangers of the outer world. Thus *echo* here is more than the recall of a silenced traumatic event of the past; it is an impenetrable silence of shadows, revenants, and ghosts that search for an echo chamber, a safe place from which to speak and be heard. It provides traces and refractions of an unspeakable historical traumatic event that Danticat narrates through a keen understanding of the complex relationships among voice, speech, and language in systems of communication.

In her 1993 Nobel Prize lecture, Toni Morrison explores the uses and abuses of all types of language systems. Discussing the nature of oppressive language as symbol of nation and cultural hegemony, Morrison asserts,

> Oppressive language does more than represent violence; it is violence; does more than represent the limits of knowledge; it limits knowledge. Whether it is obscuring state language or the faux-language of mindless media; whether it is the proud but calcified language of the academy or the commodity-driven language of science; whether it is the malign language of law-without-ethics, or language designed for the estrangement of minorities, hiding its racist plunder in its literary cheek—it must be rejected, altered, and exposed. It is the language that drinks blood, laps vulnerabilities, tucks its fascist boots under crinolines of respectability and patriotism as it moves relentlessly toward the bottom line and the bottomed-out mind. Sexist language, racist language, theistic language—all are typical of the policing languages of mastery, and cannot, do not permit new knowledge or encourage the mutual exchange of ideas.[1]

Morrison articulates the contours of what I call the nation's homogenous echo chamber, wherein the single-body, single-mind, single-voice, single-language fantasy of a dominant community thrives. It is through this fantasy that the illusion of wholeness in the national imaginary is perpetuated. In all her works, Danticat's framing of diaspora foregrounds the role of the imagination in destabilizing and denaturalizing mythic fantasy structures of the nation, whose demand for linguistic purity leads to epistemic violence. Danticat's writing pushes us to be attentive to the inner worlds and subjective experiences of individuals who do not fit nationalist fantasy structures and are perceived as a threat and contagion that must be sealed off from the nation's body politic. In this last chapter, I assert that the inscription of the experience of displacement and its affective dimensions in *The Farming of Bone*s for Danticat constitutes a diasporic imaginary wherein in the work of the imagination and fantasy entails the project of transgressing all forms of borders, including real territorial and linguistic borders that foster boundary-producing state-sanctioned narratives of nation, identity, community, and belonging to produce new language and alternative knowledge that acknowledge hybrid, multiple, and dialogic forms of communication that unsettle the rhetoric of nationalism and its corollary traditional notions of kinship, heritage, ancestry, origin, and linguistic purity.

Fantasy in the idea of diasporic imaginary also evokes traumatic forms of historical displacement. In his work on the diasporic imaginary, Vijay Mishra links fantasy to loss, lapsed enjoyment, and trauma. He argues that a reflection on diaspora in terms of negation "demands that we constantly revisit our trauma as part of an ethical relationship with the ghosts of diaspora."[2] Certainly, the psychic, haunting dimension of ghosts is prevalent in Danticat's writing and points to the intertextual links with Toni Morrison's fictional works, most prominently *Beloved*. However, in my understanding of Danticat's diasporic imaginary, fantasy is not limited to a negative, pathological relation to the past; it also has its political uses in the present and pushes us to think differently about our futures. Danticat's ghosts, as shadows, also represent creative strategies of survival and resistance and productive modes of living with the dead and the spiritual world. While ghosts invoke trauma in Danticat's work, they also represent wisdom and legacy for the future. Fantasy, when linked to the idea of agency, hope, and an ethics of justice—consistent themes in Danticat's writings—is as much about evoking past trauma as it is about imagining new worlds, searching for alternative modes of being beyond binary constructions, and striving to inhabit safe spaces

For writers like Danticat, imagining in this sense is the conscious process of the "becoming" that Toni Morrison conjures when speaking of the "work" of African American women writers in a gendered, sexualized, and racialized world.[3] This becoming of African American women writers, Morrison explains, must contend with a set of established representations in a national literary imaginary that reinforces the idea of a quintessential American identity. Indeed, to read fantasy in all of Danticat's work is to confront national stereotypes of the literary imagination and the violence national ideology promotes. Danticat's diasporic imaginary disrupts the national fantasy of an idea of America, the national fantasy of an idea of Haiti, and the fantasies that bind these two countries together despite their racial and cultural incompatibility.[4] Fantasy, in the quotidian lives of diasporic subjects, particularly those who feel marginalized and made invisible, is about redefining the contours of national identity and resisting neocolonial forms of oppression and violence that silence disenfranchised individuals and communities. In the context of *The Farming of Bones*, Danticat examines these issues through an exploration of the relationship between two countries, Haiti and the Dominican Republic, with histories of colonial and authoritarian oppression.

Morrison's framing of oppressive language then must be juxtaposed to her understanding of the simultaneous workings of fantasy and memory in the black diasporic imaginary. Articulations of the search for wholeness and belonging as part of a collective in African diasporic narratives in particular also involve a keen awareness of the critical role of fantasy and memory in the construction of alternative homelands. As Toni Morrison asserts, "The act of imagination is bound up with memory."[5] It is through memory and re-memory that black women writers in particular explore and re-create the untold interior lives of black people and their ancestors. Gaining access to an absent interior life requires, Morrison claims, a "kind of literary archaeology" and imaginative journey to a site that houses "remains" of history.[6] These remains help writers reconstruct a historical past that is often silenced. In Danticat's diasporic narratives, like those of black diasporic writers in general, fantasy and memory are also part of a social, political, and ethical project of regeneration with a subversive potential to transform violent worlds that foster ethnic absolutism.[7] The work of inscribing the experience of displacement and its affective dimensions for Danticat constitutes a diasporic imaginary wherein fantasy entails the very real project of transgressing the violence caused by boundary-producing gendered narratives of citizenship and belonging in the national imaginary. Danticat's conception of diaspora does not disavow the national imaginary that preserves the history of the Haitian people both in Haiti and in the diaspora. Instead, Danticat reworks the national imaginary through a diasporic lens, exposing the falsity of its homogeneity and undoing traditional ideas of kinship, heritage, and origin that cannot be sustained in the diasporic imaginary.

Displacement in the Historical Novel

In *The Farming of Bones,* the danger that lies in the material and external world coats itself in the language of nationalism. The Dominican national imaginary in the early part of the twentieth century and under the regime of Generalissimo Rafael Leónidas Trujillo Molina (1930–61) is most prominent and sets the stage for Danticat's critique of nationalism and binary narratives that construct a racially pure nation-body and depend on a uniform monologic voice that speaks in chronological time and thrives in dualism and closure, all the while silencing or destroying dialogic voices that speak in fragments and lend themselves to opacity, ambiguity, and indeterminacy. More specifically, Danticat explores the sociospatial and cultural impact of the geopolitical border that divides Haiti and the Dominican Republic, two nations that share the same island and similar histories of colonialism, occupation, and oppressive totalitarian regimes but are divided by linguistic, racial, and cultural distinctions that are produced and reproduced through the construction of mythic fantasies of a national imaginary. For Danticat, the interlocking historical, economic, and social relations between Haiti and the Dominican Republic reveal the complex inner workings of the imagination in the naturalization of the relationship between race, nation, language, and cultural identity. Danticat's diasporic imaginary, as evident in all her works, involves the conscious act of working through and against imaginaries that construct the fantasy of a unified monolithic national body, voice, and language. Danticat's diasporic imaginary thus relies on a reservoir of refracted images and symbols that disrupt the single-body, single-mind, single-voice, single-language fantasy.

The Farming of Bones is a historical novel that explores a silenced history from the perspective of Amabelle Désir, an eighty-year-old fictional character who tells the story of her life and struggles in a border town. The novel begins with a twentysomething Amabelle living on a Dominican sugar plantation in a fictional village called Alegría ("Joy" in Spanish) and working as a servant to a wealthy Dominican family around the time of the 1937 massacre that killed thousands of Haitians living near the border between Haiti and the Dominican Republic. Amabelle is dependent on her mistress, Señora Valencia, and her mistress's father, Don Ignacio, a landowner from Spain who took Amabelle in as a playmate for his daughter. Already affected by the loss of both her parents, whom she witnessed drown in the river at the border at age eight—the reason for her displacement in Alegría—Amabelle clings to her lover, Sebastien, for relief and comfort in dealing with the recurrent dreams of her parents' drowning as well as visions that trigger images of her ancestors. She shares a sense of parental loss with Sebastien, who migrated to the Dominican Republic for work when his father was killed seven years earlier in a hurricane in Haiti that destroyed homes and displaced families. Unfortunately, when Amabelle loses Sebastien (who is later presumed dead at the end of the novel) to the 1937 massacre, Amabelle sinks into a prolonged paralysis and profound sense of loss and disassociation from the external world. After she recovers from her physical injuries at the border clinic, Amabelle returns to her hometown of Cap-Haitien with Yves, Sebastien's friend and roommate, who embarks on a journey for survival with Amabelle when the massacre begins. Saddened and burdened by the ghosts of those who were killed on the journey, the two live separate lives and harbor feelings of guilt in silence. To console themselves, they both choose a life of work, but while Yves tries to forget the slaughter by working his father's land, Amabelle chooses to remember by living her body's sadness every day. She resigns herself to a "living death."[8]

Throughout the novel Amabelle is consumed by an anxiety of displacement not only because she is orphaned and away from her Haitian homeland but also because of the sociospatial barriers that marginalize the Haitian migrant labor force as well as Haitian descendants living on the sugarcane plantations in Danticat's Alegría. In reality, these territorial and imagined boundaries between Haitians and Dominicans stimulate the denigration of Haitian black bodies and voices and encourage ethnic discrimination against Haitian migrants. Danticat takes up this history as backdrop in the novel to explore the suppression of Amabelle's body and voice and, by extension, the belittling of her ethnic identity, which escalates into epistemic violence and torture at the hands of Rafael Trujillo, who would rule the Dominican Republic until his assassination in 1961, where the last scenes of the novel take place. The regime's nationalist rhetoric of Dominican identity and culture encouraged a national fear of Haitian contamination that resulted from the growing presence of the Haitian labor force in the Dominican Republic, a presence ironically desperately needed for Dominican nation-building since the country's entry into the world sugarcane industry in the nineteenth century. The novel ends with a return to the Massacre River, the site of the historical trauma, on the twenty-fifth anniversary of the slaughter, with Amabelle floating and "looking for the dawn" (310).

Some scholars have remarked that *The Farming of Bones* diverges from Danticat's interest in migration.[9] But this second novel is framed by the historical backdrop of Haitian migration to the Dominican Republic during the 1930s, when Haitians were being exploited as cheap labor and worked in the sugarcane fields under harsh physical conditions while facing discrimination at the hands of Dominicans. Thus I argue that in taking up the task of tracing and mapping the geography of violence at the border between Haiti and the Dominican Republic in the 1930s, Danticat brings forth, once again, pertinent issues of migration and displacement in ways that both foreground the contemporary global plight of the statelessness of migrants as a major social justice issue and echo the Haitian refugee crisis in the United States and the Dominican Republic in the 1990s, around the time the novel was published. In the novel, the coupling of Haiti and the United Sates is not made as explicit as the coupling of Haiti and the Dominican Republic—there are mentions of yanki sugarcane mills, the yanki occupation, and khaki uniforms that function as remnants of the occupation of the entire island of Hispaniola by the United States and implicate the country and its role in the world sugar industry. In an article in which she is quoted in 1999, a year after the publication of *The Farming of Bones,* Danticat explains, "The more I read the testimonies [of survivors of the massacre], the more I heard the voices from the past, the more drama I saw in it. The idea of flight, which is still active today, people leaving Haiti to come to the United States by boat. It is very dramatic. It strikes me as very dramatic that you do have this island, the first place Columbus saw in what he called the New World, and it is one island, and the French and the Hispanics fought over this land, and split it. So you have this history back and forth and this drama in itself."[10] In Danticat's diasporic imaginary, the contemporary migration crisis involves historical recall of multiple events and diverse diasporic experiences that delineate interrelated and circular histories of colonialism, imperialism, neocolonialism, and transnational forms of global capital designs. Danticat recalls the 1937 Haitian massacre not only to tell a dramatic story but also to raise awareness in the US consciousness about the plight of a new generation of Haitian migrants who must confront discriminatory immigration practices and laws. She also addresses Haitians and Haitian Americans by redressing historical silencing on the part of the Haitian nation that produces collective amnesia and frames the dynamics of a Haitian diasporic consciousness. Yet in *The Farming of Bones,* this recall of history stages the tragic drama of the intertwined national body politic of both the Dominican Republic and Haiti to expose the fiction of linguistic singularity and wholeness. If *The Dew Breaker,* as I argue in chapter 4, is an instance of intertextual diversity, then *The Farming of Bones* is an instance of linguistic hybridization.

Migration of Haitians to the Dominican Republic

In her analysis of *The Farming of Bones,* April Shemak asserts that the power of the novel "is that it speaks as much to the present day situation in the Dominican Republic as it does to the 1937 massacre."[11] Danticat states that for her the "saddest" part of the experience of writing the novel "was seeing how that event is so linked with what's going on today. We still have our people working in the cane fields in the Dominican Republic. It really isn't a memory; it's an event that has a continuing relationship. And the massacre is something that people always fear can happen again."[12] Shemak and Danticat allude to the massive expulsions of Haitians from the Dominican Republic in the latter half of the twentieth century. Any critical analysis of *The Farming of Bones* must situate the novel within the context of contemporary Haitian-Dominican relations grounded in historical tensions.

In the 1990s, the Dominican Republic deported hundreds of thousands of Haitians to Haiti. Massive expulsion during this period was not limited to undocumented Haitians but also encompassed undocumented Domínico-Haitians, Haitians born on Dominican soil who are guaranteed citizenship under Article 11 of the 1865 Dominican Constitution. Anyone who "looked Haitian" was also vulnerable to these arbitrary expulsions, which not only disrupted lives but severed families and communities. The impetus for the removal of Haitians was increasing pressure from domestic and international human rights groups after an ABC-TV news broadcast, *Primetime Live,* reported on the inhumane conditions of forced child labor practices in the Dominican Republic.[13] The report, which aired on May 2, 1991, sheds light on the maltreatment of Haitian migrant workers and their children, which included forced recruitment to sugarcane plantations by buscones, scouts hired by the State Sugar Council to recruit workers throughout Haiti.[14] Ironically, despite a presidential decree (417–90) the year before that promised reforms that in the end only slightly improved conditions of migrants in the Bateyes, communities of sugarcane cutters living in shanty-town camps and hidden from Dominican life, it did not eradicate child labor. Moreover, many of the reforms were not implemented.[15] In response to international criticism and condemnation, which was followed by congressional hearings in the United States, then eighty-four-year-old president Joaquín Balaguer, who would serve for a total of six terms in office until 1998, defiantly ordered the repatriation of "Haitian foreigners" under age sixteen and over age sixty working and living on state-run and privately owned sugarcane plantations. The decree came only seven weeks after the United States, the Dominican Republic's largest trading partner and principal purchaser of Dominican sugar, decided to continue to grant Generalized System of Preferences trade benefits to the Dominican Republic after completing a two-year review of Dominican labor rights practices. The decree (233–91) led to an infamous wave of abusive expulsions that began in June 1991, conveniently at the end of zafra (the harvest season), and ended with the exile of Aristide—the result of a military coup—on September 30, 1991. Denied the fair immigration hearing guaranteed by the Dominican Constitution, six to eight thousand Haitians were rounded up and bused across the border to Haiti within three months. Many thousands left voluntarily to avoid random military roundups and maltreatment by Dominican soldiers. An estimated fifty thousand Haitians returned to Haiti during this period.[16]

Known as political heir of the thirty-one-year authoritarian regime of Dominican dictator Rafael Trujillo, Balaguer received national support for the decree by reiterating a long-standing narrative of Dominicanidad that depends on an anti-Haitian ideology, an ideology Balaguer himself helped to develop and institutionalize as one of the leading intellectuals of the Trujillo regime. Influenced by Nazism and other racist discourses of the period aimed to promote racial homogeneity, the ideology offers a representation of Haitians as a threat to national sovereignty and racial and cultural identity. The persistent concern and narrative of a "peaceful invasion" that, in the Dominican national imaginary, describes the anxiety of an increasing Haitian presence through labor migration stems from both the history of the Haitian occupation of the Dominican Republic between 1822 and 1844 and the fear that Haitian migration would lead to the Africanization and Haitianization of Dominicans. As Edward Paulino states, the expulsion of Haitians in 1844 became "the seed of Dominican nationhood" and the Dominican nation based its identity on the rejection of Haiti.[17] This led to the construction of an imagined monoethnic national community that necessitated not only the naturalization and geopolitical reproduction of territories and boundaries to demarcate distinctions between Dominicans and Haitians but also discriminatory sociospatial practices of othering that continue to affect the lived experiences of Haitians and Haitian Dominicans in the Dominican Republic.

Indeed, it has been reported that since 2000, an estimated twelve thousand Haitians have been deported annually through police roundups.[18] These expulsions have been critiqued as both domestic and international human rights violations. But in 2004, the government introduced a migration law (285–04) that expanded the definition of "foreigners in transit" to include children of undocumented Haitian immigrants born and raised in the country. This gave the government the right to deny Haitians birth certificates and ID cards, which, prior to the law, was an informally acknowledged practice. Lack of birth certificates and ID cards allows the government to curtail access to education, health care, and other basic human rights to which Haitians are entitled. The law was upheld as constitutional by the Dominican Supreme Court in 2005, despite the Inter-American Court of Human Rights ruling the practice a violation of the Dominican Constitution and the American Convention on Human Rights just months before the decision was made.[19] In August 2005, two thousand people were deported to Haiti for "looking Haitian."[20] Thirteen racially motivated murders of Haitian-Dominicans were reported in the media that year.[21] In January 2006, twenty-one homes perceived as Haitian settlements were burned to the ground in retaliation for the death of a Dominican soldier who was actually murdered by another Dominican.[22] In 2009, the United Nations High Commissioner for Human Rights estimated that in previous years between twenty and thirty thousand Dominicans and immigrants were expelled annually. In 2010 a constitutional reform eliminated birthright citizenship. A few years later, on September 23, 2013, the Dominican Constitutional Tribunal court handed down judgment TC 168–13, ruling anyone born in the Dominican Republic to Haitian migrant workers after 1929 noncitizens.[23] This ruling retroactively rescinded the citizenship and nationality of over 200,000 Dominicans of Haitian descent. President Danilo Medina, who took office in 2012, tried to mitigate the court ruling in 2014 with a naturalization law (169–14) that recognizes the citizenship of those already registered with the state.[24] But the pitfalls of Dominican immigration laws and recent constitutional reforms continue to put hundreds of thousands at risk of denationalization and statelessness.

The contemporary condition of the statelessness of Haitians in the Dominican Republic echoes the experiences of Haitians in the 1930s that Danticat imaginatively narrates. In *The Farming of Bones*, Amabelle's identity as an orphan, her psychic alienation from her environment as a result of sociospatial boundaries of plantation life, and her own description of her experience after the slaughter as a "living death" are a literary representation of the psychic sense of alienation and dehumanization of Haitians in the Dominican Republic that amounts to neocolonial expressions of social death. Through the novel Danticat shows that if Haitians are not being physically killed and made to disappear, their presence must be symbolically camouflaged and made invisible in the national body politic, their bodies used and abused for nation building, and their voices muted and their speeches altered by the illusion of national language.

Anti-Haitian Sentiments and Mythic Fantasies of Origin

Some of the dialogue that Danticat imaginatively recalls in *The Farming of Bones* could very well be said by Haitian migrants living in the Dominican Republic today. For example, when rumors of the killings are heard by members of the Haitian community on the sugarcane plantations, Sebastien makes a distinction between the *vwayaje,* the cane cutters, and the *non-vwayaje,* Haitian descendants whose families had been in Alegría for generations, with some enjoying the privilege of land ownership. The non-vwayaje are perceived as "a people who had their destinies in hand" (68). But this distinction is immediately disrupted by the dialogue between parents walking their children to school and complaining about "the limitations on their children's education" (69). One parent, a woman with a "mix of Alegría Kreyol and Spanish" says, "I pushed my son out of my body here, in this country. . . . My mother too pushed me out of her body here. Not me, not my son, not one of us had ever seen the other side of the border. Still they won't put our birth papers in our palms so my son can have knowledge placed in his head by a proper educator in a proper school." This statement is followed by the explanation of another parent, a man who "responded in Kréyol": "This makes it easier for them to push us out when they want to" (69). Contemplating the dialogue between the parents, Amabelle becomes unsettled: "I found it sad to hear the non-vwayaje Haitians who appeared as settled in the area as the tamarind trees, the birds of paradise, and the sugarcane—it worried me that they too were unsure of their place in the valley" (70). Amabelle also accepts this identification as a vwayaje, even though she has been living in Alegría since childhood. Not only are there differences and nuances in the linguistic patterns of oral speech, but the dialogic exchange between the parents and Amabelle's intimate thoughts show that the binary distinction between the vwayaje and the nonvwayaje cannot fully be maintained.

At the same time, Sebastien's identification of the cane cutters as vwayaje is a way of creating new narratives of identity, a counternarrative against that of orphanhood and homelessness that workers internalize when they are working in the cane fields and feeling demoralized. In an earlier exchange, Sebastien tells Amabelle, "Sometimes the people in the field, when they're tired and angry, they say we're an orphaned people. . . . They say we are the burnt crud at the bottom of the pot. They say some people don't belong anywhere and that's us. I say we are a group of vwayaje, wayfarers. This is why you had to travel this far to meet me, because that is what we are" (56). The cane cutters reveal what Frantz Fanon describes as a third-person consciousness that reflects the Dominican perception of Haitians.[25] This third-person consciousness as a negative activity results from the act of stepping outside of oneself to view one's image in the eyes of the oppressor. Fanon asserts that when the oppressed is constantly forced to view himself in the eyes of the oppressor, he eventually gains the perception of his oppressors. The cane cutters are very much aware of how they are being perceived and debased by the Dominicans, and this awareness negatively affects their own sense of identity. Contrarily, Sebastien's third-person consciousness allows him to construct a first-person narrative that offers more fruitful and liberatory articulations of the Haitian migrant experience. Sebastien uses his imagination to create a positive story that accounts for both the collective migratory experience and sense of displacement of Haitians on the sugarcane plantations as well as the individualized love story that is a central focus of the story that Amabelle narrates in *The Farming of Bones*.

One of the main functions of the love story in *The Farming of Bones* is to counter the dehumanization of Haitians influenced by the promulgation of anti-Haitian sentiments that feed on the plight of the cane cutters specifically and Haitians more broadly in the Dominican imaginary. Amabelle reveals some of these sentiments when she encounters Dominican strangers after the massacre begins. When Amabelle reaches a cathedral in Dajabon with Yves in an attempt to cross the border to escape the massacre, she overhears the conversations between Dominicans nearby: "Some of the Dominicans who were closest to us gave us looks that showed they pitied us more than they despised us. Others pointed us out to their children and laughed. They told jokes about us eating babies, cats, and dogs" (190). Interestingly, in the novel, the nationalist rhetoric that engenders these derogatory stereotypes is artificially and mechanically transmitted. For example, the characters in the novel only hear the voice of the generalissimo via the radio, which transmits only "fragments from a series of old speeches" (97) that for Amabelle sound "as shrill as a birdcall" (97): "A buzzing hum intruded at many points, and some words, sometimes even whole phrases, were lost to the distance the transmission had to travel to Papi's radio" (97). While Amabelle's body and those of other characters in the novel are overwhelmingly visible, Trujillo can only be represented as a national disembodied voice that can only be ventriloquized. The radio transmits the voice of Trujillo, albeit not completely, to a community of listeners who can imagine themselves as a unified collectivity. The radio serves a similar function for Papi, the father of Señora Valencia's father, whom Amabelle serves. Like Amabelle, he experiences displacement and raises concerns about nationalist tendencies. But Amabelle perceives him as an exiled patriot "fighting a year-and-a-half old civil war in Spain by means of the radio" (43). In the novel, it is the radio that transmits the nationalist voice of the nation. But because the national voice requires an artificial vessel to transmit the message, the singular voice that represents the nation loses authority. Ironically, while the radio sustains an imagined community, because it transmits imperfectly in fragments, it also forecloses any illusion of wholeness. If the radio is the vessel for the voice of the nation, the artificial and mechanical reproduction, transmission, and dissemination of the all-knowing authoritative disembodied voice is not completely effective. Consequently, people are forced to take the place of the radio and become organic instruments of the singular voice of the nation that ventriloquizes Dominican propaganda through coercion. What happens when people become an echo chamber for the homogenized national voice?

The most clear anti-Haitian nationalist rhetoric in the novel is ironically filtered through the voice of a minor character, Father Romain, a young Haitian priest from Cap-Haitien with a parish school in Alegría. When he is introduced in the novel, he is described as someone who promotes and embraces cultural heritage. He participates in creating community by reminding his Haitian congregants of common ties such as "language, foods, history, carnival, songs, tales, and prayers" (73) that can be enriching resources for remembering the homeland, Haiti. Because kinship ties have been broken by the experience of migration and displacement, Romain promotes alternative methods of community to re-create the sense of unity and collectivity and in so doing relies on willful memory to activate community. Amabelle explains, "His creed was one of memory, how remembering—though sometimes painful—can make you strong" (73). Romain speaks of a collective memory that is meant to unite and promote solidarity and healing. Romain eventually learns that memory can also cause discord, alienation, and aggravation.

During the massacre, Father Romain is caught smuggling members of his parish back to Haiti. For this, he is imprisoned, tortured, and forced to forget the very things he encouraged Haitians to remember. Experiencing profound amnesia as a result of the state-sanctioned torture, Father Romain goes mad and loses his own consciousness, the consciousness that relies on memory. When Amabelle finally visits him in Cap-Haitien after the massacre, Father Romain is babbling, repeating Dominican propaganda like a "badly wound machine" (261). In an act of ventriloquisms, he mouths the words he was forced to memorize in the prison:

> On this island, walk too far in either direction and people speak of different language. . . . Our motherland is Spain; theirs is darkest Africa, you understand? They once came here only to cut sugarcane, but now there are more of them than there will ever be cane to cut, you understand? Our problem is one of domination. Tell me, does anyone like to have their house flooded with visitors, to the point that the visitors replace their own children? How can a country be ours if we are in smaller numbers than the outsiders? Those of us who love our country are taking measures to keep it our own. (260)

Father Romain continues, "We as Dominicans must have our separate traditions and our own ways of living. If not, in less than three generations, we will all be Haitians. In three generations, our children and grandchildren will have their blood completely tainted unless we defend ourselves now, you understand?" (261). In his analysis of *The Farming of Bones*, Martin Munro describes Father Romain's words as "mechanical echoes" that represent traumatized memory.[26] These mechanical echoes must be distinguished from what I perceive as the "ghostly echoes" that find their way into Amabelle's inner world and subconscious. The echoes of the inner world are memory and voice that cannot be silenced, erased, or manipulated by nation-state language and the fantasy of the nation's echo chamber.

As mechanical echoes, Romain's voice and speech are displaced and replaced by another speech to advance Dominican nationalism on all bodies that inhabit the nation. But in using the body of Romain to promote Dominican ethnic exceptionalism, the logic that sustains the idea of group identity along biological claims of kinship is both heightened and disrupted. All bodies, regardless of visibly marked differences, are incorporated into the body politic of the nation to advance the illusion of a singular, homogenized identity. All bodies can embody a national language, even its visible markers of diversity and multiplicity. Thus a single set of linguistic codes can be inhabited in different bodies. This not only puts into question biological and ethnic claims to national identity; it also complicates the relationships among memory, body, and lived experience. Alison Landsberg uses the term "prosthetic memory" to examine new definitions of memory affected by technologies of reproduction. She asserts, "Memory remains a sensuous phenomenon experienced by the body, and it continues to derive much of its power through affect. But unlike its precursors, prosthetic memory has the ability to challenge the essentialist logic of many group identities."[27] I would add that this out-of-body experience of memory means that people can also embody ideologies in which they do not believe. People can also embody someone else's discourse intentionally or unintentionally, such as the affinity between nationalist imaginings and religious imaginings achieved through strategic forms of forgetting and remembering. Father Romain's mechanical discourse and the displacement of his speech that results in extreme amnesia reveal that the idea of kinship in linguistic sets of relations are not only oppressive in the context of nationalism but also expose the falsity of linguistic singularity and purity.

Dominican nationality and cultural identity relies on a fantasy of Spanish heritage based on purity of blood and glorification of Spain as homeland. The indigenismo literary movement at the beginning of the twentieth century refines and shifts the narrative of Dominican identity and culture to make room for the existence of pre-Columbian inhabitants of Hispaniola, the Taino-Arawak Indians. The discursive shift creates a double origin narrative whose essential function is to erase any sign of blackness and African ancestry. As Ernesto Sagas asserts,

> Even though the Amerindian population of Hispaniola was exterminated in less than a century, the pro-Hispanic Dominican elites portrayed the Dominican people as the descendants of these brave Indians and the Spanish colonists, deliberately obviating the black element in Dominican society. For most Dominicans, both the elites and the masses, it was a greater honor to have a rebellious Indian (like Enriquillo) as a predecessor than an African Slave. Their fabricated Indian ancestry also created a mythological national past, with deep roots in the prehistory of the island, which gave the Dominican nation a sense of continuity and helped it repress its traumatic colonial history.[28]

With the new double origin narrative, Dominican identity remains grounded in anti-Haitianism and antiblackness. In *The Farming of Bones* Danticat complicates the rhetoric of origin by both appropriating and disturbing this history and notion of genealogy based on bloodline in the novel. In the novel, kinship and heritage are reconsidered through the strategy of twinning. Danticat makes use of the Marassa motif that is pervasive in all her work to symbolically couple Haiti and the Dominican Republic as twins. As Chancy astutely observes, "Through the ingenious use of the Marassa trope, she has used elsewhere, Danticat signals the necessity of achieving balance between bipolarized racial identities, the unification of male and female, and that of dead spirits with those living."[29] When Señora Valencia is introduced in the novel, she is in labor and Amabelle unexpectedly has to play the role of midwife. Señora Valencia bears twins, who are immediately and explicitly distinguished by their gender, color, and size. The twin son, Raphael, named after the Generalissimo, is of "coconut-cream colored" complexion like his mother (9), and the twin girl, Rosalinda, who is named after Señora Valencia's mother, appears "much smaller than her twin, her skin a deep bronze" (11). Señora Valencia already creates a narrative of the twins that fits well within the Dominican national discourse of double heritage. She tells Amabelle, "See what we've brought forth together, my Spanish prince and my Indian Princess" (29). With the umbilical cord curled around her neck, Rosalinda appears to be the weaker and the most vulnerable twin. A metaphor for the two interconnected countries, Raphael embodies the Dominican nation, while Rosalinda is a presentation of Haiti and the vulnerability of Haitians in the Dominican Republic. The position of the umbilical cord also portends danger for the Haitians and the challenge of cohabitation of both nations. But while Señora Valencia interprets the caul covering Rosalinda's face as a curse, the "thin brown veil" (10) can also be interpreted as a natural barrier of protection against danger. Rosalinda's darker complexion already puts her in jeopardy. Señora Valencia asks Amabelle, "What if she's mistaken for one of your people?" (12). Señora Valencia already begins to create a narrative of resilience for her daughter to protect her against the harsh realities of the world she will inhabit. She tells Amabelle, "My daughter is a chameleon" (11). The fantasy of racial purity is unsustainable. Señora Valencia's narrative stabilizes and destabilizes the double origin myth. On the one hand, twin tales are narratives that explicate the established order of the dialectal world and the struggle with the divided self that leads to a double consciousness. The death of one twin must occur to remedy the pathology of double consciousness and the anxiety of twoness. But Danticat chooses to kill Raphael, the prized son who receives all his father's attention, and to give Rosalinda a fighting chance. On the other hand, twins are associated with the disturbance of genealogy and the transgression of borders. They function as symbols of borrowings and crossings, of cross-border cooperation and ideal union. Twins are the signifiers of a Marassa consciousness that promote the hybrid space of the border. Shemak argues that through the lens of Marassa consciousness, "Danticat's text reworks the genealogy of the island by symbolically erasing the border between the nations and revealing their single origin."[30] In my reading of the novel, the border never disappears. Like Danticat's notion of kinship, the border is porous. Very much in keeping with the Marassa consciousness, Danticat reworks the double origin myth to both familiarize and defamiliarize the border. Restating the binary between the two nations through the figure of the twins, Danticat exposes the opposing constructs of the border to show the complex machinations in the Dominican imaginary. But the border remains a sociospatial construct that seeps into the consciousness of both Haitians and Dominicans and works to sustain the divide between the two nations.

Sociospatial Border Consciousness

In her essay on Hispaniola, Marie Rendon states that no other island in the world is divided so neatly. After describing the physical contours of the border between Haiti and the Dominican Republic, Rendon adds, "We are dealing with a porous and sinuous border that zig-zags across territory. There is nothing natural about it, reminding us that it is a political, and not a physical, construction."[31] With a focus on the lives of migrants at the border, Danticat's novel evokes the significance of the border image on the individual and collective psyche of Haitian people. The border between Haiti and the Dominican Republic in the Haitian diasporic consciousness becomes a symbol for the harsh realities of displacement, the impact of colonialism on the black body, and the consequences of global capitalism that continue to force people to migrate and put their bodies on the line. But Danticat pays keen attention to sociospatial expression of anti-Haitian sentiments and actions in the novel that also reveal the policing of social borders and process of national socialization that engender formation of sociospatial consciousness[32] involved in the process of othering the ethnic body. It also demarcates public and private spaces and limits or obviates intimacy between Haitians and Dominicans. But borders also create borderlands. In *Bordering and Ordering the Twenty-First Century,* Gabriel Popescu describes the social construction of borders and their transnational elements: "The concept of borderlands poses that a border, because of its influence over the surrounding areas (known as 'border effect'), creates its own distinctive region. As a consequence, a border can serve not only as an element of division in space, but also a vehicle of creating new territorial realities. Therefore, in order to make sense of state borders, there is a need to go beyond the preoccupation with border lines themselves and to take into account broader areas—border-lands—where social processes induced by borders, such as perceptions, stereotypes and actions, are experienced and reproduced" (20).[33] Iron-ically, borders produce borderlands that in essence transgress borders. Borderlands create cohabitation and shared space and become bridges for opportunities for cross-border cooperation and articulation of alternative sociospatial models.

Social borders influence the movement and interaction of the charac-ters in the novel. These social borders induce what Anssi Paasi defines as a "socio-spatial consciousness" that "represents a broader form of collec-tive consciousness which reflects the ideological and hegemonic structures of the society and hence also the power relations which emerge from the social division of labor."[34] In *The Farming of Bones*, Amabelle has to be very careful not to transgress into the intimate spaces of the people she works for. This is evident very early in the novel. When Amabelle converses with Dr. Javier, she is very conscious of her body: "Dr. Javier followed me to the pantry. As he passed through the doorway, a sus-pended bundle of dried parsley leaves brushed his scalp, leaving behind a few tiny stems in his hair. I reached up to flick them away but stopped myself in time. It would be too forward of me to touch him; he might misunderstand. Working for others, you must always be on your guard" (18). This is echoed when Señor Pico Duarte arrives to meet his newborn children for the first time. Amabelle observes, "Working for others, you learn to be present and invisible at the same time, nearby when they need you, far off when they didn't, but still close enough in case they changed their minds" (35).

The sociospatial conditions of the plantation system create a twofold consciousness that makes Amabelle very aware of the limitations of her body and movement in space. She not only has to police her own body to maintain the social order but she also needs to be very aware of the presence of other bodies, including those that are othered. Later, Señora Valencia must also police her own body to maintain the social division that sustains her privilege. But in her moment of grief after burying her newborn son, Rafi, she transgresses these established barriers. She invites the cane workers "for un cafécito with her" (114). Kongo—one of the older cane workers and a father whose son was killed in a car accident at the hands of Señor Pico—reaches the parlor to take a look at Rosa-linda, the twin girl who survived. But when he attempts to touch her face, "Señora Valencia reache[s] up and block[s] Kongo's hardened old fingers" (115). Consciousness of the body is a part of the nationalization process that is meant to limit the space of intimacy between the Dominicans and the Haitians. When Señora Valencia informs her husband, Señor Pico, a military officer with strong nationalist sentiments, of the gathering with the cane workers at the house, he rectifies this act of transgression: "He did not scold her, but once he discovered that she had used their imported orchid-patterned tea set, he took the set out of the yard and, launching them against the cement walls of the house latrines, he shattered the cups and saucers, one by one" (116). Señor Pico fully embraces the rhetoric of contagion that is critical to the mechanism of othering in the Domin-ican national imaginary. In this scene he performs a Dominican nation-alism that is at the same time a performance of his masculinity. If she is unable to police her body and social space for her own protection, he must do it for her on behalf of the nation. Danticat's critique of nationalism attends to the racial, class, and gendered borders that function as tools of nationalism.

Danticat defines the border as "neutral space."[35] Interestingly, in Dan-ticat's diasporic imaginary, the border is not erased but becomes a floating signifier. In *The Farming of Bones,* Danticat imagines a borderland that offers the opportunity for spatial and symbolic reconfiguration. These borderlands allow room for an alternative and "new consciousness that could ultimately redraw national borders."[36] For those with insider/out-sider status, this is the consciousness of the diasporic subjects who strad-dle between two worlds. It is no coincidence that Amabelle chooses to return to the Massacre River at the end of the novel, where she offers her silent address to Metrès Dlo, the mistress of water in the vodou religion. The river is a natural barrier that stands at the crossroads between life and death. It is an ambiguous and open-ended space that frees Amabelle from the prism of unnatural borders.

Uncovering the Silenced Story of the Haitian Massacre of 1937

Edwidge Danticat was only twenty-two years old when Balaguer ordered the first round of deportations in 1991. But by then an estimated 500,000 Haitians were living permanently in the Dominican Republic.[37] The plight of Haitian migrants was already an issue of concern for a young Danticat, who, as mentioned in chapter 1, was very much aware of the conditions of Haitian refugees and asylum seekers in the United States. Danticat was also familiar with the story of the Haitian massacre of 1937.[38] Between October 2 and October 8 of 1937, under the command of Trujillo, the Dominican army, with the participation of civilians, killed between fifteen and thirty-five thousand Haitians with machetes, bayonets, and clubs at the Dominican Republic–Haitian border.[39] These weapons were intentionally used to hide the state's involvement in what Haitians call "Kout Kouto"—the stabbing—and Dominicans call—"El Corte"—the cutting.

The slaughter of Haitian men, women, and children is infamously named Operación Perejil (the Parsley Massacre) because Dominican soldiers carried sprigs of parsley to identify and distinguish Haitians from Dominicans. Soldiers would ask those who "looked Haitian" to pronounce *perejil,* the Spanish word for parsley. Ethnic Haitians who pronounce the word with a French or Creole accent would supposedly not be capable of trilling the *r.* The Haitians who failed the test would be immediately captured, tortured, and executed.[40] In *The Farming of Bones,* Amabelle and those traveling with her to escape the slaughter do not even have an opportunity to take the test, as their black bodies already mark them as other. When Amabelle is confronted with the possibility of being tested, she thinks,

> At the moment I did believe that had I wanted to, I could have said the word properly, calmly, slowly, the way I often asked "perejil?" of the old Dominican women and their faithful attending granddaughters at the roadside gardens and markets, even though the trill of the r and the precision of the j was sometimes too burdensome a joining for my tongue. It was the kind of thing that if you were startled in the night, you might forget, but with all my senses calm, I could have said it. But I didn't get my chance. Yves and I were shoved down onto our knees. Our jaws were pried open, and parsley stuffed into our mouths. My eyes watering, I chewed and swallowed as quickly as I could, but not nearly as fast as they were forcing the handfuls into my mouth. (193)

Language is used to publicly perform nationalism and linguistic purity at the expense of an entire ethnic community. For Amabelle, the utterance of the word *perejil* depends on specific social contexts. In this instance, Amabelle's voice was forcibly silenced, foreclosing the possibility of language. While the parsley test for Amabelle is the silencing of voice under oppressive conditions, for Odette, one of the characters who die at the river, it is the very circumstances of oppression and subjugation that elevates voice and the act of voicing as tools of resistance and acts of defiance:

> With her parting breath, she mouthed in Kreyol, pesi, . . . no effort to say 'perejil' as if pleading for her life. Speak to me of the things the world has yet to truly understand, of the instant meaning of each bird's call, of a child's secret thoughts in her mother's womb, of the measured rhythmical time of every man and woman's breath, of the true colors of the inside of the moon, of the larger miracles in small things, the dear mysteries. But Parsley? Was it because it was so used, so commonplace, so abundantly at hand that everyone who desired a sprig could find one? We used parsley for our food, our teas, our baths, to cleanse our insides as well as our outsides. Perhaps the Generalissimo in so larger order was trying to do the same for his country. (203)

For Odette, language, which has the capability of expressing mysteries and articulating unspeakable things, is reduced to the symbolic realm of master signs that do not neatly represent lived experiences. Parsley as universal metaphor of linguistic purity and singularity elides the actual and multiple uses of parsley in social contexts and individualized experiences. While parsley is presented as an image and sign that demarcates linguistic purity through othering, it is refracted to expose the materiality of linguistic diversity and hybridization.

While no one knows exactly how many Haitians were indeed massacred, it has been documented that between 1935 and 1950 the Haitian population in the Dominican Republic declined drastically, from 52,627 to 18,772.[41] Bodies of the victims were burned and buried unceremoniously in unmarked graves or dumped in Massacre River.[42] In an interview, Danticat asserts that she had known about the story of the massacre since childhood:

> I became interested in that story, the story of the massacre, as we were approaching the fifty-year anniversary of the massacre, in 1987. I started thinking about it, and then I met in the early 1990s a painter, Ernst Prophète, who painted the event in this incredible painting called *My Grandmother Told Me That the Massacre River Runs with Blood*. My wonderful friend Jonathan Demme recently gave me that painting as a gift, the painting that inspired the book. It was a wonderful gift for more reasons that I can even express. So after 1987, I started doing research, just reading about the massacre, and I was trying to read it from both sides, the points of view of both Dominicans and Haitians, but it was really hard to find much documentation on the Hai-

tian side. I tried to find everything that was written about the massacre, and I traveled to both Haiti and the DR a couple of times, to actually see the physical places and to just talk to people on the border and in the area, in Dajabon, the area that I wanted to set the book in. At some point you really had to let the imagination take over. I also liked the idea of testimony, because I felt that in the research that I was doing, that's what was lacking. People were saying, "You know, there are few direct testimonials," and that's where I felt I needed to create these testimonials in the novel, because that's almost what I wished I had when I started.[43]

The process of investigating this historical event and searching for testimonials led Danticat to the discovery of a number of books on the subject, one of which, *Blood in the Streets,* exposed her to the real story of a Haitian female servant murdered at the hands of the family whom she served.[44] The story is the inspiration behind the creation of Amabelle as the central fictional character in *The Farming of Bones.* As Danticat explains,

> Amabelle's character is based on an actual story that I had heard, of a woman who worked all her life in the home of a military man, a colonel, and this woman, while serving supper, was stabbed at the dinner table by her employer. I knew I wanted to write about someone like that who was sort of treading, as you said earlier, who was working these borders, these social borders, who knew both sides and felt like, somehow, she belonged to both sides but really didn't. I wanted to write about someone like that, but I wanted her to tell the story. I wanted her to live.[45]

The story of the woman killed by a colonel at a dinner table finds its way into the novel when the community begins to share rumors of groups of Haitians being killed (114).

With this story, Danticat's imagination is activated to reconstruct the interior life of a displaced Haitian female migrant who is lost to history and official written narratives. The process of reconstructing an interior life and unearthing a buried story involves the activity of remembering, what Annette Kuhn calls memory work, that functions like archaeology and entails "working backwards—searching for clues, deciphering signs and traces, making deductions, patching together reconstructions out of fragments of evidence."[46] For Danticat, memory work is a central component of articulating the in-between status that structures diasporic subjectivity and imaginary. She explains, "I think memory is that great bridge between the present and the past, between here and there, even between life and death. Even people who are stripped of everything material still have something left when they have their memories. It is what helps us rebuild and start over in another country. It is what helps us reconstruct our lives."[47] Through memory work writers restore a historical past that is often silenced and buried.[48]

The work of memory, as mentioned at the beginning of this chapter, is fundamental to Toni Morrison's understanding of the black diasporic imaginary. But Morrison makes a distinction between memory and the imagination. More than memory, the act of imagination gives total access to "unwritten interior life" that allows a writer to refashion a world and revaluate a "kind of truth."[49] This memory work for Morrison begins with an image that inevitably conjures other images, some of which manifest in dreams and visions. The role of the writer is to penetrate the silences and crystallize these images through language and narrative. Memory work also means deciphering the world of dreamscapes and the unconscious that releases a reservoir of images. As Annette Kuhn asserts, "'the unconscious does not operate with the language of logic but with images'—functioning in the same way as the dream work, with its condensations, its displacements, gaps, non-causal logic and discontinuous scenes."[50] This explains the dual narrative structure in the novel. A number of scholars have already analyzed the double-voiced nature of the novel's narrative structure, which is divided between a dream sequence that offers entry into an interior and fragmented poetic voice in present tense and a first-person voice that narrates the external world chronologically in past tense.[51] What Danticat calls the "voice of dreams" is in bold type and appears in the odd chapters, and the straight linear narrative, which appears in the even chapters, is in regular type.[52] Some of these images point to a site of trauma and haunt both the writer and the character's interior life. In the black diasporic imaginary, these images often represent what Brenda Mehta describes as colonial and neocolonial diasporic wounds.[53] They represent textual wounds in the narrative, an act of echoing in the dream sequence that presents memory as unconscious language and an impossibility in the conventional linear narrative.[54]

In Sugar Land, Sugar Is Made from Blood

Discussing the title of the novel, Danticat explains, "'The farming of bones' the first source of it, comes from my conversations with people who work in the cane. I was talking to a man who said, 'I work the land, I'm working the land to grow bones.'"[55] Bones in the novel are recognized "as last material remains of the dead" (40). But the novel also pushes us to think about what to do with the spiritual remains. The answer exposes the centrality of telling untold stories. From the very title of Danticat's novel, *The Farming of Bones* reveals the impossibility of narrating a story about the migration and displacement of Haitians without evoking the particular story of the sugar industry on the island of Hispaniola that led to the forced displacement and enslavement of millions of Africans in the New World and the double displacement of their descendants. As Chancy asserts, "Sugar is a binding agent in the history between Haitians and Dominicans."[56] Indeed, as a geographically unified space, the island of Hispaniola was the first place where sugarcane was planted in the Americas, with the Spanish side of the island producing sugar for export in the sixteenth century.[57] Spain pioneered the sugar industry and the plantation system when the cane was first shipped back to Europe as early as 1516.[58] This was shortly followed with the importation of African slave labor to the Americas to meet the growing demand for sugar.[59] Colonialism and imperialism in the Spanish New World also transformed the character of European sugar consumption. But the Hispanic sugar industry was considered a failed experiment,[60] as it did not endure beyond the sixteenth century.[61] During this time, Spain was losing control of the seas to French, Dutch, and British forces, who began to establish Caribbean plantations, and in 1697, through the treaty of Ryswick, Spain ceded the western part of Hispaniola to France, after French settlers began to occupy the area. In the seventeenth century, the French colony of Saint-Domingue prospered on the backs of enslaved Africans, producing a large quantity of sugar for Europe. By the eighteenth century it became known as the "Pearl of the Antilles," not only for its natural beauty but also for its place as France's richest colony and biggest colonial producer. Spanish Santo Domingo's main economy in the seventeenth century was cattle ranching, and fewer slaves were imported to the colony.[62] The decay of the sugar plantation system in the Spanish colony of Hispaniola led to indiscriminate poverty. This played a role in racial integration that explains the emergence of the "mulatto" class in the Dominican Republic.[63] The loss of the French colony of Saint-Domingue after the Haitian Revolution followed by a series of wars toward the end of the century negatively affected world sugar production. Migration of French colonists to Cuba after Haitian independence helped make Cuba the foremost sugar producer of the period. Indeed, in the nineteenth century, Cuba and Brazil were recognized as centers of New World production.[64] The Dominican sugar industry resumed large-scale production in 1875 when refugees fleeing Cuba and political persecution in the struggle for independence from Spain—known as the Ten Years'

War (1868–78)—arrived in the Dominican Republic and established sugar mills.[65] Falling prices of sugar during this period gave the United States an entry into the market with a US-Dominican trade agreement signed in 1891 that reduced tariffs on Dominican sugar entering the United States.[66] The United States quickly became the principal importer of Dominican sugar as the new sugar industrialist. The First World War resulted in an economic downturn and freeze on wages, which resulted in local labor shortage. Sugar industrialists turned to China, India, and the British West Indies, who provided the majority of cheap labor at the turn of the twentieth century. The migration of Haitians and Cocolos, non-Spanish-speaking immigrants from the British Isles, for work were occurring simultaneously as sugarcane production expanded in the Dominican Republic and was under the control of the United States, which maintained complete dominance of the Dominican sugar industry through an occupation between 1916 and 1924. Haiti was concurrently under US control, occupied by the emerging world power from 1915 to 1934. But by the 1930s, with the global business crisis that led to the Great Depression and restrictive anti-immigration laws,[67] Haiti became the main source of labor, which increased with the systematic recruitment of braceros,[68] followed by forced coercion in the 1940s that came with the modernization of the sugar industry and establishment of territorial borders to intercept and control the undocumented.[69] The first mutually accepted border agreement between Haiti and the Dominican Republic was ratified in 1936,[70] six years after Trujillo began to rule the country and take control of the sugar industry as a family enterprise. Trujillo owned mills that produced two-thirds of country's sugar.[71] A 1952 accord with braceros nationalized the sugar empire after the assassination of Trujillo in 1961. By 1966 the Haitian government was being paid to develop recruitment centers. When the Dominican Republic was occupied again by the United States in 1965, the Dominican sugar industry thrived until the 1970s but declined again in the 1980s.[72] Thereafter tourism became the profitable alternative for sugar export.

It is not surprising, then, that a number of images that represent sugarcane plantation life consume *The Farming of Bones*. In fact, the novel begins and continues at various moments with vivid descriptions of bodies scarred and mutilated by sugarcane work. On the very first page of the novel, which introduces the lyrical dreamscape and narrative voice, which is differentiated from the linear straightforward narrative, Amabelle describes her lover's body: "He is lavishly handsome by the dim light of my castor oil lamp, even though the cane stalks have ripped apart most of the skin on his shiny black face, leaving him with crisscrossed trails of furrowed scars. His arms are as wide as one of my bare thighs. They are steel, hardened by four years of sugarcane harvests" (1). Then later, in one of the straight linear narrative chapters, Amabelle describes the environment near the stream where Haitian women gather. She says, "There were women in the stream who were ancient enough to be our great-grandmothers. Four of them were nearby, helping a few of the orphaned girls to wash themselves. Among the oldest women, one was missing an ear. Two had lost fingers. One had her right cheekbone cracked in half, the result of a runaway machete in the fields" (61). Kongo, one of the elders mourning the loss of his son Joel who was killed in car accident as Señor Pico was rushing to meet his newborn twins, describes plantation life: "In sugar land, a shack's for sleeping, not for living. Living is only work, the fields. Darkness means rest" (107). Physical labor, injuries, and scars function as images and evidence of exploitation at the border that relies on the bodies of Haitians for national and transnational economic development. Danticat makes these bodies, as flesh, overwhelmingly present to turn people lost to history into mausoleums and materialized testaments.[73] This is most poignant when Amabelle realizes how the slaughter has affected her own body: "Now my flesh was simply a map of scars and bruises, a marred testament" (227).

The most prominent image that points to this form of trauma is the sugar woman. Beyond the issue of narrative style, the question is what story does the recurring image of the sugar woman in Amabelle's dreamscape narrative tell? Amabelle's dreamscape of the sugar woman, like the other dreamscape sections in the novel, is a fragmented narrative, an attempt at articulating an impenetrable silence. But it does tell a story, the story of the sugar industry as a primal source of displacement. In her analysis of *The Farming of Bones,* Semia Harbawi writes that the dreamscape of the sugar woman is "an imaginative psychic silhouette reminiscent of African slaves toiling on the Caribbean sugar plantations."[74] The image of the sugar woman is a representation of a marred testament to colonial and neocolonial past and appears in Amabelle's dream as a residual echo of a traumatic ancestral past marked by colonial structures. It symbolizes a primary and gendered wound of diaspora, the result of epistemic violence and social death. Right before the dream narratives abruptly stop in the novel, Danticat dreams of the sugar woman. The dreamscape narrative begins with a description:

I dream of the sugar woman. Again.

As always, she is dressed in a long, three-tiered ruffled gown inflated like a balloon. Around her face, she wears a shiny silver muzzle, and on her neck there is a collar with a clasped lock dangling from it. (132).

The sugar woman appears dancing the kalanga and wearing chains on her ankles. When Amabelle, whose voice is that "of an orphaned child at the stream," asks the sugar woman what is on her face, the sugar woman replies, "Given to me long time ago, this was, so I'd not eat the sugarcane" (132). Amabelle follows up with another question, "Why are you here?" to which the sugar woman responds, "Told you before . . . I am the sugar woman. You, my eternity" (133). Later in the novel, fragments of the sentence are repeated when the narrative integrates the dreamscape of Amabelle's inner world with the straight narrative voice of her outer world. This time it is the image of her mother arriving in her dreams to console her and offer words of comfort. The exchange between mother and daughter is profound. Amabelle tells her mother, "I will never be a whole woman . . . for the absence of our face" (208), to which her mother responds, "You will be well again ma belle, Amabelle. I know this to be true. And how can you have ever doubted my love? You, my eternity" (208). This powerful exchange in the dreamscape, which occurs when Amabelle is recovering at the border clinic from the blows she received during the massacre, exposes Amabelle's own fantasy of primordial wholeness that results from separation from the mother. The return to the mother narrative both reinforces and disrupts national imaginaries of home and their emphasis on origin and ancestry. It evokes a desire for union and reconnection with an idealized safe place. Thus, Danticat's exploration of the pitfalls of nationalism does not disavow discourses of wholeness and union, reunifications that are said to reference the stuff of nation. This desire for wholeness is reiterated twenty-five years later when Amabelle returns to the river. On the very last page of the novel, Amabelle expresses a need to "raise my body and carry me into the river, into Sebastien's cave, my father's laughter, my mother's eternity" (310).

In an interview with Myriam Chancy, Danticat explains the objective of *The Farming of Bones:*

> The most important goal of this book for me was to create a chain of memory. Each person who read the book I felt was getting a chance to honour the memory of a life, gain a living memory of one or of the many lives who had perished this way. The book to me is a memorial, and when people read it and are touched by it then their hearts become one more memorial to not only the past pain but also to the living pain we're in. And since there are no actual memorials to those who died in the 1937 massacre, we must have the living memorials in our hearts.[75]

In *The Farming of Bones,* Amabelle's final return involves communion with the dead as projects of reclamation, regeneration, and memorialization of lost voices that manifest in the present as echoes that allow a writer like Danticat to imagine an interior life and textualize "unspeakable" dreams for a poetics of remembering, an offering to those who have not had a proper burial. Danticat's poetics of remembering the dead is not only a reclamation of lost lives and a call for new narratives that help to reconstruct lives in the diaspora but a recognition that the heterogeneity of the echo chamber in the diasporic imaginary expands to the realm that transgresses all language. The direct address to Metrès Dlo in *The Farming of Bones* allows for a redefinition of the border zone that foregrounds the zone of spirituality. In Danticat's diasporic imaginary, the border is transformed into a site of mourning and memorialization, a space beyond language, a way of communing with the ancestors and listening to their voices, an intentional process of returning dignity to the dead without tombs, without names, through the very act of writing and relating to other texts.

Epilogue

Toward a Globalectical Imagination

The lesson is that a plural, multiplying, fragmented, identity is no longer given or thought as a lack of identity but rather as a huge opening and new opportunity of breaking open closed gates.
—Édouard Glissant, "The Unforeseeable Diversity of the World"

Works of imagination refuse to be bound within national geographies; they leap out of nationalist prisons and find welcoming fans outside the geographic walls. But they can also encounter others who want to put them back within the walls, as if they were criminals on the loose.

—Ngũgĩ wa Thiong'o, *Globalectics*

ONE OF the most wrenching diasporic stories of the relation between mourning and memorialization in Danticat's treatment of voice as echo is found in "Water Child," the third story of *The Dew Breaker*. In chapter 4, I briefly discuss the story in the context of intertextual links and the trope of the puzzle. I return to this story now to foreground a striking image, the image of the voice box that binds Danticat's fictional texts to her two memoirs, *Brother, I'm Dying* and *The Art of Death*. The voice box image reveals much about the origins of Danticat's preoccupation with embodied and disembodied voices and the workings of the trope of echo and its double, ventriloquism, in Danticat's oeuvre.

In "Water Child," Danticat presents the character Nadine, a thirty-year-old nurse who works overtime to wire money to her parents in Haiti. Because her parents sacrificed everything to put their daughter in nursing school and offer her a better life, Nadine feels a responsibility to repay her parents and, as a result, defers her own dreams of seeing the world. As in the first story of *The Dew Breaker*, Danticat shows that her Haitian characters are also being transformed by the crossings of cultures and languages as a result of globalizing processes. They embrace and incorporate other cultural beliefs in their lives to cope with trauma.

This cultural hybridization is established in the very title of the story. "Water child" is the literal translation of the Japanese word *mizuko,* which means dead fetus, or dead baby. Nadine is struggling with the loss of a "nearly born child" (56) she aborted two months after conception. Nadine creates an altar to honor her child's memory. She appropriates the Japanese way of honoring an unborn child: "She had once read about a shrine to unborn children in Japan, where water was poured over altars of stone to honor them, so she had filled her favorite drinking glass with water and a pebble and had added that to her own shrine, along with a total of now seven microcassettes with messages from Eric, messages she had never returned" (57). The altar is transformed not only by the mingling of cultures but also by the mingling of tradition with modernity, represented as the framed drawing she had made herself and microcassettes from the answering machine. "Water Child" is linked to the preceding story in *The Dew Breaker,* through the character Eric, the night manager who, the reader learns, is Nadine's ex-boyfriend and "near father of her nearly born child" (56). Eric is both overwhelmingly present and absent in this story. He is only a captured voice in an answering machine, a voice that is unacknowledged, since Nadine never responds to the messages Eric leaves. When she finally decides to speak to him, his telephone has been disconnected.

Nadine, who lives alone in a one-bedroom condo in Canarsie, Brooklyn, works in the ear, nose, and throat department of a hospital; she deals with post-op patients who have lost their voice as a result of total laryngectomies. When she is home, she likes the sound of white noise: "Nadine was greeted by voices from the large television set that she kept on twenty-fours a day. Along with the uneven piles of newspapers and magazines scattered between the fold-out couch and the floor-to-ceiling bookshelves in her living room, the television was her way of bringing voices into her life that required neither reaction nor response" (56). When she hears the one message on her answering machine (a message from her ex-lover, Eric), she is reminded of the "electively mute, newly arrived immigrant children whose worried parents brought them to the ward for consultations, even though there was nothing wrong with their vocal cords" (56). Nadine "removed the microcassette from the answering machine and placed it on the altar she had erected on top of the dresser in her bedroom" (57). It is at this moment that the reader makes the connection to the story "Seven," the story of Eric, Nadine's ex-lover. The link is further acknowledged when the reader learns that Nadine has a total of seven microcassettes with messages from Eric that find their way onto the altar.

As she does in *The Farming of Bones,* Danticat explores the relationship between voice and technologies of reproduction.

Aside from the lack of communication between Eric and Nadine, communication that is further curtailed by the fact that Eric can no longer be reached because he has changed his number to sever ties with the women he has been with in the United States while waiting for his wife to join him, the issue of silence and lack of vocal agency becomes even more poignant with Nadine's engagement with her patient, Ms. Hinds, a twenty-five-year-old nonsmoker who is recovering from a laryngectomy and must write to communicate to others. At one point in the story Ms. Hinds writes down the words "I can't speak," to which Nadine verbally responds, "That's right. . . . You can't" (61). Nadine recommends an artificial larynx, a voice box, and a speech therapist. But Nadine knows that this will not appease the fear of being voiceless:

> Nadine was tempted to warn Ms. Hinds that whatever form of relief she must be feeling now would only last for a while, the dread of being voiceless hitting her anew each day as though it has just happened, when she would awake from dreams in which she'd spoken to find that she had no voice, or when she would see something alarming and realize that she couldn't scream for help, or even when she would realize that she herself was slowly forgetting, without the help of old audio or videocassettes or answering machine greetings, what her own voice used to sound like. She didn't say anything, however. Like all her other patients, Ms. Hinds would soon find all this out herself. (65–66)

In the story, Ms. Hinds functions as Nadine's relational double, a distorted image of Nadine's self imposed silence and inability to articulate the trauma of the abortion. But Nadine is in the end a refracted image of Edwidge Danticat. This refracted relation between Nadine, the character, and Danticat, the author, is made abundantly clear not in the story itself, but in Danticat's memoir, *Brother, I'm Dying.*

Described as a family memoir, *Brother, I'm Dying* explores the separate but intertwined lives of her two "fathers," Andre Miracin, Danticat's actual father, a cabdriver who left Haiti thirty years ago, and Joseph, Danticat's uncle, who is painted as a charismatic Baptist pastor who is committed to his community in Bel Air and only visits New York to see his brother sporadically. Like the figure of Antigone, Danticat emerges in the memoir as a daughter caught between two deaths, the death of her uncle and the death of her father. And like Antigone, Danticat wants to honor these two lives and return dignity to them in death. In a 2009 interview, Danticat was asked about the difficulty of writing the memoir.

She responded, "It was a book I felt I had to write, for my uncle who died in immigration custody as well as for my father who died at around the same time and for the future generation, including my daughter, who was born in the midst of all that. It was indeed very therapeutic to write. I've said this before, I think of *Brother, I'm Dying* as not a me-moir, but a nou-moir, a we-moir; it's not just my story but all these stories intertwined."[1] It was also a book, that, as she states in another interview, allowed her to address the issue of male influences in her work.[2] In this "we-moir," Danticat tells her uncle's story. The uncle's story is intertwined with the story of Danticat's father, who used to sell used clothes in Haiti for an Italian émigré boss, a recounting of her grandma Melinda's death woven within a Rapunzel-like tale and an exploration of kinship beyond blood ties via the saga of her cousin Marie Micheline, Uncle Joseph's adopted daughter. In the memoir, Danticat reactivates the name-of-the-father motif, displacing it from the symbolic order, replacing in the lived experiences of her own childhood and her family's histories of migration and displacement.

Danticat explains the significance of her patrilineal history and the influences of the men in her life:

> I write these things now, some as I witnessed them and today remember them, others from official documents, as well as the borrowed collections of family members. But the gist of them was told to me over the years in part by my uncle Joseph, in part by my father. Others in great detail. What I learned from my father and uncle, I learned out of sequence and in fragments. This is an attempt at cohesiveness, and at re-creating a few wondrous and terrible months when their lives and mine intersected in startling ways, forcing me to look forward and back at the same time. I am writing this only because they can't.[3]

Danticat understands that in order to retell the story, she must begin with fragmented pieces and then work her way into a desired cohesion. The narratives she puts together become part of a diasporic archive. In this diasporic narrative, Danticat explains that her uncle, at the age of fifty-five, had a radical laryngectomy in New York during one of his visits to the United States:

> While my uncle was not the only mute person in Bel Air—there was a boy who was born voiceless and an old woman who'd suffered a stroke—he was the only one with a tracheotomy hole in his neck. People were so curious about the hole that they kept their eyes on it throughout entire one-way conversations with him. I too was intrigued by this narrow abyss that seemed to lead deep

into his body. A perfect circle, it was salmon pink like our house and convulsed outward when he sneezed. (63)

This passage recalls one of the earliest interviews with Danticat that reveals the impact of her uncle's laryngectomy on her childhood experiences and her relationship with voice. In a 1996 interview with Renée H. Shae, Danticat explained,

> My uncle, who was living in Haiti, came back to the states to have this operation, and when he returned, this man who is a minister all of a sudden couldn't speak. I could see his sadness. My uncle is one of the most amazing people I know, and he was so sad. I spent more time with him than other people, getting things for him, doing errands. I was ten. Slowly, I picked up what he was saying. He would move his lips, and I would figure it out. At first, he would write things down, but as he wrote them, he would also mouth them, I realized what he was saying, so he would take me everywhere with him. He would say things, and I would say them out loud. It's a bit presumptuous of me to say that I was his voice, but for a while, I felt like I was an extension of his voice.[4]

For eight formative years, starting at the age of four, Edwidge was left under the care of her uncle. Danticat explains that her uncle Joseph had a specific relationship to the dead. He kept track of cadavers by listing the names of victims in a small notepad that he carried in his jacket pocket. Danticat further explains, "Before my uncle's operation, a big part of his job was to eulogize the dead. And even after his operation, he faithfully attended all church funerals, and believing that children shouldn't be shielded from either the idea or the reality of death, he often brought Nick, Bob and me with him. So the sight of a corpse was not new to us" (72). Thus, through her relationship with her uncle, Danticat has a very unique experience with voice that explicates her articulation of the quest for voice and the experience of voicelessness in diaspora.

The epigraph to the memoir, a quote from Paul Auster's *The Invention of Solitude,* also provides a clue to Danticat's own understanding of the relationships among voice, death, and the writing process: "To begin with death. To work my way back into life, and then, finally, to return to death. Or else: the vanity of trying to say anything about anyone." The *Invention of Solitude,* published in 1982, is a memoir, divided into two parts: the first part explores the death of the author's father and his relationships with his father and his son; the second part then shifts to a meditation on the nature of absence. The epigraph alone establishes the presence of death even in life. As if that were not enough, the first sentence of Danticat's book reads, "I found out I was pregnant the same day that my father's rapid weight loss and chronic shortness of breath were positively diagnosed as end-stage pulmonary fibrosis" (3). Danticat begins the memoir with the suspension between the living and the dead. It is the theme of death and its ability to silence a generation that worries Danticat here. Birth, on the other hand, signals the necessity to pass on the stories that mark a generation so that there is continuity between the living and the dead, between the past and the future, between listening, reading, and writing. In her latest book, *The Art of Death,* Danticat returns to the theme of death, exploring, through anecdotes, the way other writers approach the topic to tell the story of her mother, Rose, who passed away from ovarian cancer in 2014. In *The Art of Death,* Danticat writes, "We write about the dead to make sense of our losses, to become less haunted, to turn ghosts into words, to transform an absence into language."[5] Danticat's two memoirs expose the ways in which her understanding of voice is tied to her articulation of death. Voice, for Danticat is also about memorializing the dead, giving voice to those who are muted in death, and offering fruitful ways to commune with the dead in this polyvocal and heterogeneous echo chamber.

Between Postcoloniality and Globalization

There is a substantial amount of literary criticism that places Danticat and her treatment of voice within the framework of the postcolonial, including my earlier work on the writer. Indeed, the debate about voice, the muted voices of colonized subjects who regain agency by "coming into voice" or the undoing the authoritative voice of the colonizer, grounds the field and centers the work of postcolonial emigrant writers. But this book does not fit neatly into a postcolonial frame. It does, however, offer an interdisciplinary approach that places the field of postcolonial studies in conversation with global studies. As I outlined in the introduction, I am reading the global and analyzing the use of the echo and the trope of the echo chamber in relation to recent articulations of diaspora and globalization that are presented in Danticat's work. I do not begin with the assumption that Danticat is doing something that is different from postcolonial writers or something new that is called *globalization.* Eschewing this disciplinary binary, I see Danticat as a postcolonial writer as well. But I do want to differentiate between a postcolonial imaginary and a diasporic imaginary, although there is a relation between the two. This book moves beyond certain terms and metaphors of migrancy, nomadism, exile, tourism, and hybridity that are specific to "postcolonial consciousness" and language particular to postcolonialism as a field. In this respect, I embrace Glissant's notions of the imaginary, relationality, and polyvocality because they are transportable, able to move through these discursive fields even though they evoke the workings of an Antillean imaginary. Furthermore, they push us to explore the relationship between theories of postcolonialism and theories of globalization. My reading of Danticat both within our understanding of the emergence of globalization and transnationalism in the latter half of the twentieth century, as well as the experiences of migration and the formation of diasporic communities (particularly the Haitian diaspora in the 1970s through the 1990s), recalls colonial and neocolonial histories that expose oppressive globalizing processes. This necessarily involves awareness of the workings of the colonial imaginary and its articulations in literary productions.

World Literature and the Globalectical Imagination

Writing about the multiplicity of US literature as "rainbow literature" that results from migration, Ngũgĩ wa Thiong'o asserts, "No matter the definition, it is clear that globality as much as coloniality are the constant features in the postcolonial even when the latter refers exclusively to those societies and peoples impacted by imperial colonialism."[6] Furthermore, the postcolonial, he writes, "is at the heart of World literature, which in its vastness offers the possibility of a balance between the national and the global, the preservation of the 'particularity of a national literature' that also caters to the 'global reach and appeal.'"[7] Thiong'o describes his vision of world literature:

> World literature would be like the sea or the ocean into which all streams from all corners of the globe would flow. The sea is constituted of many rivers, some of which cross many fields, but the rivers and their constituent streams do not lose their individuality as streams and rivers. The result is the vastness of the sea and the ocean. Confronted with the possibility of that reality, and quite frankly, its vastness, it is easy for organizers of literary knowledge to stop in fright and stay within a national boundary, taking comfort in the certainty of the structures already tried and passed on as tradition. The traditional organization of literature along national boundaries is like bathing in a river instead of sailing in the ocean, or trying to contain a river's flow within a specific territory.[8]

Such vision seems applicable to Danticat's work, which reveals a strong presence of ocean imagery. What, for example, can be said about the evocation of Metrès Dlo in Danticat's diasporic imaginary? How can we explore the imaginary space of Danticat's small coastal village in *Claire of the Seal Light* (2013), the only book Danticat has produced that is set exclusively in Haiti. What does it reveal about the diaspora's relationship with the local context of the homeland and the presence of "revenants" in island spaces or in what might be called a sacred imaginary? Understanding the worldliness of any text, as I have tried to do with the writing of Edwidge Danticat, necessitates what Thiong'o calls the "globalectical imagination." To read globalectically "is a way of approaching any text from whatever times and places to allow its content and themes to form a free conversation with other texts of one's time and place, the better to make it yield its maximum to the human."[9] It involves a reading that should bring "into mutual impact and comprehension the local and the global, the here and there, the national and the world."[10] The present study reveals that the world, for Danticat, is a global site of displacement that gets enacted in localized spaces. It is, to borrow Glissant's phrase, an écho-monde in polyphonic communion and communication.

What has interested me over the years as a scholar fascinated by diaspora as a phenomenon and a reader of immigrant literature is the way writers and individuals perceive, interpret, and reimagine the world from a diasporic lens. I have attempted to explore Danticat's relationship to the imaginary through her publications and not just the collective imaginary discussed by African diaspora and global studies scholars. It should be noted that Danticat's diasporic imaginary cannot be fully separated from the reader's imaginary. In fact, this is part of the complexity of the echo and the echo chamber, especially when it is explored within notions of intertextuality and rewriting, which I discuss throughout the book. Like the dialogics between nation and diaspora, the relation between the reader and Danticat is significant to comprehending Danticat's understanding of diaspora and investment in breaking down monologic epistemologies. World literature in the context of globalectic imaginary is a mode of reading and listening to the polyphonic voices of echo subjects scattered, like the mountain nymph, all over the world. How we gather their dismembered and disremembered parts is of the utmost significance.

The Missing Pieces

A great deal has been said here about Danticat's work, but there is still much more to say. For example, Danticat's activism is beyond the scope of this project. I believe the extensive interview I conducted with Danticat during the summer of 2017 (included as an appendix in this book), much like her op-ed pieces, offers a glimpse into her political mind, particularly in the area of US immigration policies. It is evident that the recent immigration policies under the Trump administration that demonize disadvantaged poor immigrants are weighing heavily on Danticat's mind. I hope that there will be a book devoted to exploring Danticat's political engagement and social justice activism in recent years. Danticat's growing reputation as an activist is an important factor to understanding not only migration policies that affect the lives of diasporic communities but also her global appeal in the twenty-first century.

Danticat is a prolific writer who is nowhere near ready to throw in the towel. She already has a book of short stories that will be out around the time of her fiftieth birthday. It is my hope that another scholar will publish a full-length study on Danticat that looks at existing works I have not delved into for this project, such as her children's books and young adult novels and forthcoming publications. In the meantime, I am positive that Danticat will continue to perfect her craft as a writer and use her pen and her imagination to fight on behalf of immigrants and against a monologic idea of America that is anathema to her own identity and diasporic imaginary.

Appendix

Interview with Edwidge Danticat

NADÈGE T. CLITANDRE: Edwidge, thank you for taking the time to do this interview with me. I can't believe it has been almost twenty years since we first met. I was working on my master's thesis on *Breath, Eyes, Memory* at the University of Chicago at the time. I believe you were in town for a reading. Of course I went and took the liberty of giving you a draft of my paper, which you generously read. I still have the card you sent after reading it. You probably don't remember that, but I was starstruck and so impressed by your graciousness and openness. I still am.

EDWIDGE DANTICAT: I do remember. I also remember when you were kind enough to host Junot Díaz and me at Berkeley. This does feel like a full circle moment after close to a quarter of a century now. I'm not sure there are that many people who have been reading me for such a long period of time. I thank you for your interest and I thank you for remaining interested.

NTC: I thank you for your oeuvre, Edwidge. It has been a pleasure reading your work. I want to begin with your first book. When *Breath, Eyes, Memory* was published, I was in my last year of high school. I don't remember when I read the book exactly, but it must have been while I was a freshman in college. However, I do remember the impact. I remember recognizing myself and my own experience of migration for the first time in a way I hadn't with any other text I had read prior to yours. And like you I was an avid reader. In a 1998 interview, you said that you write for the person you were at fifteen, for the girl looking for an image of herself. There is a whole generation who appreciates this novel because you gave us just that. Of course I am speaking broadly about your articulation of the experience of migration and description of the Haitian community in the United States. You have written a few young adult books since your first novel, including *Untwine,* which was published in 2015. But I want to know if in all your work you still write for that person, that fifteen-year-old girl looking for an image of herself.

ED: Absolutely. I've never stopped writing for that girl. When I came to the United States at age twelve, I initially could not read any of the English-language books at the library. So I read all the Haitian literature that was available at the Brooklyn Public Library branches near me. Actually, that's when I read your dad's, Pierre Clitandre's, incredible novel *Cathédrale du mois d'août.* I also read Marie Vieux Chauvet at that time, Jacques Roumain, Jacques Stephen Alexis, J. J. Dominique, Dany Laferrière. I read these books to go home, to return to Haiti in my imagination. They opened a whole new world to me since I had not been taught Haitian literature when I was in school in Haiti. I had been to the *certificat* exam early—at age ten— so I was kind of an advanced reader for my age, and though I had been given excerpts of Voltaire and Zola and a few other French writers to read—and certainly LaFontaine to recite—I don't remember being taught any Haitian literature. Maybe it was a failure of the school I went to—I'm not sure. But it was wonderful to read books that were set in Haiti and see that whole range of possibilities and that whole range of experiences, from urban to rural, from poor to rich characters. It also taught me a lot about how stories that I was somehow already familiar with, stories set during the American occupation or during the dictatorship, for example, could be told and retold from different perspectives and points of view.

After I exhausted the stockpile of Haitian and French literature books at the library, as soon as I learned to read English—even with a dictionary—I began reading every single book there was with a little girl on the cover. Or anything resembling "girl" in the title. That's how I found Maya Angelou's *I Know Why the Caged Bird Sings* and Rosa Guy's *The Friends,* Paule Marshall's *Brown Girl, Brownstones,* Toni Morrison's *The Bluest Eye,* and many others. I was looking for myself in those books. Later that search would extend to books like Amy Tan's *The Joy Luck Club* and Maxine Hong Kingston's *Woman Warrior* and Julia Alvarez's *How the Garcia Girls Lost Their Accents.* Part of me still reads like that fifteen-year-old girl, and no matter what the genre, I'm still writing for that fifteen-year-old girl who was so desperate to find herself, or some version of herself, and her life in print. I think the fact that I sought and found those narratives also made it seem possible for me to tell my own story and eventually become a writer. It moves me so much when people say that my book has done something similar for them. Lately I've been running into grown women who got in trouble a lot when they were young. Some were in the system. Some were in foster care after reporting their parents for disciplining them the way they would have been disciplined in Haiti, notably the rigwaz or marinèt. And these young women told me that they took *Breath, Eyes, Memory* with them from home to home or juvenile place to juvenile place, because some teacher or well-meaning adult had given it to them. They found solace, and some even found a voice in it. Every time I hear something like this, I want to cry.

NTC: Thanks for sharing this story. It is just one example of the positive impact of *BEM* on young women who read it. I remember reading somewhere that you received hate mail after the publication of *BEM* for "outing" the custom of testing a girl's virginity, which Martine, the mother of the protagonist, Sophie, gives to her daughter. So many immigrant writers are heavily critiqued for "airing dirty laundry." And some face death threats because of what they write. The fatwa against Salman Rushdie for his book *Satanic Verses*, for example, has never been officially lifted, and recently there was a new bounty for his death. *BEM* was your first book and you were young. How did you feel at the time? Did that experience influence your writing in any way? What you wrote and how you wrote it? How do you now deal with writing about matters that may be sensitive to the Haitian community? I wonder: Did anything like that come up when you wrote/published *The Dew Breaker* or any of your other work?

ED: Luckily there was no fatwa, but there was some backlash. I think part of the reason some people reacted so negatively to the portrayal of the mother's testing the girl's virginity is how writers of colors are read in general. It was clear, in my mind, that though this was something that happened to some people in Haiti as elsewhere—I've met women from the Middle East and parts of Asia that this has happened to—it was clear to me that I was writing fiction, and I believed that people would read it that way. But they read it as anthropology, and when I was interviewed, that's all the interviewers wanted to talk about. I never even saw it as "dirty laundry" on the community. I saw it as something that happens in this family, and that's obviously not a good thing to have happened because it hurts the family. But it was read as my saying that this happens in all Haitian families and some people got very mad at me for "telling lies" in my fiction. I felt really besieged at the time and somewhat ashamed of myself. I did not want to be one more person contributing to a "negative" image of Haiti, so the fact that my book was seen in that light by some made me sad. When the book was picked for Oprah's book club in 1998, I wrote an afterword to explain. Some scholars then told me that I had "defaced" the text, but that's how embarrassed I was that I had somehow further tarnished the image of Haitians. I wouldn't say it affected my writing too much, though. Usually by the time I publish something, I try to have something else finished or far along so that no matter what the reaction to the newly published thing, I can still find the courage to go on. That advice was given to me by my first editor, Laura Hruska at Soho Press, and I still try to keep it up today. So by the time *Breath, Eyes, Memory* was out and being discussed I had already finished writing *Krik? Krak!*, my story collection. I did go back and reread it with the "controversy" in mind, and though I tried to be less general about certain things, I did not really change much else. This is the way I've gone forward from that time; I try to be sensitive, but I am writing my own truth or my characters' truth. I know that's not going to make everyone jump for joy. There are always going to be people who think you're getting it wrong. I do my best, but I can't not say certain things because they make us look bad. Otherwise, I'm really lying and it's not worth it at all. I might as well pack it all up and go home. Every book I've had since has had some unexpected reaction, but not as much. There are always countrymen and -women of mine who want me to stop writing about poor people and show the beaches—even though *Claire of the Sea Light* is set on a beach, but the people on the beach are poor, so that doesn't count. *The Farming of Bones,* some thought I was too easy on the Dominicans. For *The Dew Breaker,* some told me to forget about the dictatorship already and come to the present. Again, you can never please everyone.

NTC: The afterword to *BEM* is powerful. I would like to ask about the theme of separation in the novel. You and I have similar experiences of separation from family. My father was exiled during the Duvalier dictatorship when I was three years old, and my mother followed him to Brooklyn, New York, when I was five years old. We, my older brother, younger sister, and I, were left with our paternal grandfather, but he disappeared shortly after, never to be found again. My maternal grandmother had to step in and take charge of us. One of the most fascinating things about *BEM* is the way you highlight the consequence of migration in terms of familial separation and its affective dimensions. Families get separated for all kinds of reason. In your opinion, is there something particular about separation through migration?

ED: I'm glad you liked the afterword. In terms of writing about the dictatorship, your grandfather's story and the stories of others who disappeared during the dictatorship is why we can't move on from the dictatorship. It haunts us inside our families. It's hard in those cases to just say, "Let bygones be bygones." This is what I always tell the people who want me to move on from it as a subject. Looking at current cases of migration, cases where children are in detention centers in Miami, for example, children who were put on a boat in hopes of having them be reunited with a parent. Or the cases we see in the news of people packing boats to cross the Mediterranean with their babies in their arms or people stranded in refugee camps or in "jungles" across Europe. When I look back now, my case feels relatively mild. I think now that my parents made the right choice to leave me behind when they first moved here. When I did join my parents in Brooklyn at age twelve, I realized that it was a very hard life. I don't know what it would have been like for me and my brother sooner. Even at age twelve, I had to become a substitute mother for my younger brothers. We almost died in an apartment fire during that time. So my parents made a very difficult choice that I think now was the right one. But familial separation through migration definitely alters the family dynamic. In some families, it creates a hierarchy between the US-born, often younger, children—the *ti ameriken*—the little Americans and the Haitian-born children. I know some siblings for whom that chasm has never healed because they felt less loved because they were left behind. I know some who were never able to feel close again to their parents. One of the things that are not really discussed in public debates of emigration is how much emigrants sacrifice emotionally for the opportunities they are seeking. Fiction does that best, I think, because you can go very deeply into someone's heart to explore those kinds of tears and scars.

NTC: Yes, this is why I love teaching novels and examining the issue of migration through literature. I am fascinated by the impact of migration on individual lives, and fiction has a way of delving "deeply," as you say, into the affective dimensions of migration. Our family also has an apartment fire story in Brooklyn that nearly killed us during the early years of our migration experience. I left Haiti when I was seven years old. My older brother, like you, was twelve years old. He has vivid memories of Haiti. But I only remember feelings—mostly an overwhelming sense of being loved by my grandfather. Do you think there is a correlation between the way we remember Haiti and the way we reconnect to it? Not all individuals and writers stay connected to the homeland. What do you think makes you stay connected to Haiti, not only in terms of imaginary returns, but also physical returns?

ED: My brother, I think, is a lot like you. He was ten when we arrived. Those two years made a big difference for us. I also was a kind of *ti granmoun,* a little old woman. I was always scared and nervous. I observed a lot. I had to take a lot of mental notes, etc., about different situations, get the lay of the land, if you will, to keep myself safe. So I was very observant. Not much was lost on me. I find too that the older child has to be more observant, more vigilant, to keep the younger one safe, or to make the younger one feel safe. So you tend to be more mature in that way. You replace, for your younger sibling, the parent who is not there. Like you, my younger brother remembers a lot of sensations and some very vivid moments. I feel as though I remember everything. Even though that is probably not true. It might also have to do with the work I do. The writing forces you to pull things from deep inside your subconscious, so there is that as well. I think based on what we remember we might either want to connect or not. Some people need to let go for their sanity. I can't let go, because I think I'm trying to understand. I'm trying to make sense of things. I find myself confused sometimes about the present moment, but I am always trying to understand. If I feel like I know what's going on too well, then I don't write about something well. I stay connected to Haiti first because I love the country. And sometimes when you say that people will say, "Well, then, go live there," and my love feels reduced. But every word I write is to pay homage to that love and to try to understand it, and Haiti as much as I can manage.

NTC: Your love for Haiti shows in all your work. And it's not blind love; it's the kind of love that fully accepts all the good and the bad. That kind of love is too powerful to be reduced.

Another fascinating aspect of *BEM* is your subversion of Western myths of displacement and privileging of African diasporic mythology. Were you conscious of that at the time? Did you read a lot of Greek mythology as a child and when you came to the United States? African mythology? As I am asking the question, I can't help but think of your primal connection to storytelling. Myths are, after all, collective stories that get passed down and retold.

ED: I started reading Greek myths like most kids, in middle school. There's one particular Greek mythology book that I think many middle schoolers get. When I read about those Greek gods and goddesses, it struck me how some could be Haitian *lwas*. The place of mortals between smaller deities and God—*Gran mèt la*—is fascinating to me and sometimes a lot of the ways we fail or celebrate ourselves and each other seems to me connected to the sense that there's a hierarchy and we're somewhere between the absolutely divine and plant life. I think most belief systems involve trying to find exactly where we belong in that scheme. I love the way African mythology and many Haitian folktales try to explain how some things in the world came to be. That origin-based storytelling is very fascinating to me. It's somewhat comforting in migration as well to have collective stories that are passed on even though we are no longer living in the place the stories originated from. It says you weren't always here. This is where you came from. This is how we think our peoples came into existence. It gives, in my view, every story a presumed beginning, as we eventually try to figure out the middle and ending.

NTC: After all, the collective stories are sometimes the only things we can take with us in the journey to another country. But there are those who do not have stories to pass on and go searching for them elsewhere. Your books are full of stories, replete with voices that help us understand our complex history and culture and the challenges we face as Haitian immigrants. In my reading of your work, there are indeed many voices, but you have elsewhere talked about a primal voice. Is that the voice of Grandmè Melina, who was with you in Bel Air? Grandmè Ifé, the character in *BEM*, represents that voice. What does that primal voice sound like to you in your mind? Does it evoke a specific feeling or memory? Has it evolved over the years? When do you hear it the most now?

ED: That voice has definitely evolved as I have gotten older. Initially, I realize now, it's a voice I was missing. It was my mother's voice, which was there the first four years of my life, then was gone the next eight, until I was twelve. As I listened to my aunt and grandmothers tell stories when I was a child, I would imagine what it was like for my mother to tell me those stories. Initially, when I began writing my first short stories, as well as *Breath, Eyes, Memory*, they were things in the stories and in the novel that I had no idea I knew. The older people in my family would ask how I knew them and I could not answer. I must have absorbed them sometime in very early childhood, an age before I even had conscious memory, but I used to think of these stories as my mother's stories. I even wrote that in the acknowledgments page to *The Farming of Bones*. Later my mother resisted that. She suffered a bit too from the *Breath, Eyes, Memory* backlash, since people from her church and other friends of hers believed I was writing about her, that she was Martine, the mother in the book. So she would tell me not to write about her. This was a good thing in the end because I had to now assume full responsibility for what I was writing. I think this happened around the time after *The Farming of Bones* was published. She kind of rejected the mantle I gave her. She refused to be my shield, the person to whom I gave credit because I felt I had no right to certain stories. So I had to now step out and say these stories are mine. This voice is mine. And because these stories are mine, some of them have to be new stories. That's when I went to Jacmel to write a narrative of carnival called *After the Dance*. Then I started writing *The Dew Breaker*, which was a view from the present on the aftermath of the Duvalier dictatorship and what it's like for a family living in its shadow as both victim and perpetrator in Brooklyn. That was really a stepping out on my own kind of story, and the primal voice at that point became my own. Writers often talk about when they found their voice. This is when I found my voice.

NTC: Speaking of primal voices, the end of *BEM*, the moment when Sophie is beating the cane stalk, is like a primal scream, one that acknowledges histories and consequences of slavery and colonialism and connects to your own family genealogy of resistance. Although you published the book at the age of twenty-five, which is still quite young, you started writing it at eighteen. Your collection of short stories, *Krik? Krak!*, also evokes these histories and memories of the transatlantic slave trade and its aftermath. Where do you think your consciousness of historical trauma comes from? How has that consciousness developed over the years?

ED: This is a bit of what I was saying before. I don't think I was intellectually aware of what I was doing back then. I didn't consciously set out to write those things. I think they were a part of me that maybe if I didn't write I might never have expressed openly but would have felt somewhat, maybe in the way I carry myself or something like that. I really think I was born with all of this somewhere in me; then it was tapped into with the writing. Maybe it's like being a natural dancer—and I've seen a few in my time—your body just knows it. Or maybe it was spoken of around me when I could barely speak. I remember when I was in high school being shocked when learning about certain things—like the Middle Passage for example—I felt like I already knew about it somehow but could not pin it down. Maybe it was in the stories I was told in my childhood, but I couldn't pin it down to any particular story I could recite to someone. I don't want to make it sound too mysterious. Of course I read a lot as a young person, but I think there were kernels of knowledge in me that somehow felt unacquired. Maybe that's what creativity is overall, the ability to capture something out of the air that you do not quite understand.

NTC: There is knowledge that one acquires and knowledge that one inherits. Sometimes what we capture creatively is also ancestral memory. But since we are on the subject of history, let's transition to your second novel, *The Farming of Bones*. I love this novel for so many reasons, and I learned a lot about relations between Haiti and the Dominican Republic because of it. I don't recall having any knowledge of the Haitian massacre at the border until I started reading the book. Elsewhere, you have talked about your visit to the Massacre River as the inspiration behind this book. I love the interview you did with Eleanor Wachtel, where you discuss how struck you were by the "ordinariness of life" at the border there. Since you have published this book, have you thought about the complexities of life at the border of other places? In your travels, have you been to other places where you were struck by the lack of memory, the lack of event in the physical environment, places where there are no markers to commemorate an event?

ED: Of course, borders are more complex than ever these days. Not just because of the Trump era, where if you live in America you're always hearing about walls being built and immigration being curtailed, etc., but because the things that drive people to borders, conflicts, environmental problems, are more and more visible to us because of all the ways people now have to record and communicate. Before I started writing the book, I decided I had to step foot in the river. I had read two Haitian novels touching on this subject, *Compère Général Soleil* by Jacques Stephen Alexis and René Philoctète's *[Le peuple des] des terres mélées,* and I felt like they'd helped me to go there in my imagination, but I wanted to put my hand in the water, feel the sand underneath the water. Of course you build up a huge thing in your mind where you think you're going to a memorial site because such a bloody thing happened there. But as with many such sites in Haiti, they are also utilitarian and functional spaces. People need the water to drink and wash their bodies and their clothes and for their animals to drink. It remains a border crossing. People naturally use the river the way it is meant to be used, the way it has been used both before and after the massacre. The trauma was a mere interruption because if you make the river entirely a memorial, you're cutting off a useful resource. People can't just come and look at it and take pictures with it when they need to use it in their daily life. It reminds you too of the luxury of being able to have such memorials. We come from a place where trauma is piled upon trauma and, as a friend of mine once said, if we turned every place of trauma in Haiti into an official memorial, there would be no places left for people to actually live their lives. But I was still expecting a plaque, something that I later found out, when I asked an area official about putting one somewhere, would take government action. No government we've had so far has seemed interested. Maybe the president will go and lay a wreath this year on the eightieth anniversary of the massacre. In the case of lack of markers, you have no choice but to see the life carrying on as its own kind of memorial. The living and their bodies become the memorial. One of the characters in the book says nature has no memory. It has no choice but to move on. We are its memory.

NTC: In the novel, your characters are divided not just by the physical border that separates the two countries that share one island but also by deeply entrenched social borders. I believe in a 2007 interview with Nancy Raquel Mirabal, you talked about the ways in which globalization brings us closer together and offers opportunities for exchange and exposure. I think you framed it in the context of villages coming closer together and acknowledged this as a positive aspect of globalization. In the era of globalization, do you think these borders are being dismantled or reinforced? What about the negative aspect? I am glad you brought up the Trump era. I can't help but think of our current president's desire to build a great wall between Mexico and California. I am also thinking of the lack of security in Port-au-Prince that has led to the construction of fences and walls to secure individual homes and properties. This has created a whole new relationship with neighbors. In our current (global) state of affairs, what do you think of this desire to reinforce both physical and social borders?

ED: I think I was asked to think of a positive aspect of globalization, and this was one I could think of. Rather than borders falling away now, we see more coming up and the poorest of the poor being locked on the other side. That's of course the negative impact. That money, as the late Édouardo Galeano has written, can cross borders, and human beings cannot. Nativists often cite the saying "Good fences make good neighbors." It is said in the Dominican Republic and it is said here. In the Trump era, countries that hate immigrants and want to push them out use Trump's vitriol against immigrants to empower themselves to do it. In today's Dominican Republic, for example, expulsions are happening more and more and in more brutal ways because they believe that if Trump can do it the way he's doing in America by scapegoating so-called bad hombres, then they can do it too. So the legacy to the massacre is that it's still with us and more than ever it's a cautionary tale on what can happen when you scapegoat immigrants and the children and grandchildren of immigrants. So we certainly seem to be moving toward more insularity, but as Trump's evolving immigration policy is showing, that wall is not between the United States and Canada. It is between the United States and Mexico. The United States is closing itself off against poor brown and black people. As was announced today, skilled white people who already speak English are always going to be welcomed to come and stay.

NTC: This reminds me of Randolph Bourne's 1916 article, "Transnational America." In the essay he critiques the idea of Americanization at the time as "Anglo-Saxonization." Under this proposed Reforming American Immigration for Strong Employment Act endorsed by the president, people like you and me would not be here, Edwidge. The United States would not be able to claim you as one of its great contemporary writers. We are indeed moving away from the definition of American that includes the promotion of freedom and democracy at home and abroad. As we speak, the State Department is considering eliminating the promotion of democracy from its mission statement. This is all madness to me. Certainly anathema to your work, which promotes heterogeneity and multiplicity and exposes both the dignity and contributions of poor immigrants who have to overcome insurmountable challenges and sacrifice so much to live the "American dream." With this bill, the Trump administration is also officially demonizing low-wage workers who are fundamental to our nation's service economy.

In *BEM* you had such clarity about the transnational contours of the Haitian community in New York. It makes us think about the issue of assimilation that Bourne found problematic in 1916. It is interesting that we are returning to this version of Americanization a century later. In *Farming,* one of the major themes you tackle is nationalism. You have mentioned elsewhere the idea of "imagination" as a different way of thinking about nation. The novel is critical of the discourse of nationalism. In fact all of your work engages in some way with the pitfalls of the language of nationalism and the way it creates fixed identities and archetypes that leave no room for the nuances you are so committed to exploring. How has Haitian nationalism been influenced by migration? In your mind, is there a distinction between nation building and nationalism? In other words, can we build a nation without the discourse of nationalism? Is there another language for nation building?

ED: Haitian immigrants face nationalism in such brutal ways in many of the places we go. In the United States, we face it as part of a block of immigrants, particularly black and brown immigrants, but in the Caribbean, nationalists often aim their rage directly at Haitians. We must be precise and say poor Haitians. The way immigration policies are shaped in the Dominican Republic or in the Bahamas, for example, you get a sense that their immigration policies are only for Haitians. So you can't help but feel the hypervulnerability of Haitian migrants to nationalistic language and sometimes even violence in our own region, even as their labor is being exploited. Are we ourselves nationalistic? We have national pride, certainly. We have great pride in our history. But it seems to me that anyone can come and go in Haiti. Some are very sensitive to issues of sovereignty, but a lot of outsiders of different stripes get away with doing a lot in Haiti. Look how long the United Nations forces were there. Even after all the raping they did of both men and women, boys and girls and introducing of cholera, nothing's happened to them. They refuse to take responsibility. How can you build a nation in situations like that? How can you build a nation when you were straddled with a massive debt form the start of that nationhood? I think Haitians would probably use the language and method of the *lakou* for nation building, if we were interfered with less, if we were allowed. In many rural areas, there is very little presence of a state to speak of. Yet people take care of each other in a family-based lakou system. Maybe our internal nation building would look like a lakou. I am not an expert, but this seems to me one possible way it could be done.

NTC: And all of these issues have intensified after the earthquake. I have been following the cases of sexual abuse by UN soldiers. As for the cholera, it took the UN six years to make an official apology for its role in the cholera outbreak. It's all quite appalling. The plight of Haitian migrants in the Dominican Republic is also terrible. Since we are now discussing *Farming* and regional discrimination against Haitians, let's talk a little bit about Haitian-Dominican relations. A lot has happened to the Haitian community in the Dominican Republic since you published *The Farming of Bones*. Can you give me your own assessment of the current plight of Haitians in the Dominican Republic? Have you been back to the border?

ED: I have not been to the border in a few months, but I know people who have been and they see a lot of the same people there. They are people who cannot return to the Dominican Republic and have no one in Haiti, so they live in dusty stretches on the border in a terrible situation. Sadly, I don't think it will get better for Dominicans of Haitian descent or Haitian migrants in the Dominican Republic anytime soon. We recently found out that even people who were granted citizenship in the Dominican Republic under a new law that was meant to modify the way Dominicans of Haitian descent were rendered stateless after the constitutional decision in 2013 have a limited kind of citizenship. Some had had their birth certificates modified to make them foreigners. And as we have seen in the past, their birth certificate can be pulled at any time and be declared fraudulent because they have a Haitian-sounding name. It's a very bad situation and one that I fear in this age of global xenophobia will only get worse.

NTC: There is indeed a lot to be anxious about when it comes to immigration policies under the Trump administration and in the international arena. The chaos and constant leadership changes in the

White House make it hard for people to really follow the issues. Let's move on and talk a little bit about your relationship with the Haitian Dominican writer Junot Díaz, which has really blossomed over the years. I am glad you mentioned the conference a group of us organized as graduate students that brought the two of you to campus. I was responsible for your visit. We were so proud of that conference but also quite nervous. We were also very naïve and made a few mistakes along the way. I think we overworked the two of you, for example. I hope you both have forgiven us for that. Can you talk about the work you two do together to improve relations between Haitians and Dominicans? I know you have done a lot of activist work to shape immigration policies toward Haitians. Can you talk a little bit about your involvement with organizations dealing with the question of immigration and the plight of stateless people?

ED: I don't remember being overworked. I think of it as a rather positive experience. With every writer friend, your private relationship is somewhat different from when you're put in front of a bunch of people to have a conversation. What he and I have both done, both together and alone, over the years is try to support organizations that are doing this very important work on both sides of the island and in the United States. The thing is, he and I both know some real activists. We know people who put their bodies and their safety and their peace of mind on the line every day for this cause, so I'm always hesitant to call myself an activist in light of people I know who are doing the real work. I believe I can speak for both of us when I say we try to support the people who are doing the work in whatever way we can, whenever we can, with our presence and with our voice, because essentially we are not merely talking about the ideological. This is a situation where people's lives are in danger, where they are losing everything, so it's not an intellectual exercise.

NTC: We can never lose sight of actual bodies in the line of fire. But as you suggest in *Create Dangerously* on the relationship between the text and the world, and as I try to teach my students, the ideological informs the praxis and vice versa. You often cite a wonderful quote by Toni Cade Bambara: "Writing is how I participate in the struggle." But you have engaged in a lot of "activism" that takes you out of the "writing space" over the years. I believe that the writing informs your activism, but does the activism inform your writing in any way?

ED: I love that quote and I love her. I should say writing is *one* of the ways I participate in the struggle. That was also true for her. There are so many ways now and there is so much need, from working with kids to filling out immigration forms to being a translator to being what James Baldwin called a witness. Though I try not to be too preachy in the fiction writing, what I write even in that space is informed by what is happening in the world. I can't forget, for example, that the Haitian characters I write today have the specter of a very anti-immigrant America hanging over their heads. So even when that is not openly in my writing, it is there.

NTC: It is indeed there. Political oppression is the backdrop of many of your novels. It is also very present in your op-ed pieces, where you speak directly about these issues and push for social change. There are different forms of activism, and your op-ed pieces are in my opinion activist work. I remember reading something you wrote where you mentioned visiting Haitian detainees at the Brooklyn navy yard when you first arrived in the United States. That in itself is an early form of activism, guided by your father. Did the stories you heard during those visits ever find their way into your writing over the years? I am thinking of *Krik? Krak!* as an early example, maybe? Do you still think of these stories in the work you do with various organizations? Do they resurface in your later writing?

ED: Absolutely. Frankly, I am still in awe at these visits and that my parents, who considered themselves very apolitical, used to even do that. Those visits were extremely eye opening for me. The essential message of these visits from my parents was that these are our people. They are us. They are family. I have never forgotten that. Later, when I was at Brown University, I used to spend time with families who came by boat in the 1990s. The stories I heard them tell and translated for them inspired "Children of the Sea," the first story in *Krik? Krak!* My parents also went with my brothers and me to the big march against the US Food and Drug Administration blood ban for Haitians. They went to marches with us when Abner Louima was brutally assaulted, because my parents were friends with his parents. My brothers and I also went to marches when Yusef Hawkins was killed, and they encouraged us to go to those. I think the biggest lesson I learned from my parents in terms of what they did is that you don't have to be holding a bull horn. You don't have to be up front to be present, as long as you're doing what you can.

NTC: My family and I were also at that march across the Brooklyn Bridge. We were living in Flatbush at that time and it felt like every Haitian we knew was at that march. That was indeed an experience.

How does it feel to know that a number of people who make up your audience have learned about Haitian culture and history by reading your books? Does this knowledge affect your writing in any way? Does this responsibility empower you or create anxiety?

ED: They say the Brooklyn Bridge shook that day, and I believe it. What an incredibly unifying day that was. As we discussed with *Breath, Eyes, Memory,* people learning about Haiti from me can be a double-edged sword. I often meet people who say, "I went to Haiti because of you." "Great," I say, "as long as I encourage you to learn more." I don't want people to take my version of things as the only one. That would make me anxious. That's why I've edited anthologies, etc.: I want people to go beyond me, to explore further, to read more. I hope to at least encourage that.

NTC: Speaking of anthologies, in *The Butterfly's Way,* one of your main objectives as editor of the anthology, I believe, was to show the complexity and diversity of the Haitian diaspora. You have also talked about the idea of diaspora as a lens through which one can explore gray places, blank spaces, the spaces in between. How do you define the Haitian diaspora today? Do you find that there are new patterns emerging that may change the contours of the diaspora in the United States, for example? A lot has changed in the United States in the past fifteen years.

ED: The Haitian diaspora today, in my view, is very big and complex. You now have a lot of Haitian-born millennials who are adding another very important layer to the conversation. Some of them are in media, and what is highlighted about them is not even that they're Haitian. They're just out there excelling and doing their thing. Sadly, we also have a lot of problems in the poor communities within the diaspora. In Miami, for example, we have a lot of young Haitians in prisons and new arrivals in detention centers. The parents of some school-age children are older and are rather perplexed by what's happening with their children. So while some of us are doing really well, we have a lot of children in our communities being left behind.

NTC: I would like to ask a few more questions about diaspora and identity, Edwidge. What do you think the literature of the diaspora offers to contemporary Haitian literature in Haiti in terms of themes and aesthetics? Did you get a lot of feedback on the book from writers living in Haiti?

ED: I think since we have so much migration out of Haiti, dyaspora writing can offer a lot of insight to Haitians in Haiti on what it's like to live outside of Haiti. Our work can show both the difficulties and advantages of that life from up close. Perhaps readers in Haiti can learn as much about our realities as we can learn about theirs. Tangentially, I'll tell you something funny. A year ago, I was speaking to some kids in Martissant, a poor neighborhood in Port-au-Prince, and they asked me why Haitian writers can't write some science fiction or something. "Why always politics?" they asked. And they were talking about writers who live in and outside of Haiti. But in terms of other feedback, earlier feedback, when I was first published, I felt some tensions between the literatures of the diasporas and the work being published in Haiti. And it wasn't just the Anglophone diaspora. What people seemed to be saying, some to my face and some not, was that there were better writers in Haiti, but mediocre writers were being published and marketed abroad. I still hear that. Someone once sent me a link to a public forum where scholars were debating whether enough had been written about me and it was time to move on to others. I'd be the first person to say move on to others. My own literary education began with Haitian writers. I think I have tried to promote Haitian writers. I just don't like the false dichotomies that in order to praise one group of writers we have to trash others. This part has gotten a lot better, but when I just started writing, I would go to conferences and would sit in the audience and listen to people debate whether I was a Haitian writer or not, whether I had any talent or not, or was some creation of the blans, because of course the blan so desperately needed a Haitian writer that they had to create me. At the same time, I was reading criticism of my work by white people who said that the American literary establishment was pandering to people like me and giving us prizes because of multiculturalism. So at some point, I just had to stop traveling so much and really just concentrate on my work and my personal life. Otherwise I would have lost all desire to go on. I was just tired of defending my right (my write) to exist. I just have to let the work do it, make its own way without me. Again, most writers I have personal relationships and friendships with, we don't talk too much about work. That tends to be across nationalities, Haitian or not. I am not seeking that from them, and they are not seeking that from me. But one thing I notice with writers with similar immigrant backgrounds: they've faced a similar kind of situation. One of Julia Alvarez's wonderful essays in her book *Something to Declare*—the essay is called "Doña Aída, with Your Permission"— speaks perfectly about being in that place initially where you might be rejected by both sides.

NTC: How do you engage with non-Haitian writers who write about the diasporic experience in the contemporary moment and the immigrant experience in the United States? What do you learn from these writers that may be different from your experience? Or do you find more similarities than distinctions? Here I am thinking about your other edited volumes, such as *The Beacon Best of 2000,* and *The Best American Essays of 2011.*

ED: I learn a lot from them. And as I mention above, they make me realize that I'm not alone. I often have the experience of saying to a reader from the home country of a writer I love how much I love that writer, only to get a tirade from that reader about how much the writer gets wrong. Even that makes me feel less alone. Things that I think are unique to my experience these writers also face. The way we're talked about in this country is also similar. I remember when Jhumpa Lahiri did a "By the Book" column in the *New York Times* in 2013, and she said that there's no such thing as immigrant fiction. "What do we call the rest?" she said. "Native fiction? Puritan fiction?" "All American writing is immigrant writing," she said. I found that very empowering. So it's wonderful to know that there are other "dyasporic" writers of different ethnicities on this journey as well. These anthologies certainly brought us together under a different tent than I'm used to being put in. If you say "Best American," then based on your choices, you broaden the definition of even what it means to be American.

NTC: Over the years, you have talked a great deal about being both insider and outsider. I find that the concept of duality and notions of the double are prominent in your work but are used to blurring a number of binaries, including the binary between who is insider and who is outsider. I also think this complicates the divide between the homeland and the host country, between the nation and its diaspora. What do you think?

ED: I think I have multiple identities in which I fold myself. I am Haitian. I am black. I am a woman. I am Caribbean. I am a black woman Caribbean writer. I think I hold on to multiplicities. When I was first published in the period that I was talking about, people used to talk a lot about authenticity. I often felt very inauthentic because I was writing about Haiti in English, so I would say I am the least authentic writer ever, just to free myself from the burden of it. But in the inauthenticity I was claiming, I always saw a kind of welcomed multiplicity.

NTC: You have traveled to Haiti a lot since the publication of your first book. And you made the move to Miami from Brooklyn sometime before *Dew Breaker* was published, I believe. Haiti is no longer just a memory, and you no longer have to read books to go back home. What is the role of nostalgia in your work? Does living in Miami make a difference? Can you talk about your first return and what that felt like? As I ask this question, I am reminded of the fact that you were a part of my own first return experience to Haiti in 2000 through the UMASS summer study abroad program with Professor Marc Prou. I think we first saw you riding on a horse in Montrouis, where we were staying. It felt so surreal. But back to my question. Do you find that your relationship with Haiti shifts and evolves with every return, or do you feel like you have a more stable relationship with Haiti? "Stable" may not be the right word here.

ED: I first returned to Haiti in my twenties after leaving at age twelve. I describe it a bit in my memoir, *Brother, I'm Dying.* There were things that, of course, became foreign to me. And others that seemed to have not changed at all. People were my compass. My loved ones were my anchors. People often read my work as nostalgic, but it is always so present for me in the moment of writing that I never think of it as nostalgic. Now that so much time has gone by—*Breath, Eyes, Memory* is almost twenty-five years old—it might read like nostalgia. I have just written some stories set in Miami; I could not do that before. I was not used to writing about the present of a place I was living in. Miami is closer physically to Haiti. There are a lot of Haitians here, but it's a community I had to learn as well, both the physical landscape and the people of Miami. I remember that experience of seeing you in Haiti. I think I later fell off that horse. Symbolic, uh? I didn't realize it was your first time. I think I put you in your dad's novel, and before we knew each other, I felt like you had always lived

there. My returns to Haiti are now different because many of the
people who knew me there when I was a child have died. A whole
upper layer of my family there is gone. Most of the people who've
known me my whole life are dead. And some of the physical places I
used to return to were either destroyed in the 2010 earthquake or are
inhabited by other people. So now when I go to Haiti, the familial
place is often my mother-in-law's place in the country. So that return
is sowing seeds for my daughters as well as creating new connections
for me. Sometimes I go with friends who work there, and I go and see
their projects, and that's another kind of visit, but I am often in the
same familial plane as my daughters now. I am seeing their father's
past, and when I walk through the places where I grew up, I don't
have as many relatives to point to as I used to have in the past.

NTC: Speaking of the past, in 2004–2005 a lot happened. Nina Rastogi
calls the year your "annus horribilis," wherein you experienced the
death of your uncle in November 2004, the birth of your daughter
four months later in 2005, followed by the death of your father in
2005 after suffering from a painful lung disease that left him bed-
ridden for nine months. Your 2007 memoir, *Brother, I'm Dying*, is a
way of working through these life-changing moments. I would like to
talk briefly about *Brother, I'm Dying*. My father confessed to me that
when I was born, he was full of anxiety and afraid that he would pass
that on to me. He was only twenty-three years old at the time and
was already deeply involved in politics during the Duvalier regime.
I do remember myself feeling a burden beyond myself, beyond my
own childhood comprehension. I thought of this when reading your
memoir. I also thought about the workings of ancestral memory,
memory that gets passed down from one generation to another quite
naturally. What do you think about this idea of inheriting a parent's
pain and fears?

ED: Annus horribilis indeed. I had the same feeling as your father when
my oldest daughter was born, especially since she was born in the
middle of so much upheaval in my family. She gets her name, Mira,
from my father's nickname. She was born a month before he died,
a few months after my uncle who raised me died. So I really was
worried that she would be "damaged" by all the anxiety I had while
pregnant with her. I know someone who was in the World Trade
Center on September 11, 2001, while she was six months pregnant
and escaped, and people attribute her daughter's nervous ways to

that. It's possible that the adrenaline in the mother's body might have affected the fetus—I don't know. But I was very worried that all my mourning and all the shock of my losses during my "annus horribilis" were going to affect my daughter, because I do believe that you can inherit a parent's pain, not necessarily by osmosis but by observation. Children are very perceptive, so they can experience that pain for you and from you.

NTC: You testified before House Judiciary Committee at a congressional hearing on detention centers in the fall of 2007, I believe. I am curious: Did the committee read your book *Brother, I'm Dying?* What was that experience like? Did it provide a whole new context for understanding immigration policies here in the United States? After that experience, do you believe that your work can influence policies toward Haitian immigrants?

ED: I don't think they read the book, but I am always hoping that immigration officers will be made to read it as part of their training. At least that's my hope. It was a surreal experience. I hoped that my uncle's story would prevent other tragedies like that from happening, and this felt like a step in that direction, though soon after we got a Republican Congress, which tried to eliminate the few gains that had been made. I wrote an opinion piece for the *Washington Post* at that time and it was put into the record at another congressional hearing.

NTC: You have written over ten books since your first publication in 1994, and I am not even counting the books you have written for children. Which of these books challenged you the most personally? And why? As for the children's books, what is it like to write specifically for a child?

ED: I find the nonfiction most challenging. The older I get, the harder it is to talk about my personal stuff. Camus wrote that the writer is in the amphitheater. These days the amphitheater feels a lot bigger. One also feels more vulnerable because people's loyalties are so precarious. They can be cursing a writer today that they loved yesterday because she said the "wrong" thing in the wrong way. I love writing the work for children because my children can read them. I feel like I am closer to writing for my daughters' fifteen-year-old selves.

NTC: *Claire of the Sea Light,* which was published in 2013, was, I believe, the first work of fiction you wrote since becoming a mother. You just mentioned your two girls, Mira and Leila. How old are they now? It is interesting that you are returning to the theme of parental separation that grounded your first book. How has your idea of motherhood changed with the birth of your girls? Does being a mother influence the kind of stories you choose to write now? Did your relationship with your own mother change after the birth of your first child?

ED: Mira is twelve and Leila is eight. I didn't realize until a friend pointed it out to me that I was revisiting the theme of parent-child separation now from the point of view of a mother rather than a daughter. That friend, who knows me very well, thought that *Claire of the Sea Light* was my way of reprocessing that material from this new perspective of being a mother. Now that I am a mother, I feel like I am able to write more nuanced mothers. That comes partly from the double perspective of having been both daughter and mother. Just like it's easier for me now to understand some of my mother's choices throughout my life.

NTC: *Claire* is about a father's wrenching decision to give his seven-year-old daughter away so that she could have a better life. So you are also able to write more nuanced fathers. This novel was also your first publication since the earthquake in 2010, although you started working on it in 2005. The book is as much a reflection on motherhood as it is about a small seaside town. You have disclosed somewhere that half of the book was published before the earthquake, while the other half was published afterward. Did the earthquake have an impact on the direction of the book in any way? Did you feel an urge to preserve a particular image of small-town living because of the disaster that destroyed specific communities?

ED: The book is set right before the earthquake. The townspeople don't realize what is going to happen. That part came into the story right after the earthquake. It seemed to me strange to write a book that had no presence at all—or in this case no prescience—of the earthquake. I was not ready to write a book about the earthquake, but I wanted to implant some signs in the book, and in the place, that one might be coming. It was strange to me to reread *The Farming of Bones* after the earthquake and see mentions of tremors in that book. I must have discovered that in the research. This made me realize that in some ways earthquakes have always been a part of our dormant reality.

NTC: You seem to have a profound relationship with death. You learned about it early on through your uncle, who presided over funerals as a minister. You also have had a number of experiences with death in the past thirteen years, the most recent being the death of your mother in 2014 from ovarian cancer. You just mentioned that you have a better understanding of the choices your mother made. Can you talk about your new book, *The Art of Death: Writing the Final Story,* which focuses on your mother's story and your own grieving process? Do you think a little differently about what it means to be a woman and a mother after her death? I was initially struck by the subtitle. What do you mean when you say "final story"?

ED: *The Art of Death* is part of a series by Graywolf Press where writers discuss craft issues. I was really glad to have that framework to work with. I am writing about my mother but also what it's like to write about death and grief. For some reason death has always fascinated me. I think part of it has to do with my uncle having been a minister who presided over many funerals that I attended when I was young. In the book I talk about a lot of literature about dying, some of which is written by dying writers. Thus the subtitle. Of course when you lose a parent, every moment you spent together is revised through that lens. I'm glad I don't have much regret about what I said or didn't say to my mother. Just like with my father, there was some time between her diagnosis and her death for me to speak to her and resolve many things.

NTC: I am glad you had the time, those precious moments with both your parents before their passing. My condolences to you for these losses.

ED: Thank you. I realize that this is a privilege not everyone has. It's made grieving a bit less complicated for me.

NTC: You often cite another great writer, Ralph Ellison: "Who knows but that, on the lower frequencies, I speak for you?" It makes me think of your investment in magnifying voices of marginalized individuals who are not heard, who cannot speak of themselves, or who are often silenced when they do speak. I would like to end with a couple of questions on the relationship between voice and silence, which I think is a prominent theme in all your work. Are you aware of how much that dominates your writing?

ED: I wasn't really aware of it until someone pointed it out. I think it was after *Brother, I'm Dying* came out and someone made the connection between my uncle having had cancer surgery to remove his larynx and the fact that I used to speak for him and my work as a writer. That felt like a revelation to me. Then I could see it clearly. I realize now that this is why that Ellison quote speaks so powerfully to me. It's not saying with all certainly that I speak for you, but it says, Who knows? I think this is why I write. You never know. The thing I am writing about might also ring true for someone else.

NTC: You know, I did think of your uncle's surgery when I read that quote by Ralph Ellison. I think becoming your uncle's voice when he literally lost his after the removal of his larynx is critical to understanding your relationship with voice and silence. You touch on this experience again in the story "Water Child" through the character Nadine, the Haitian American nurse who works with patients who have lost their voice as a result of total laryngectomies. Voice, and lack thereof, is indeed a dominant theme in your work. Every time I think of you and read your work, the phrase that comes up is "daughter of a voice." There is always a spiritual aspect to this voice in my mind. In rabbinic literature the term *bat kol* means daughter of a divine voice, and that voice is often described as a small but powerful echo. In my analysis of your oeuvre, I talk about the significance of the echo as recall and repetition of voices that get amplified to be heard. Do you see a relationship between spirituality and voice? How do these small voices come to you?

ED: Of course, voice is very spiritual. When one creates, one becomes a kind of vessel. That's why you often hear artists say that they're unsure where the work comes from. Writers might say that the character takes over. There's something very deeply spiritual, even mystical, about an act of creation, of putting out in the world something that was not there before. Voices come to me in dreams. Sometimes they come to me while I'm reading. Sometimes they are actual voices I happen to overhear speaking and appropriate for my work.

NTC: In *Create Dangerously* you write, "Maybe that was my purpose, then, as an immigrant and a writer, to be an echo chamber, gathering and then replaying voices from both the distant and the local devastation." I was so struck by that statement that I framed my book about your works on this notion of the echo chamber and its relationship to voice. Did you know you were evoking Marguerite Duras and Roland Barthes? You do cite Barthes in *Create Dangerously*. Were you conscious of how the phrase was being used by writers before you?

ED: These are of course questions that many writers wrestle with, so I'm not surprised that they've been brought up before. In terms of evocation, I'd say Barthes more than Duras. Though Duras's writing is extremely evocative. She is a kind of distant model. I think Barthes's notion of the death of the author is certainly one that's intrigued me. Especially in this most recent book, *The Art of Death,* where he's not as much cited as felt.

NTC: As in *Create Dangerously,* you make reference, albeit more subtly, to a lot of books in *The Dew Breaker.* In my analysis of this book, I explore the significance of intertextuality and argue that it is a particular kind of echo. Of course Barthes is one of the major theorists of intertextuality who stresses the role of the reader. Is it a conscious effort on your part to expose your audience to other books and writers that have come before you? That have influenced your work? I learned so much about how you write and your "source texts" by reading these two books.

ED: A lot of my wok is "in conversation" with other Haitian books. *The Farming of Bones* is in conversation with *Compère Général Soleil* by Jacques Stephen Alexis and René Philoctète's *[Le peuple des]des terres mélées. The Dew Breaker* is in conversation with Jacques Roumain's *Gouverneurs de la rosée (Masters of the Dew).* The stories in *The Dew Breaker* are what happens when we stop being masters of the dew, as Roumain seemed to be encouraging us to be. We then destroy everything as the *shoukèt laroze,* or the "dew breakers" did. I discuss more of my recent source texts in *The Art of Death.*

NTC: This book is a testimony to what an avid reader you are. I have added a few more books on my reading list after reading *The Art of Death.* In this most recent book, which was published less than a month ago, you mention long-time influential writers like Albert Camus, Zora Neal Hurston, Toni Morrison, and Gabriel García Márquez, who passed away in 2014.

Without giving away any spoilers, you open up in your most recent book in ways you would not have if your parents were alive. It is interesting you say that you feel more hesitant to share personal stuff the older you get. Having read *The Art of Death,* I do feel you are being vulnerable in ways you had not with your other nonfictional books. Are you in a place in your life where you can tell stories you were perhaps not ready to tell before?

ED: I have a writer friend who always says that there are things that she could not write until her mother died. I certainly write things in *The Art of Death* that I would not have written if my parents were still alive. This felt very liberating to me to write. Even more so because I could write it without hurting them. Still I find myself being happy when I read reviews of the book and no one mentions it. It's something I'm still processing. Yet it is the only thing that I feel I could not have written when my parents were still alive. Everything else was fair game. Maybe that's why I'm more reluctant to reveal after this. It feels like I have no more secrets.

NTC: I want to return to the echo. When people evoke the term today, they are speaking of like-minded folks, a homogenous community. Your echo chamber is a heterogeneous community, the space of inclusion and expansion, of myriad and diverse voices. How do you define the echo chamber? Is it the writer's memory? Is it the experience, or space, of diaspora? Is the echo chamber a new way of writing new realities outside the homeland? Is there new knowledge in the echo chamber?

ED: It's very hard to separate it from something negative these days, especially in this age of alternative facts, and people in power always want to hear what they want to hear. I think if a writer were to say that they're in an echo chamber now it would be hard to separate it from all of that. What I could go back to is that Greek myth and the echo there. That always reminds me of being in the mountains of Léogâne as a child and shouting out a name and hearing that name repeated back to me in dozens of voices that I was never fully sure were mine. I think that's what I think of as a positive when I hear the words *echo chamber.*

NTC: That's exactly the image that comes to my mind when I think of you and this idea of the echo chamber: you in the mountains of Léogâne as a child. One last question, Edwidge. You will be turning fifty soon! That is a milestone birthday, and you have accomplished so much already. I am sure there is a lot more to come. Any new projects in the pipeline? Do you have an idea of how you will celebrate?

ED: I will be fifty in a year and a half. After witnessing so much death up close, of both my parents and close friends, I feel vulnerable in a way I did not in the past. Frankly, my big plan is to try to stick around and see my daughters grow up, to watch them become young women, then see them launch into their own lives. That more than anything is what I would love to be granted, *Si Dye vle,* God willing. In the meantime, I want to continue writing, maybe try different forms of writing. I have a book of short stories coming out in a while, probably in my fiftieth year. That will be the celebration, writing-wise. When I'm fifty, I will be eternally grateful that I would have had a twenty-five-year career and journey as a writer, something I never would have thought possible as a little girl. I'll be grateful that I'm still writing, and that I still want to write. That's a great blessing.

NTC: Sounds like a wise plan for a wise woman. Would you mind describing briefly this new book of short stories?

ED: They're right longish stories dealing with friendship, family, romance. All eight (love) stories are about people searching for a once-in-a-lifetime love they may or never find.

NTC: I hope that in between all this writing there will be dancing.

ED: Yes, there is always dancing. Though not always in public.

NTC: Thank you, Edwidge, for your time. It really has been an honor to get to know Haiti through your writing.

ED: Thank you. *Mèsi anpil.*

Notes

Preface

1. Bellamy, review of *Edwidge Danticat: A Reader's Guide,* by Martin Munro.

Introduction

1. Davies, *Black Women, Writing, and Identity,* 4.

2. Bakhtin, *The Dialogic Imagination.*

3. Mercer, *Welcome to the Jungle,* 65.

4. See, for example, the work of Homi Bhabha, Paul Gilroy, James Clifford, Stuart Hall, and Arjun Appadurai.

5. As James Clifford asserts in "Diasporas," nations and nation-states are not identical.

6. See, for example, Chow, *Writing Diaspora;* and Radhakrishnan, *Diasporic Mediations.*

7. Robertson, *Globalization;* Giddens, *The Consequences of Modernity;* Appadurai, *Modernity at Large.*

8. Danticat, "Dyasporic Appetites and Longings," 30.

9. Robertson, *Globalization,* 8.

10. Giddens, *The Consequences of Modernity,* 64.

11. Appadurai, *Modernity at Large.*

12. Steger, *The Rise of the Global Imaginary,* 179.

13. Sassen, "The Global Inside the National."

14. Braziel and Mannur, "Nation, Migration, Globalization," 7.

15. Danticat, *Create Dangerously,* 159.

16. See, for example, Peter Doyle's analysis of Deleuze's notion of territorialization and deterritorialization in his examination of the relationship to music and space. Doyle, *Echo and Reverb.*

17. See Chude-Sokei, *The Sound of Culture.*

18. G. Bloom, *Voice in Motion.*

19. See *Bulfinch's Mythology.*

20. See, for example, Vinge, *The Narcissus Theme.*

21. See, for example, Cowart, "Haitian Persephone, Danticat's *Breath, Eyes, Memory,*" in *Trailing Clouds.*

22. Alexander, *Mother Imagery,* 13.

23. T. Walters, *African American Literature.*

24. Marassa, also spelled *Marasa,* in the vodou religion is a twin spirit. I use the spelling *Marassa* to be consistent with Danticat's spelling in *Breath, Eyes, Memory.* A number of scholars have attended to this matter. See, for example, Mardorossian, 'Doubling, Healing, and Gender"; Gerber, "Binding the Narrative Thread." VèVè Clark's analysis of the "marasa" as reading strategy moves beyond the binary coexistence of opposites. Clark, "Developing Diaspora Literacy." See also A. Mills, "The Interplay of Doubles."

25. See Lacan, *Écrits,* on the distinction between the symbolic, the imaginary, and the real.

26. Anderson, *Imagined Community,* 4–6.

27. Taylor, *Modern Social Imaginaries,* 23.

28. Steger, *The Rise of the Global Imaginary.*

29. W. Walters, *At Home in Diaspora,* xxii.

30. Glissant, *Poetics of Relation,* xxii.

31. Glissant, *Poetics of Relation,* 170.

32. Glissant, *Poetics of Relation,* 151.

33. Glissant, *Poetics of Relation,* 27.

34. Glissant, *Poetics of Relation,* 33.

35. Glissant, *Poetics of Relation,* 18, 19.

36. Glissant, *Poetics of Relation,* 33.

37. Glissant, *Poetics of Relation,* 169.

38. In pushing for more relational modes of thinking, my work is aligned not only with Bakhtin's dialogic principle and Glissant's poetics of relation but also the work of recent scholars such as Carine Mardorossian, who, in calling for new aesthetic and strategies of reading and writing practices that helps us rethink postcolonial approaches to literature, exposes the ways in which a new generation of Caribbean writers "contribute to the study of interrelatedness of identity categories" and articulate a "poetics of location that does not hinder relation." Mardorossian. *Reclaiming Difference,* 19, 4. My analysis also complements the work of Mary Gallagher, who foregrounds Glissant to examine the relationship between globalization and literary studies and addresses the question of inter-textuality to explore processes of globalization and its effects on contemporary writing. See, for example, Gallagher, *World Writing.*

39. Glissant, *Poetics of Relation,* 93.

40. Glissant, *Poetics of Relation,* 93–94.

41. See, for example, Said, *Out of Place.*

42. Bhabha, *The Location of Culture.*

43. Said, "Intellectual Exile," 381.

44. Said, "Voice of a Palestinian," 48.

45. Gikandi, *Writing in Limbo*.

46. Mardorossian, "From Literature of Exile to Migrant Literature," 15–16.

47. Mardorossian, "From Literature of Exile to Migrant Literature," 15–16.

48. Ludden, "Writing in Exile Helps Authors."

49. Ménard, "The Myth of the Exiled Writer."

50. Lahens, "Exile," 736.

51. Lahens, "Exile," 745.

52. Chancy, *Framing Silence*, 13.

53. Chancy, *Framing Silence*, 10.

54. Munro, *Exile and Post-1946 Haitian Literature*, 37.

55. Edmondson, *Making Men*, 13.

56. Kaplan, *Questions of Travel*.

57. Kaplan, *Questions of Travel*, 2.

58. Braziel and Mannur, "Nation, Migration, Globalization," 3.

59. Gilroy, "Diaspora and the Detours of Identity," 330.

60. Gilroy, "Diaspora and the Detours of Identity," 330.

61. Gilroy, *The Black Atlantic*, 110.

62. Gilroy, *There Ain't No Black in the Union Jack*, 155.

63. Gilroy, "Diaspora and the Detours of Identity," 318.

64. Gilroy, "Diaspora and the Detours of Identity," 329.

65. Hall, "Cultural Identity and Diaspora," 236.

66. Hall, "Cultural Identity and Diaspora."

67. Mishra, 'The Diasporic Imaginary and the Indian Diaspora."

68. Mishra, 'The Diasporic Imaginary and the Indian Diaspora," 433–34.

69. See Brubaker, "The 'Diaspora' Diaspora."

70. See, for example, Butler, "Defining Diaspora"; Tololyan, "The Nation-State and Its Others; and Brubaker, "The 'Diaspora' Diaspora."

71. Brubaker, "The 'Diaspora' Diaspora," 1.

72. Bauman, "Diaspora," 315.

73. Sell, introduction, 10.

74. See, for example, W. Walters, *At Home in Diaspora*.

75. Brah, *Cartographies of Diaspora*.

76. Said, *Orientalism*.

77. Brennen, *Wars of Position*.

78. Chow, *Writing Diaspora*.

79. See, for example, Davies, *Black Women, Writing, and Identity*; and Edmondson, *Making Men*.

80. Danticat, "'The Past Is Not Always Past.'"

81. Charles, "Gender and Politics in Contemporary Haiti," 139.

82. Alexander, "M/othering the Nation," 387.

83. Davies, *Black Women, Writing, and Identity*, 49–50.

84. Gourdine, *The Difference Place Makes,* 102.
85. See, for example, Wallace, *Black Macho;* Collins, *Black Feminist Thought;* and hooks, *Ain't I a Woman.*
86. Wallace, *Invisibility Blues,* 148.
87. Danticat, "'The Past Is Not Always Past.'"
88. Wright, *Becoming Black,* 133.
89. Wright, *Becoming Black,* 133.
90. Stephens, *Black Empire,* 16.
91. Pinto, *Difficult Diasporas.*
92. Pinto, *Difficult Diasporas,* 5.
93. Dayal, "Diaspora and Double Consciousness."
94. See, for example, JanMohamed, "The Economy of Manichean Allegory."
95. Mardorossian, "Doubling, Healing, and Gender."
96. See, for example, A. Mills, "The Interplay of Doubles."
97. See Clifford, "Diasporas."
98. In his essay "Diasporas in Modern Societies," William Safran defines diaspora as an intellectual enterprise. He writes, "The Gypsies have had social and economic grievances . . . , but they have not been asking themselves questions about 'the Gypsy problem' in the way that the Jews have thought about a 'Jewish problem.'" (87).
99. Jackson, *Geographies of the Haitian Diaspora,* 12.
100. Lavie and Swedenburg, *Displacement, Diaspora, and Geographies of Identity,* 14.
101. Clifford writes, "Diasporist discourses reflect the sense of being part of an ongoing transnational network that includes the homeland, not as something simply left behind, but as a place of attachment in a contrapuntal modernity." Clifford, "Diasporas," 311.
102. Clifford, "Diasporas," 194.
103. Jackson, *Geographies of the Haitian Diaspora,* xxv.
104. Coupeau, *The History of Haiti,* 121–22.
105. Coupeau, *The History of Haiti,* 183.
106. See, for example, Pierre-Louis, *Haitians in New York City.*
107. Laguerre, *Diaspora, Politics, and Globalization,* 45
108. Clitandre, "Reframing Haitian Literature Transnationally," 94.
109. Khachig, "The Nation-State and Its Others," 6.
110. Clifford, "Diasporas," 307.
111. Basch, Schiller, and Blanc, *Nations Unbound.*
112. Basch, Schiller, and Blanc, *Nations Unbound,* 5.
113. See, for example, Laguerre, *Diasporic Citizenship,* 173.
114. Clitandre, "Reframing Haitian Literature Transnationally," 94.
115. Appadurai, *Modernity at Large,* 31.
116. Grewal and Kaplan, *Scattered Hegemonies.*
117. Shackleton, "Haitian Transnationalism," 16.

118. Braziel, "Edwidge Danticat."
119. Yuval-Davis, *Gender and Nation*, 65.

1. Recall

1. Clifford, "Diasporas," 319
2. Scott, *The Fantasy of Feminist History*, 53.
3. Chude-Sokei, *The Sound of Culture*.
4. On the relationship between history and memory, see, for example, Nora, "Between Memory and History."
5. Danticat, "A Conversation with Edwidge Danticat" (Wachtel), 107.
6. Trouillot, *Silencing the Past*, 27.
7. Trouillot, *Silencing the Past*, 26.
8. Trouillot, *Silencing the Past*, 48.
9. Trouillot, *Silencing the Past*, 27.
10. Trouillot, *Silencing the Past*, 107.
11. Trouillot, *Silencing the Past*.
12. Buck-Morss, *Hegel, Haiti, and Universal History.*.
13. Fischer, *Modernity Disavowed*.
14. Dash, *Haiti and the United States*.
15. Nesbitt, *Universal Emancipation*.
16. Nesbitt, *Voicing Memory*, 211.
17. Kaisary, *The Haitian Revolution in the Literary Imagination*; Munro and Walcott-Hackshaw, *Reinterpreting the Haitian Revolution*.
18. Braziel, "Re-membering Défilée," 59.
19. Chancy, *Framing Silence*, 16.
20. Chancy, *Framing Silence*, 17
21. Chancy, *Framing Silence*, 13.
22. Edmondson, *Making Men*.
23. Lahens, "Haitian Literature after Duvalier."
24. Danticat, *Create Dangerously*, 5. Subsequent references to this source cited parenthetically by page number in text.
25. Danticat, "A Conversation with Edwidge Danticat" (Wachtel), 112.
26. Danticat, "Horror, Hope & Redemption," 21.
27. Laguerre, *Diasporic Citizenship*, 2.
28. Laguerre, *Diasporic Citizenship*, 3.
29. Zéphir, *The Haitian Americans*, 17.
30. Lawless, "Haitians."
31. Lawless, "Haitians," 26.
32. Catanese, "Haitians," 57.
33. Zéphir, *The Haitian Americans*, 15–16.
34. Zéphir, *The Haitian Americans*.
35. See, for example, Gallagher, *Soundings in French Caribbean Writing*, 265.
36. Dejean, *The Haitians in Quebec*, v.

37. Dejean, *The Haitians in Quebec,* 8–11.

38. S. Mills, *A Place in the Sun.*

39. S. Mills, *A Place in the Sun,* 23.

40. S. Mills, *A Place in the Sun,* 55.

41. S. Mills, *A Place in the Sun,* 83.

42. S. Mills, *A Place in the Sun,* 74.

43. S. Mills, *A Place in the Sun,* 89.

44. Desroches, "Uprooting and Uprootedness," 205–6.

45. Dany Laferrière recently became the first Haitian, the first Canadian, and the second black person inducted into the Académie française.

46. S. Mills, *A Place in the Sun,* 134.

47. Dejean, *The Haitians in Quebec,* 65.

48. Dejean, *The Haitians in Quebec,* 81.

49. See, for example, Lahens, "Exile: Between Writing and Place."

50. Pierre-Louis, *Haitians in New York City,* 64.

51. See Pierre-Louis, *Haitians in New York City,* 30.

52. Danticat, "Dyasporic Appetites and Longings," 29.

53. Schuller, *Killing with Kindness,* 46.

54. Farmer, *The Uses of Haiti,* 115.

55. Shamsie, "Export Processing Zones," 656.

56. Dewind and Kinley, *Aiding Migration,* 61.

57. Corten et al., "Five Hundred Thousand Haitians in the Dominican Republic," 99.

58. Corten et al., "Five Hundred Thousand Haitians in the Dominican Republic," 99.

59. Payne and Sutton, *Modern Caribbean Politics,* 73.

60. Buss, *Haiti in the Balance,* 97.

61. Sassen, *The Global City.*

62. Pierre-Louis, *Haitians in New York City,* 31.

63. Abbott, *Haiti.*

64. Plummer, *Haiti and the United States.*

65. Danticat, "AHA!," 40.

66. Danticat, "Not Your Homeland."

67. Zéphir, *The Haitian Americans,* 18.

68. "Haiti," mongabay.com.. The exodus to the Bahamas is the backdrop of Pierre Clitandre's novel *Cathedral of the August Heat.*

69. Zéphir, *The Haitian Americans,* 18.

70. Zéphir, *The Haitian Americans,* 50–51.

71. Zéphir, *The Haitian Americans,* 50–51.

72. Wasem, "US Immigration Policy on Haitian Migrants," 4.

73. Stepick, "Unintended Consequences."

74. Commonly known as the "4H club," the groups indicated were homosexuals, heroin addicts, Haitians, and hemophiliacs.

75. Lawless, *Haiti's Bad Press.*
76. Ollivier did not view the Haitian community living abroad as a diaspora but as dislocated individuals in "new Haitian spaces." See Munro, *Exile and Post-1946 Haitian Literature;* and Ollivier, *Passages.*
77. Zéphir, *The Haitian Americans,* 52–54.
78. Ferguson, "The Duvalier Dictatorship," 80–81.
79. Gavigan, "Migration Emergencies and Human Rights in Haiti."
80. See, for example, Gavigan, "Beyond the Bateyes."
81. Gavigan, "Beyond the Bateyes."
82. Mark Potter, "Boatload of Haitians Swarms Ashore in Florida."
83. French, "U.S. Starts to Return Haitians."
84. Sciolino, "Clinton Says US Will Continue Ban on Haitian Exodus."
85. Braziel, *Diaspora,* 152.
86. Pierre-Louis, *Haitians in New York City,* 6.
87. Zéphir, *The Haitian Americans,* 54.
88. Abner Louima is a Haitian immigrant who was assaulted, brutalized, and forcibly sodomized with a broken broomstick by New York City police officers in a bathroom of a precinct station in Flatbush, Brooklyn, after being arrested outside a Brooklyn nightclub in 1997. Patrick Dorismond is a Haitian American whose sealed juvenile records were released after he was shot and killed by an undercover police officer.
89. Danticat, "Haiti."
90. Danticat, "Haiti," 5.
91. Danticat, "Haiti," 6.
92. Haitian Canadian geographer George Anglade is recognized as one of the first people to use the term "dixième département." See Jackson, *Geographies of the Haitian Diaspora.* Between 1986 and 2003, the tenth department was recognized symbolically as an overseas territory. As of the time of this writing, Haiti is divided into ten departments, after Nippes became a department in 2003, making the diaspora technically the eleventh department.
93. Jean-Pierre, "The 10th Department," 195.
94. Pierre-Louis, *Haitians in New York City,* 67.
95. Danticat, *Brother, I'm Dying,* 140.
96. Fouron and Schiller, "Haitian Identities."
97. Schiller and Fouron, "Transnational Lives and National Identities," 149.
98. Laguerre, *Diaspora, Politics, and Globalization,* 166.
99. A staunch critic of the Duvalier regime and tactics that suppress the voices of the Haitian people.
100. Danticat, *The Butterfly's Way,* xiv.
101. Wucker, *Why the Cocks Fight.*
102. Rosenblum, "US Immigration Policy."
103. Danticat, foreword to *We Are All Suspects Now,* by Tram Nguyen, xi.
104. Danticat, "Out of the Shadows."

105. Danticat, "A Very Haitian Story."
106. Danticat, "The Most Important Story of Her Life," 42.
107. See Schiller and Faist, *Migration, Development, and Transnationalism.*
108. Danticat, "AHA!," 42.
109. See, for example, the work of Saskia Sassen, in particular her article "The Global inside the Nation."

2. Echo Chamber in *Create Dangerously*

1. See Jamieson and Cappella, *Echo Chamber,* 75–76.
2. Camus, "Create Dangerously," 251.
3. Danticat, "We Are All Going to Die."
4. C. Dayan, review of *Create Dangerously,* 266.
5. C. Dayan, review of *Create Dangerously,* 266.
6. C. Dayan, review of *Create Dangerously,* 265, 266.
7. Duras and Gauthier, *Woman to Woman,* 141.
8. Gunther, *Marguerite Duras.*
9. Noonan, *Echo's Voice,* 59.
10. Danticat, "Edwidge Danticat" (interview by Cadogan), 107.
11. Barthes, *Roland Barthes,* 74.
12. Barthes, "From Work to Text," 159–60.
13. Barthes, "From Work to Text," 66.
14. See Barthes, "The Grain of Voice."
15. Barthes, *The Pleasure of the Text,* 64.
16. Barthes, "The Death of the Author," 148.
17. Barthes, "The Death of the Author," 159.
18. See H. Bloom, *The Anxiety of Influence.*
19. Ovid, *Metamorphoses,* ll. 339–558.
20. Ovid, *Metamorphoses,* ll. 462–77.
21. Ovid, *Metamorphoses,* ll. 513–16.
22. Segal, *Narcissus and Echo,* 6.
23. Daly, *Heroic Tropes,* 20.
24. Spivak, "Echo," 186.
25. Brunel, *Companion to Literary Myths,* 384.
26. Baptiste, "Back to Dark Days in Haiti."
27. Herbert, "In America; Betrayal."
28. Morrison, *Beloved,* 43.
29. Braziel, "Re-membering Défilée," 69.
30. Braziel, "Défilée's Diasporic Daughters," 89.
31. Braziel, "Défilée's Diasporic Daughters," 89.
32. Braziel, "Re-membering Défilée," 84.
33. Danticat, "Interview with Edwidge Danticat," (Lyons), 192–93.
34. Latortue, "The Woman in the Haitian Novel," 39.
35. Ménard, *The Occupied Novel.*

36. Shelton, "Haitian Women's Fiction," 770.
37. Zane, "Edwidge Danticat's Top Ten List." See also Zane, *The Top Ten*, 55.
38. She divorced Pierre after this incident.
39. Danticat, "Edwidge Danticat" (interview by Cadogan), 108.

3. Haitian Echoes

1. Chinosole, *The African Diaspora & Autobiographics*, xii.
2. Chinosole, *The African Diaspora & Autobiographics*, 135.
3. Chinosole, *The African Diaspora & Autobiographics*, 138.
4. Chinosole, *The African Diaspora & Autobiographics*, 140.
5. See Danticat, "Haiti," 2.
6. Du Bois, *The Souls of Black Folk*, 5.
7. Clark, "Developing Diaspora Literacy and Marasa Consciousness," 14.
8. Clark, "Developing Diaspora Literacy and Marasa Consciousness," 12.
9. Clark, "Developing Diaspora Literacy and Marasa Consciousness," 11.
10. Anzaldúa, *Borderlands / La Frontera*, 101–2.
11. In 1990, Danticat graduated from Barnard College with a degree in French literature. She was offered a full scholarship to Brown University's masters of fine arts in creative writing program.
12. Danticat, "The Dangerous Job of Edwidge Danticat," 382.
13. Danticat, "Interview with Edwidge Danticat" (Alexandre and Howard), 161. See also Alexandre and Howard, "My Turn in the Fire."
14. For a review of both texts, see, for example, Balutansky, "Review."
15. Agha-Jaffar, *Demeter and Persephone*, 9.
16. T. Walters, *African American Literature*, 19, 28.
17. Cowart, *Trailing Clouds*, 127.
18. Cowart, *Trailing Clouds*, 134.
19. Morris, *Close Kin and Distant Relatives*, 85, 86.
20. Braziel, "Daffodils, Rhizomes, Migrations," 113.
21. Cowart, *Trailing Clouds*, 127.
22. See T. Walters, *African American Literature*, 21.
23. See Dowing, *The Long Journey Home*, 3.
24. Dowing, *The Long Journey Home*, 53–54.
25. T. Walters, *African American Literature*, 27.
26. Dowing, *The Long Journey Home*, 2.
27. Dowing, *The Long Journey Home*, 4.
28. T. Walters, *African American Literature*, 28.
29. Agha-Jaffar, *Demeter and Persephone*, 59–60.
30. Agha-Jaffar, *Demeter and Persephone*, 60.
31. Danticat, *Breath, Eyes, Memory*, 46. Subsequent references to this source cited parenthetically by page number in text.
32. Dowing, *The Long Journey Home*, 59.
33. See William Wordsworth's poem "I Wandered Lonely as a Cloud."

34. For a literary analysis of the daffodil as trope of Englishness, see Edmondson, *Making Men.*

35. Pyne-Timothy, "Language, Theme and Tone," 129.

36. Christophe, "Truth, Half-Truths and Beautiful Lies," 99.

37. Braziel, "Daffodils, Rhizomes, Migrations."

38. Alexander, "M/othering the Nation," 377.

39. Mardorossian, *Reclaiming Difference,* 134.

40. Clitandre, "Reframing Haitian Literature Transnationally," 97.

41. Clitandre, "Reframing Haitian Literature Transnationally," 98.

42. Walcott-Hackshaw, "Home Is Where the Heart Is," 81.

43. Nichols, "'Poor Visitor,'" 199.

44. Nichols, "'Poor Visitor,'" 199.

45. Nichols, "'Poor Visitor,'" 200.

46. Donovan, *After the Fall,* 2.

47. For a discussion of cultural narrative of motherhood, see Hewett, "Mothering across Borders."

48. Sarthou, "Unsilencing Defile's Daughters," 103.

49. Ovid, *Metamorphoses,* ll. 637–39. Subsequent references to this source cited parenthetically by line number in text.

50. T. Walters, *African American Literature,* 23.

51. Kadushin, *The Rabbinic Mind,* 262.

52. N'Zengou-Tayo, "Rewriting Folklore," 137.

53. Pressley-Sanon, "One Plus One Equals Three," 123.

54. Christophe, "Truths, Half Truths, and Beautiful Lies," 99.

55. Christophe, "Truths, Half Truths, and Beautiful Lies," 100.

56. Mardorossian, *Reclaiming Difference,* 129.

57. Danticat, "The Dangerous Job of Edwidge Danticat," 385.

58. Danticat, "The Dangerous Job of Edwidge Danticat," 386.

59. Danticat, "The Dangerous Job of Edwidge Danticat," 385.

60. Lorde, *Zami,* 78.

61. J. Dayan, "Erzulie," 43.

62. J. Dayan, "Erzulie," 35.

4. *The Dew Breaker* **as Écho-Monde**

1. Morrison, Nobel lecture; Bernabé, Chamoiseau, and Confiant, *Éloge de la Créolité;* Walcott, *The Antilles.*

2. Danticat, "Haiti," 6.

3. Danticat, "Haiti," 8.

4. Danticat, "Horror, Hope & Redemption," 21.

5. Glissant, *Poetics of Relation,* 94.

6. Landsberg, *Prosthetic Memory,* 50, 55, 61.

7. In fact, the collection was initially entitled "Seven" and came out of the idea of publishing seven stories. See Danticat, "Bearing Witness," 15.

8. Danticat, *The Dew Breaker,* 20. Subsequent references to this source cited parenthetically by page number in text.

9. Jennifer E. Henton, "Danticat's *The Dew Breaker.*"

10. Henton, "Danticat's *The Dew Breaker,*" 2.

11. Henton, "Danticat's *The Dew Breaker,*" 2.

12. Henton, "Danticat's *The Dew Breaker,*" 3.

13. Henton, "Danticat's *The Dew Breaker,*" 4.

14. Henton, "Danticat's *The Dew Breaker,*" 4.

15. Henton, "Danticat's *The Dew Breaker,*" 4.

16. Henton, "Danticat's *The Dew Breaker,*" 5.

17. Henton, "Danticat's *The Dew Breaker,*" 6.

18. Jacques Lacan presents three main moments of the psyche that structure an individual's development: the imaginary order, the symbolic order, and the real. The symbolic is the order of language and narrative.

19. Henton, "Danticat's *The Dew Breaker,*" 8

20. Lacan, *Écrits,* 6–7.

21. Lacan, *Écrits,* 13.

22. Lacan, *Écrits,* 7.

23. Valerie Kaussen, *Migrant Revolutions,* 199.

24. Machado Sáez, *Market Aesthetics,* 188.

25. Glissant, *Poetics of Relation,* 11.

26. See Deleuze, *A Thousand Plateaus.*

27. Glissant, *Poetics of Relation,* 15.

28. Glissant, *Poetics of Relation,* 18.

29. Glissant, *Poetics of Relation,* 14.

30. Glissant, *Poetics of Relation,* 18.

31. Glissant, *Poetics of Relation,* 19.

32. Glissant, *Poetics of Relation,* 19.

33. Glissant, *Poetics of Relation,* 16.

34. Glissant, *Poetics of Relation,* 33.

35. Glissant, *Poetics of Relation,* 62.

36. Glissant, *Poetics of Relation,* 93.

37. Glissant, *Poetics of Relation,* 93.

38. Glissant, *Poetics of Relation,* 93.

39. Glissant, *Poetics of Relation,* 62.

40. Glissant, *Poetics of Relation,* 92.

41. Glissant, *Poetics of Relation,* 94.

42. Davis, "Oral Narrative as Short Story Cycle," 71.

43. Misrahi-Barak, "'My Mouth Is the Keeper,'" 2.

44. Misrahi-Barak, "'My Mouth Is the Keeper,'" 3.

45. Misrahi-Barak, "'My Mouth Is the Keeper,'" 3.

46. Misrahi-Barak, "'My Mouth Is the Keeper,'" 5.

47. Minor, review of *The Dew Breaker,* 774.

48. Gallagher, "Concealment, Displacement, and Disconnection," 148.

49. Gallagher, "Concealment, Displacement, and Disconnection," 151–52.

50. Gallagher, "Concealment, Displacement, and Disconnection," 157.

51. Misrahi-Barak, "Exploring Trauma through the Memory of Text," 164.

52. Misrahi-Barak, "Exploring Trauma through the Memory of Text," 173.

53. Wilson C. Chen, "Narrating Diaspora in Edwidge Danticat's Short Story Cycle in *The Dew Breaker*" *Literature Interpretation Theory* 25 (2014) 222.

54. Duboin, "Reprises textuelles dans *The Dew Breaker*"

55. Dash, "Danticat and Her Haitian Precursors," 36.

56. See, for example, Walcott-Hackshaw, "Home Is Where the Heart Is."

57. Cobham, "The Penance of Speech."

58. This story can be found on page 360 of *Papa Doc and the Tonton Macoutes.*

59. Lemoine, *Fort-Dimanche,* 13.

60. See Danticat, "An Interview with Edwidge Danticat" BookBrowse.com.

61. Dash, "Danticat and Her Haitian Precursors," 26–27.

62. Said, *The World, the Text and the Critic,* 113.

63. Said, *The World, the Text and the Critic,* 135.

64. Said, *The World, the Text and the Critic,* 136.

65. Roumain, *Masters of the Dew,* 80.

66. Roumain, *Masters of the Dew,* 122.

67. Danticat, introduction to *Love, Anger, Madness.*

68. Roumain, *Masters of the Dew,* 124.

69. Roumain, *Masters of the Dew,* 181.

70. Glissant, *Poetics of Relation,* 52.

71. Roumain, *Masters of the Dew,* 45.

72. Roumain, *Masters of the Dew,* 75.

73. "An Interview with Edwidge Danticat" (BookBrowse.com).

74. See Cobham, "The Penance of Speech," 3.

75. Danticat, "Dyasporic Appetites and Longings," 33.

76. Greene, preface to *The Comedians.*

77. Bogues, "Tell the Minister We Are Human Too."

78. Alexis, *General Sun, My Brother,* 23.

79. Danticat also creates literary affiliation with Alexis through the character Anne, in "The Book of Miracles," who like Alexis' Hilarion, is epileptic. Anne's enchanted world in "The "Book of Miracles" formed out of a belief in faith, mysteries and the supernatural, echoes Alexis's theory of "marvelous realism." On Alexis' marvelous realism, see the work Michael Dash, Jacques Stephen Alexis, 1975

80. Bellamy, "More than Hunter or Prey," 180.

81. For an analysis on the significance of food and cooking in diasporic forms of resistance, see Loichot, "Edwidge Danticat's Kitchen History."

82. Danticat, "Horror, Hope & Redemption," 21.

83. Danticat, "A Conversation with Edwidge Danticat" (Wachtel), 114.

84. See Walcott-Hackshaw, "Home Is Where the Heart Is," 79.

85. Morrison, *Beloved,* 273–74.

86. Shae, "Teaching Edwidge Danticat's 'The Funeral Singer.'"

87. Machado Sáez, *Market Aesthetics,* 189.

88. Machado Sáez, *Market Aesthetics,* 190.

89. Machado Sáez, *Market Aesthetics,* 191–92.

90. For an analysis of the figuration of Antigone in Danticat's work, see Angela A. Ard's chapter on Danticat, "Storytelling as Diasporic Consciousness," in *Words of Witness.*

91. See Danticat, "Bearing Witness," 16. In this interview with Renee Shae, Danticat states that she wanted to write about "people who are dealing with life problems, more than immigration problems."

92. Ortiz "Re-membering the Past," 66, 75

5. Voices from beyond the (Unmarked) Grave in *The Farming of Bones*

1. Morrison, Nobel lecture, 6.

2. Mishra, "The Diasporic Imaginary and the Indian Diaspora," 7.

3. Morrison, *Playing in the Dark.*

4. Dash, *Haiti and the United States,* xiii.

5. Morrison, "The Site of Memory," 119.

6. Morrison, "The Site of Memory," 92.

7. Chancy, *Framing Silence,* 23.

8. Danticat, *The Farming of Bones,* 283. Subsequent references to this source cited parenthetically by page number in text.

9. Danticat, "Splintered Families, Enduring Connections," 194.

10. Trescott, "Edwidge Danticat: Personal History."

11. Shemak, "Re-membering Hispaniola," 107.

12. In Barsamian, *Louder Than Bombs,* 3.

13. See Americas Watch National Coalition for Haitian Refugees, *A Troubled Year,* 1.

14. See Human Rights Watch, "Dominican Republic."

15. Reforms included instructions to regularize immigration status of all Haitians in the Dominican Republic and provide individual work contracts specifying wages and gave workers the right to break their contracts and seek work elsewhere or return to Haiti. See Human Rights Watch, "Dominican Republic."

16. See Americas Watch National Coalition for Haitian Refugees, *A Troubled Year,* 1.

17. Paulino, "Anti-Haitianism," 269.

18. Howard, "Development, Racism, and Discrimination," 727.

19. Sawyer and Paschel, "We Didn't Cross the Color Line," 310.

20. Howard, "Development, Racism, and Discrimination," 727.

21. Howard, "Development, Racism, and Discrimination," 727.

22. Howard, "Development, Racism, and Discrimination," 735.

23. Hintzen, "Historical Forgetting."

24. Pérez, "We Are Dominican."

25. Fanon, *Black Skin, White Mask,* 11.

26. Munro, "Writing Disaster," 87.

27. Landsberg, *Prosthetic Memory,* 8–9.

28. Sagas, *Race and Politics,* 35.

29. Chancy, *From Sugar to Revolution,* 93.

30. Shemak, "Re-membering Hispaniola," 92.

31. Redon, "Hispaniola," 164.

32. Paasi, *Territories, Boundaries, and Consciousness,* 226.

33. Popescu, *Bordering and Ordering the Twenty-First Century: Understanding Borders* Lanham, Md: Rowman & Littlefield Publishers, Inc, 2012 2012

34. Paasi, "Bounded Spaces," 229.

35. In an interview Danticat states that we cross borders to reach a neutral space. See Candelario, "Voices from Hispaniola," 70.

36. Chancy, *From Sugar to Revolution.*

37. Unofficial estimates range from 500,000 to 1 million in 1993. See Gavigan, "Beyond the Bateyes."

38. The Massacre River got its name because of the Spanish killing of thirty French pirates there in 1728. See Wucker, *Why the Cocks Fight,* 200. See also Vega-González, "Sites of Memory."

39. Turits, "A World Destroyed," 615.

40. Turits, "A World Destroyed," 615.

41. Turits, "A World Destroyed," 615.

42. Turits, *Foundations of Despotism,* 162.

43. See Danticat, "An Immigrant Artist at Work," 53.

44. Hicks, *Blood in the Streets.*

45. Danticat, "A Conversation with Edwidge Danticat" (Wachtel), 108.

46. Kuhn, *Family Secrets,* 4.

47. Danticat, "An Interview with Edwidge Danticat" (Alexandre and Howard), 168.

48. Morrison, "The Site of Memory," 92.

49. Morrison, "The Site of Memory," 302.

50. Kuhn, *Family Secrets,* 160.

51. See Novak, "A Marred Testament"; and Hewett, "At the Crossroads."

52. Heather Hewett asserts that in a reading of *The Farming Bones* at Barnes & Noble in New York on September 13, 1999, Danticat described the bold text narrative as a lyrical "voice of dreams." Hewett, "At the Crossroads."

53. Mehta, *Notions of Identity.*

54. See Novak "A Marred Testament," 113.

55. Danticat, "A Conversation with Edwidge Danticat" (Wachtel), 109–110

56. Chancy, *From Sugar to Revolution,* 83.

57. See Martinez, *Peripheral Migrants;* see also Martinez, "From Hidden Hand to Heavy Hand," 61.

58. See Mintz, *Sweetness and Power,* 32.

59. Mintz, *Sweetness and Power,* 30.

60. Mintz, *Sweetness and Power,* 35.

61. Martinez, "From Hidden Hand to Heavy Hand."

62. Sagas, *Race and Politics,* 23.

63. Torres-Saillant, "Tribulations of Blackness," 134–45.

64. Torres-Saillant, "Tribulations of Blackness," 136.

65. See Gavigan, "Beyond the Bateyes."

66. CSCC, "Dominican Sugar."

67. See Martinez, *Peripheral Migrants.*

68. Martinez, *Peripheral Migrants,* 62–69.

69. Martinez, *Peripheral Migrants,* 73.

70. Derby, "Haitians, Magic, and Money," 493.

71. Martinez, "From Hidden Hand to Heavy Hand," 74; Turits, "A World Destroyed."

72. Jayaram, "Capital Changes."

73. Shae, "The Hunger to Tell."

74. Harbawi, "Writing Memory," 39.

75. Chancy, *From Sugar to Revolution,* 110.

Epilogue

1. Danticat, "Genius."

2. Danticat, "Up Close and Personal," 351.

3. Danticat, *Brother, I'm Dying,* 26. Subsequent references to this source cited parenthetically by page number in text.

4. Danticat, "The Dangerous Job of Edwidge Danticat," 386.

5. Danticat, *The Art of Death,* 29.

6. Thiong'o, *Globalectics,* 54.

7. Thiong'o, *Globalectics,* 57.

8. Thiong'o, *Globalectics,* 56.

9. Thiong'o, *Globalectics,* 60.

10. Thiong'o, *Globalectics,* 60.

Bibliography

Abbott, Elizabeth. *Haiti: A Shattered Nation.* New York: Overlook, 2011.

Agha-Jaffar, Tmara. *Demeter and Persephone: Lessons from a Myth.* Jefferson, NC: McFarland, 2002.

Alexander, Simone A. James. *Mother Imagery in the Novels of Afro-Caribbean Women.* Columbia: University of Missouri Press, 2001.

———. "M/othering the Nation: Women's Bodies as Nationalist Trope in Edwidge Danticat's *Breath, Eyes, Memory.*" *African American Review* 44 (Fall 2011): 373–90.

Alexandre, Sandy, and Ravi Y. Howard. "My Turn in the Fire." *Transition* 12, no. 3 (2002): 110–28.

Alexis, Jacques Stephen. *General Sun, My Brother.* Translated by Carrol F. Coates. Charlottesville: University Press of Virginia, 1999.

Americas Watch National Coalition for Haitian Refugees. *A Troubled Year: Haitians in the Dominican Republic.* New York: Americas Watch, 1992.

Anderson, Benedict. *Imagined Community: Reflections on the Origins and Spread of Nationalism.* New York: Verso, 1993.

Anzaldúa, Gloria. *Borderlands / La Frontera: The New Mestiza.* 2nd ed. San Francisco: Aunt Lute Books, 1999.

Appadurai, Arjun. *Modernity at Large: Cultural Dimensions of Globalization.* Minneapolis: University of Minnesota Press, 1996.

Ards, Angela. *Words of Witness: Black Women's Autobiography in the Post-Brown Era.* Madison: University of Wisconsin Press, 2016.

Bakhtin, M. M. *The Dialogic Imagination: Four Essays.* Translated by Caryl Emerson and Michael Hoquist, edited by Michael Hoquist. Austin: University of Texas Press, 1981.

Balutansky, Kathleen. "Review: Naming Caribbean Women Writers." *Callaloo* 13, no. 3 (1990): 539–50.

Baptiste, Nathalie. "Back to Dark Days in Haiti." *Nation*, 11 March 2014. https://www.thenation.com/article/back-dark-days-haiti/.

Barsamian, David. *Louder Than Bombs: Interviews from The Progressive Magazine.* New York: South End, 2004.

Barthes, Roland. "The Death of the Author." In *Roland Barthes: Image, Music, Text.* New York: Noonday, 1977.

———. "From Work to Text." In *Roland Barthes: Image, Music, Text.* New York: Noonday Press, 1977.

———. "The Grain of Voice." In *Roland Barthes: Image, Music, Text.* New York: Noonday, 1977.

———. *The Pleasure of the Text.* Translated by Richard Miller. New York: Hill and Wang, 1975.

———. *Roland Barthes.* Translated by Richard Howard. New York: Farrar, Straus and Giroux, 1975.

Basch, Linda, Nina Glick Schiller, and Cristina Szanton Blanc. *Nations Unbound: Transnational Projects, Postcolonial Predicaments and Deterritorialized Nation-States.* Amsterdam: Gordon and Beach, 1994.

Bauman, Martin. "Diaspora: Genealogies of Semantics and Transcultural Comparison." *Numen* 47, no. 3 (2000): 313–37.

Bellamy, Maria Rice. "Review of *Edwidge Danticat: A Reader's Guide,* by Martin Munro." *Callaloo* 36, no. 2 (Spring 2013): 463–66.

Bernabé, Jean, Patrick Chamoiseau, and Raphaël Confiant. *Éloge de la Créolité / In Praise of Creoleness.* Translated by Mohamed B. Taleb-Khyar. Paris: Gallimard, 1993.

Bhabha, Homi K. *The Location of Culture.* New York: Routledge, 1994.

Bloom, Gina. *Voice in Motion: Staging Gender, Shaping Sound in Early Modern England.* Philadelphia: University of Pennsylvania Press, 2007.

Bloom, Harold. *The Anxiety of Influence: A Theory of Poetry.* New York: Oxford University Press, 1997.

Bogues, Anthony. "Tell the Minister We Are Human Too! To Be Human in Today's World: Is It Possible?" opening convocation address, 2 September 2010, Brown University.

Brah, Avtar. *Cartographies of Diaspora: Contesting Identities.* New York: Routledge, 1996.

Braziel, Jana. "Daffodils, Rhizomes, Migrations: Narrative Coming of Age in the Diasporic Writings of Edwidge Danticat and Jamaica Kincaid." *Meridians: Feminism, Race, Transnationalism* 3, no. 2 (2003): 110–31.

———. *Diaspora: An Introduction.* Malden, MA: Blackwell, 2008.

———. "Défilée's Diasporic Daughters: Revolutionary Narratives of Ayiti (Haiti), Nanchon (Nation), and Dyaspora (Diaspora) in Edwidge Danticat's *Krik? Krak!*" *Studies in the Literary Imagination* 37, no. 2 (Fall 2004): 77–96.

———. "Edwidge Danticat." In *Encyclopedia of African American Women Writers,* edited by Yolanda Williams. Westport, CT: Greenwood, 2007.

———. "Re-membering Défilée: Dédée Bazile as Revolutionary Lieu de Mémoire." *Small Axe* 9, no. 2 (2005): 57–85.

Braziel, Jana, and Anita Mannur. "Nation, Migration, Globalization: Points of Contention in Diaspora Studies." In *Theorizing Diaspora: A Reader.* Malden, MA: Blackwell, 2003.

Brennan, Timothy. *Wars of Position: The Cultural Politics of Left and Right.* New York: Columbia University Press, 2006.

Brubaker, Rogers. "The 'Diaspora' Diaspora." *Ethnic and Racial Studies* 28, no. 1 (January 2005): 1–19.

Brunel, Pierre, ed. *Companion to Literary Myths, Heroes and Archetypes.* New York: Routledge, 1992.

Buck-Morss, Susan. *Hegel, Haiti, and Universal History.* Pittsburgh: University of Pittsburgh Press, 2009.

Bulfinch, Thomas. *Bulfinch's Mythology.* New York: Thomas Y. Crowell, 1913.

Buss, Terry. *Haiti in the Balance: Why Foreign Aid Has Failed and What We Can Do about It.* Washington, DC: Brookings Institute Press, 2008.

Butler, Kim. "Defining Diaspora, Refining a Discourse." *Diaspora: A Journal of Transnational Studies* 10, no. 2 (Fall 2001): 189–219.

Camus, Albert. "Create Dangerously." In *Resistance, Rebellion, and Death: Essays.* New York: Vintage Books, 1960.

Candelario, Ginetta E. B. "Voices from Hispaniola: A Meridians Roundtable with Edwidge Danticat, Loida Maritza Pérez, Myriam J. A. Chancy, and Nelly Rosario." *Meridians: Feminism, Race, Transnationalism* 5, no. 1 (2004): 68–91.

Cappella, Joseph N., and Kathleen Hall Jamieson. *Echo Chamber: Rush Limbaugh and the Conservative Media Establishment.* New York: Oxford University Press, 2008.

Catanese, Anthony. *Haitians: Migration and Diaspora.* Boulder, CO: Westview, 1999.

Chancy, Myriam J. A. *Framing Silence: Revolutionary Novels by Haitian Women.* New Brunswick, NJ: Rutgers, 1997.

———. *From Sugar to Revolution: Women's Visions of Haiti, Cuba, and the Dominican Republic.* Waterloo, ON: Wilfrid Laurier University Press, 2012.

Charles, Carolle. "Gender and Politics in Contemporary Haiti: The Duvalierist State, Transnationalism, and the Emergence of a New Feminism (1980–1990)." *Feminist Studies* 21, no. 1 (Spring 1995): 135–64.

Chauvet, Marie. *Love, Anger, Madness: A Haitian Trilogy.* Translated by Rose-Myriam Réjouis and Val Vinokur. New York: Modern Library, 2010.

Chen, Wilson C. "Narrating Diaspora in Edwidge Danticat's Short Story Cycle *The Dew Breaker.*" *Literature Interpretation Theory* 25 (2014): 220–41.

Chinosole. *The African Diaspora & Autobiographics: Skeins of Self and Skin.* New York: Peter Lang, 2001.

Chow, Rey. *Writing Diaspora: Tactics of Intervention in Contemporary Cultural Studies.* Bloomington: Indiana University Press, 1993.

Christophe, Marc A. "Truth, Half-Truths and Beautiful Lies: Edwidge Danticat and the Recuperation of Memory in *Breath, Eyes, Memory.*" Special Issue on Edwidge Danticat, *Journal of Haitian Studies* 7, no. 2 (Fall 2001): 96–107.

Chude-Sokei, Louis. *The Sound of Culture: Diaspora and Black Technopoetics.* Middletown, CT: Wesleyan University Press, 2016.

Clark, VèVè A. "Developing Diaspora Literacy and Marasa Consciousness." *Theatre Survey* 50, no. 1 (2009): 9–18.

Clifford, James. "Diasporas." *Cultural Anthropology* 9, no. 3 (August 1994): 302–38.

Clitandre, Nadège. "Reframing Haitian Literature Transnationally: Identifying New and Revised Tropes of Haitian Identity in Edwidge Danticat's *Breath, Eyes, Memory.*" *Journal of Haitian Studies* 9, no. 2 (Fall 2003): 90–110.

Cobham, Rhonda. "The Penance of Speech." Review of *The Dew Breaker*, by Edwidge Danticat. *Women's Review of Books* 21, no. 8 (May 2004): 1, 3.

Corten, Andre, Isis Duarte, Consuelo M. Soto, and Viviana Fridman. "Five Hundred Thousand Haitians in the Dominican Republic." *Latin American Perspectives* 22, no. 3 (Summer 1995): 94–110.

Coupeau, Steeve. *The History of Haiti.* Westport, CT: Greenwood, 2009.

Cowart, David. *Trailing Clouds: Immigrant Fiction in Contemporary America.* Ithaca, NY: Cornell University Press, 2006.

CSCC. "Dominican Sugar: A Macro View of Today's Industry." https://www.coca-cola.ie/content/dam/journey/ie/en/hidden/PDFs/human-and-workplace-rights/country-sugar-studies/DominicanSugarIndustry-AMacroLevelReport.pdf.

Daly, Pierrette. *Heroic Tropes: Gender and Intertext.* Detroit: Wayne State University Press, 1993.

Danticat, Edwidge. "AHA!" In *Becoming American: Personal Essays by First Generation Immigrant Women,* edited by Meri Nana-Ama Danquah. New York: Hyperion, 2000.

———. *The Art of Death: Writing the Final Story.* Minneapolis: Graywolf, 2017.

———. "Bearing Witness and Beyond: Edwidge Danticat Talks about Her Latest Work." Interview by Renée Shea. Special Issue on Edwidge Danticat, *Journal of Haitian Studies* 7, no. 2 (2001): 6–20.

———. *Brother, I'm Dying.* New York: Random House, 2007.

———. *The Butterfly's Way: Voices from the Haitian Dyaspora in the United States.* New York: Soho, 2001.

———. "A Conversation with Edwidge Danticat." Interview by Eleanor Wachtel. *Brick* 65–66 (2000): 106–19.

———. *Create Dangerously: The Immigrant Artist at Work.* Princeton, NJ: Princeton University Press, 2010.

———. "The Dangerous Job of Edwidge Danticat: An Interview." By Renée Shea. *Callaloo* 19, no. 2 (Spring 1996): 382–89.

———. "Dyasporic Appetites and Longings: An Interview with Edwidge Danticat." By Nancy Raquel Mirabal. *Callaloo* 30, no. 1 (Winter 2007): 26–39.

———. "Edwidge Danticat." Interview by Garnette Cadogan. *Bomb* 126 (Winter 2014): 104–10.

———. Foreword to *We Are All Suspects Now: Untold Stories from Immigrant Communities after 9/11,* by Tram Nguyen. Boston: Beacon, 2005.

———. "Genius: A Talk with Edwidge Danticat." Interview by Martha St. Jean. *Huffington Post,* 23 November 2009, https://www.huffingtonpost.com/martha -st-jean/genius-a-talk-with-edwidg_b_295040.html.

———. "Haiti: A Bicultural Experience." *Encuentros* 12 (December 1995): 1–9.

———. "Horror, Hope & Redemption: A Talk with Edwidge Danticat about Her Latest Novel, *The Dew Breaker.*" Interview by Terry Hong. *Bloomsbury Review* 24, no. 5 (2004): 21.

———. "An Immigrant Artist at Work: A Conversation with Edwidge Danticat." Interview by Elvira Pulitano. *Small Axe* 15, no. 3 (2011): 39–61.

———. Introduction to *Love, Anger, Madness: A Haitian Trilogy,* by Marie Chau- vet. New York: Modern Library, 2010.

———. "A Conversation with Haitian Writer Edwidge Danticat." Interview by Zita Allen. *New York Amsterdam News,* 19 November 2005.

———. "Interview with Edwidge Danticat." By Bonnie Lyons. *Contemporary Literature* 44, no. 2 (2003): 183–98.

———. "An Interview with Edwidge Danticat." By Sandy Alexandre and Ravi Y. Howard. *Journal of Caribbean Literatures* 4, no. 3 (2007): 161–74.

———. "An Interview with Edwidge Danticat." BookBrowse.com. https://www .bookbrowse.com/author_interviews/full/index.cfm/author_number/1022 /edwidge-danticat.

———. "The Most Important Story of Her Life." Interview by Nina Shen Rastogi. *Poets and Writers,* September–October 2007, 38–44.

———. "Not Your Homeland." *Nation,* 8 September 2005. http://www.thenation .com/article/not-your-homeland/.

———. "Out of the Shadows." *Progressive,* 23 May 2006. http://progressive.org /dispatches/shadows/.

———. "'The Past Is Not Always Past': A Conversation with Edwidge Danticat." Interview by Lanny More. *Aster(ix),* June 7, 2017. http://www.samposoniaway .org/literary-voices/2017/06/07/the-past-is-not-always-past-a-conversation -with-edwidge-danticat/.

———. "Splintered Families, Enduring Connections: An Interview with Edwidge Danticat." By Katharine Capshaw Smith. *Children's Literature Association Quarterly* 30, no. 2 (2005): 194–205.

———. "Up Close and Personal: Edwidge Danticat on Haitian Identity and the Writer's Life." Interview by Opal Palmer Adisa. *African American Review* 43 (2009): 345–55.

———. "A Very Haitian Story." *New York Times,* 24 November 2004. http:// www.nytimes.com/2004/11/24/opinion/24danticat.html.

———. "We Are All Going to Die." Interview by Nathalie Handal. *Guernica,* 15 January 2011. https://www.guernicamag.com/danticat_1_15_11/.

Dash, J. Michael. "Danticat and Her Haitian Precursors." In *Edwidge Danticat: A Reader's Guide,* edited by Martin Munro. Charlottesville: University of Virginia Press, 2010.

———. *Haiti and the United States: National Stereotypes and the Literary Imagination.* Basingstoke: Palgrave Macmillan, 1997.

Davies, Carole Boyce. *Black Women, Writing, and Identity: Migrations of the Subject.* New York: Routledge, 1994.

Davis, Rocio. "Oral Narrative as Short Story Cycle: Forging Community in Edwidge Danticat's *Krik? Krak!*" *Melus* 26, no. 2 (Summer 2001): 65–81.

Dayal, Samir. "Diaspora and Double Consciousness." *Journal of the Midwest MLA* 29, no. 1 (Spring 1996): 46–62.

Dayan, Colin. Review of *Create Dangerously: The Immigrant Artist at Work,* by Edwidge Danticat. *New West Indian Guide* 85, no. 3–4 (2011): 265–67.

Dayan, Joan. "Erzulie: A Women's History of Haiti." In *Postcolonial Subjects: Francophone Women Writers,* edited by Mary Jean Matthews Green. Minneapolis: University of Minnesota Press, 1996.

Dejean, Paul. *The Haitians in Quebec.* Translated by Max Dorsinville. Ottawa: Tecumseh, 1980.

Deleuze, Gilles. *A Thousand Plateaus: Capitalism and Schizophrenia.* Translated by Brian Massuni. Minneapolis: University of Minnesota Press, 1987.

Derby, Laurent. "Haitians, Magic, and Money: Raza and Society in the Haitian-Dominican Borderlands, 1900–1937." *Comparative Studies in Society and History* 36, no. 3 (July 1994): 488–526.

Desroches, Vincent. "Uprooting and Uprootedness: Haitian Poetry in Quebec (1960–2002)." In *Textualizing the Immigrant Experience in Contemporary Quebec,* edited by Susan Ireland and Patrice Proulx. Westport, CT: Praeger, 2004.

Dewind, Josh, and David H. Kinley III. *Aiding Migration: The Impact of International Development Assistance in Haiti.* Boulder, CO: Westview, 1988.

Diederich, Bernard. *Papa Doc and the Tontons Macoutes.* Princeton, NJ: Markus Wiener, 2009.

Donovan, Josephine. *After the Fall: The Demeter-Persephone Myth in Wharton, Cather, and Glasgow.* University Park: Pennsylvania State University Press, 1989.

Dowing, Christine, ed. *The Long Journey Home: Revisioning the Myth of Demeter and Persephone for Our Time.* Boston: Shambalah, 1994.

Doyle, Peter. *Echo and Reverb: Fabricating Space in Popular Music Recording, 1900–1960.* Middletown, CT: Wesleyan University Press, 2005.

Duboin, Corinne. "Reprises textuelles dans *The Dew Breaker* d'Edwidge Danticat." *Revue LISA,* 2 March 2015 http://lisa.revues.org/7173.

Du Bois, W. E. B. *The Souls of Black Folk.* 1903. New York: Penguin Books, 1989.

Duras, Marguerite, and Xavière Gauthier. *Woman to Woman.* Translated by Katharine A. Jensen. Lincoln: University of Nebraska Press, 1974.

Edmondson, Belinda. *Making Men: Gender, Literary Authority and Women's Writings in Caribbean Narrative.* Durham, NC: Duke University Press, 1999.

Fanon, Frantz. *Black Skin, White Mask.* New York: Grove, 1976.

Farmer, Paul. *The Uses of Haiti.* Monroe, ME: Common Courage, 2005.

Ferguson, James. "The Duvalier Dictatorship and Its Legacy of Crisis in Haiti." In *Modern Caribbean Politics,* edited by Anthony Payne and Paul Sutton. Baltimore: Johns Hopkins University Press, 1993.

Fischer, Sibylle. *Modernity Disavowed: Haiti and the Cultures of Slavery in the Age of Revolution.* Durham, NC: Duke University Press, 2004.

Foucault, Michel. "What Is an Author?" In *Textual Strategies: Perspectives in Post-Structuralist Criticism,* edited by Josue V. Harani. Ithaca, NY: Cornell University Press, 1979.

Fouron, Georges E., and Nina Glick Schiller. "Haitian Identities and the Juncture between Diaspora and Homeland." In *Caribbean Circuits: New Directions in the Study of Caribbean Migration,* edited by Patricia R. Pessar. New York: Center for Migration Studies, 1997.

French, Howard W. "U.S. Starts to Return Haitians Who Fled Nation after Coup." *New York Times,* 19 November 1991. http://www.nytimes.com/1991/11/19/world/us-starts-to-return-haitians-who-fled-nation-after-coup.html.

Gallagher, Mary. "Concealment, Displacement, and Disconnection: Danticat's *Breath, Eyes, Memory.*" In *Edwidge Danticat: A Reader's Guide,* edited by Martin Munro. Charlottesville: University of Virginia Press, 2010.

———. *Soundings in French Caribbean Writing since 1950: The Shock of Space and Time.* Oxford: Oxford University Press, 2003.

———, ed. *World Writing: Poetics, Ethics, Globalization.* Toronto: University of Toronto Press, 2008.

Gavigan, Patrick. "Beyond the Bateyes." National Coalition for Haitian Rights Report, 1995. https://hhidr.org/wp-content/uploads/2011/04/Gavigan-BeyondBateyes.pdf.

———. "Migration Emergencies and Human Rights in Haiti." Paper prepared for the Conference on Regional Responses to Forced Migration in Central America and the Caribbean, 30 September–1 October 1997. Organization of American States. http://www.oas.org/juridico/english/gavigane.html.

Gerber, Nancy. "Binding the Narrative Thread: Storytelling and the Mother-Daughter Relationship in Edwidge Danticat's *Breath, Eyes, Memory.*" *Journal of the Motherhood Initiative for Research and Community Development* 2, no. 2 (2000): 188–99.

Giddens, Anthony. *The Consequences of Modernity.* Stanford, CA: Stanford University Press, 1990.

Gikandi, Simon. *Writing in Limbo: Modernism and Caribbean Literature.* Ithaca, NY: Cornell University Press, 1992.

Gilroy, Paul. *The Black Atlantic: Modernity and Double Consciousness.* London: Verso, 1993.

———. "Diaspora and the Detours of Identity." In *Identity and Difference,* edited by Kathryn Woodward. London: Sage, 1997.

———. *There Ain't No Black in the Union Jack: The Cultural Politics of Race and Nation.* Chicago: University of Chicago Press, 1987.

Glissant, Édouard. *Poetics of Relation.* Translated by Betsy Wing. Ann Arbor: University of Michigan Press, 1997.

———. "The Unforeseeable Diversity of the World." In *Beyond Dichotomies: Histories, Identities, Cultures, and the Challenge of Globalization.* Albany: State University of New York Press, 2002.

Gourdine, Angeletta K. M. *The Difference Place Makes: Gender, Sexuality and Diaspora Identity.* Columbus: Ohio State University Press, 2002.

Greene, Graham. *The Comedians.* New York: Viking, 1965.

Grewal, Inderpal, and Caren Kaplan, eds. *Scattered Hegemonies: Postmodernity and Transnational Feminist Practices.* Minneapolis: University of Minnesota Press, 1994.

Gunther, Renate. *Marguerite Duras.* Manchester: Manchester University Press, 2002.

"Haiti." Mongabay.com. http://mongabay.com/reference/country_studies/haiti/all.html.

Hall, Stuart. "Cultural Identity and Diaspora." In *Colonial/Discourse/Postcolonial Theory,* edited by Patrick Williams and Laura Chrisman. New York: Columbia University Press, 1994.

Harbawi, Semia. "Writing Memory: Edwidge Danticat's Limbo Inscriptions." *Journal of West Indian Literature* 16, no.1 (2007): 37–58.

Henton, Jennifer E. "Danticat's *The Dew Breaker,* Haiti, and Symbolic Migration." *Comparative Literature and Culture* 12, no. 2 (2010). https://doi.org/10.7771/1481-4374.1601.

Herbert, Bob. "In America; Betrayal." *New York Times,* 1994. http://www.nytimes.com/1994/09/21/opinion/in-america-betrayal.html.

Hewett, Heather. "At the Crossroads: Disability and Trauma in *The Farming of Bones.*" *Melus* 31, no. 3 (Fall 2006): 123–45.

———. "Mothering across Borders: Narratives of Immigrant Mothers in the United States." *Women's Studies Quarterly* 37, no. 3–4 (2009): 121–39.

Hicks, Albert. *Blood in the Streets: The Life and Rule of Trujillo.* New York: Creative Age, 1946.

Hill Collins, Patricia. *Black Feminist Thought: Knowledge, Consciousness, and the Politics of Empowerment.* Boston: Unwin Hyman, 1990.

Hintzen, Amelia. "Historical Forgetting and the Dominican Constitutional Tribunal." *Journal of Haitian Studies* 20, no. 1 (Spring 2014): 108–16.

hooks, bell. *Ain't I a Woman: Black Women and Feminism.* Boston. South End, 1981.

Howard, David. "Development, Racism, and Discrimination in the Dominican Republic." *Develop in Practice* 17, no. 6 (November 2007): 725–38.

Human Rights Watch. "Dominican Republic." In *Human Rights Development Report 1990.* https://www.hrw.org/reports/1990/WR90/AMER.BOU-06.htm.

Jackson, Regine. *Geographies of the Haitian Diaspora.* New York: Routledge, 2011.

JanMohamed, Abdul. "The Economy of Manichean Allegory: The Function of Racial Difference in Colonialist Literature." "'Race,' Writing, and Difference." Special issue, *Critical Inquiry* 12, no. 1 (Autumn 1985): 59–87.

Jayaram, Kiran. "Capital Changes: Haitian Migrants in Contemporary Dominican Republic." *Caribbean Quarterly* 56, no. 3 (September 2010): 31–54.

Jean-Pierre, Jean. "The Tenth Department." In *Haiti: Dangerous Crossroads,* edited by Deidre McFadyen and Pierre LaRamée. Boston: South End, 1995.

Kadushin, Max. *The Rabbinic Mind.* 3rd ed. New York: Block, 1972.

Kaisary, Philip. *The Haitian Revolution in the Literary Imagination: Radical Horizons, Conservative Constraints.* Charlottesville: University of Virginia Press, 2014.

Kaplan, Caren. *Questions of Travel: Postmodern Discourses of Displacement.* Durham, NC: Duke University Press, 1994.

Kaussen, Valerie. *Migrant Revolutions : Haitian Literature, Globalization, and U.S. Imperialism.* Lanham, MD: Lexington Books, 2007.

Khachig, Tololyan. "The Nation-State and Its Others." *Diaspora* 1, no. 1 (Spring 1991): 3–7.

Kuhn, Annette. *Family Secrets: Acts of Memory and Imagination.* New York: Verso, 2002.

Lacan, Jacques. *Écrits: A Selection.* Translated by Bruce Kink. New York: Norton, 2002.

Laguerre, Michel S. *Diaspora, Politics, and Globalization.* New York: Palgrave Macmillan, 2006.

———. *Diasporic Citizenship: Haitian Americans in Transnational America.* London: Palgrave Macmillan, 1998.

Lahens, Yanick. "Exile: Between Writing and Place." *Callaloo* 15, no. 3 (Summer 1992): 736.

———. "Haitian Literature after Duvalier: An Interview with Yanick Lahens," By Clarisse Zimra. *Callaloo* 16, no. 1 (Winter 1993): 77–93.

Landsberg, Alison. *Prosthetic Memory: The Transformation of American Remembrance in the Age of Mass Culture.* New York: Columbia University Press, 2004.

Latortue, Régine. "The Woman in the Haitian Novel." PhD diss., University of Michigan, 1983.

Lavie, Smadar, and Ted Swedenburg, eds. *Displacement, Diaspora, and Geographies of Identity.* Durham, NC: Duke University Press, 1996.

Lawless, Robert. *Haiti's Bad Press.* Rochester, VT: Schenkman Books, 1992.

———. "Haitians: From Political Repression to Chaos." In *Portrait of Culture: Ethnographic Originals,* edited by Melvin Ember, Carol E. Ember, and David Levinson, vol. 2, *South and Middle America.* Englewood Cliffs, NJ Prentice-Hall, 2007.

Lemoine, Patrick. *Fort-Dimanche, Dungeon of Death.* Victoria: Trafford, 2011.

Loichot, Valérie. "Edwidge Danticat's Kitchen History." *Meridians* 5, no. 1 (2004): 92–116.

Longus. *Daphnis and Chloe*. Anthenian Society. Cambridge, Ontario: Greek Series, 2002.

Lorde, Audre. *Zami: A New Spelling of My Name*. New York: Crossing, 1982.

Ludden, Jennifer. "Writing in Exile Helps Authors Connect to Home." National Public Radio, November 15, 2010. https://www.npr.org/2010/11/15/131334555 /writing-in-exile-helps-authors-connect-to-home.

Machado Sáez, Elena. *Market Aesthetics: The Purchase of the Past in Caribbean Diasporic Fiction*. Charlottesville: University of Virginia Press, 2015.

Mardorossian, Carine. "Doubling, Healing, and Gender in Caribbean Literature." *MaComère* 12, no. 3 (Winter 2010): 17–29.

———. "From Literature of Exile to Migrant Literature." *Modern Literature Studies* 32, no. 2 (2002): 15–33.

———. *Reclaiming Difference: Caribbean Women Rewrite Postcolonialism*. Charlottesville: University of Virginia Press, 2005.

Martinez, Samuel. "From Hidden Hand to Heavy Hand: Sugar, the State and Migrant Labor in Haiti and the Dominican Republic." *Latin American Research Review* 34, no. 1 (1999): 57–84.

———. *Peripheral Migrants: Haitians and Dominican Republic Sugar Plantations*. Knoxville: University of Tennessee Press, 1996.

Mehta, Brenda. *Notions of Identity, Diaspora, and Gender in Caribbean Women's Writing*. New York: Palgrave Macmillan, 2009.

Ménard, Nadève. "The Myth of the Exiled Writer." *Transition* 111 (2013): 53–58.

———. "The Occupied Novel: The Representation of Foreigners in Haitian Novels Written during the US Occupation, 1915–1934." PhD diss., University of Pennsylvania, 2002.

Mercer, Kobena. *Welcome to the Jungle: New Positions in Black Cultural Studies*. New York: Routledge, 1994.

Mills, Alice. "The Interplay of Doubles in Edwidge Danticat's Fiction." *PALARA: Publication of the Afro-Latin/American Research Association* 8 (Fall 2004): 86–99.

Mills, Sean. *A Place in the Sun: Haiti, Haitians, and the Remaking of Quebec*. Chicago: McGill-Queen's University Press, 2016.

Minor, Kyle. Review of *The Dew Breaker*, by Edwidge Danticat. *Antioch Review* 62, no. 4 (Autumn 2004): 774.

Mintz, Sidney W. *Sweetness and Power: The Place of Sugar in Modern History*. New York: Penguin Books, 1985.

Mishra, Vijay. "The Diasporic Imaginary and the Indian Diaspora." *Textual Practice* 10, no. 3 (1996): 421–47.

Misrahi Barak, Judith. "Exploring Trauma through the Memory of Text: Edwidge Danticat Listens to Jacques Stephen Alexis, Rita Dove, and René Philoctète." *Journal of Haitian Studies* 19, no. 1 (Spring 2013): 163–83.

————. "'My Mouth Is the Keeper of Both Speech and Silence . . . ,' or the Vocalisation of Silence in Caribbean Short Stories by Edwidge Danticat." *Journal of the Short Story in English* 47 (Autumn 2006): 155–66.

Morris, Susana. *Close Kin and Distant Relatives: The Paradox of Respectability in Black Women's Literature.* Charlottesville: University of Virginia Press, 2014.

Morrison, Toni. *Beloved.* New York: Alfred A. Knopf, 1987.

————. Nobel lecture, 1993. *World Literature Today* 68, no. 1 (Winter 1994): 5–8.

————. *Playing in the Dark: Whiteness and the Literary Imagination.* Cambridge, MA: Harvard University Press, 1992.

————. "The Site of Memory." In *Inventing the Truth: The Art and Craft of Memoir,* edited by William Zinsser. Boston: Houghton, 1987.

Munro, Martin, ed. *Edwidge Danticat: A Reader's Guide.* Charlottesville: University of Virginia Press, 2010.

————. *Exile and Post-1946 Haitian Literature: Alexis, Depestre, Olivier, Laferrière, Danticat.* Liverpool: Liverpool University Press, 2007.

————. "Writing Disaster: Trauma, Memory, and History in Edwidge Danticat's *The Farming of Bones.*" *Ethnologies* 28, no. 1 (2006): 81–98.

Munro, Martin, and Elizabeth Walcott-Hackshaw, eds. *Reinterpreting the Haitian Revolution and Its Cultural Aftershocks.* Jamaica: University of the West Indies Press, 2006.

Nesbitt, Nick. *Universal Emancipation: The Haitian Revolution and the Radical Enlightenment.* Charlottesville: University of Virginia Press, 2008.

————. *Voicing Memory: History and Subjectivity in French Caribbean Literature.* Charlottesville: University of Virginia Press, 2003.

Nichols, Jennifer J. "'Poor Visitor': Mobility as/of Voice in Jamaica Kincaid's *Lucy.*" *Melus* 34, no. 4 (Winter 2009): 187–207.

Noonan, Mary. *Echo's Voice: The Theatres of Sarraute, Duras, Cixous and Renande.* London: Modern Humanities Research Association and Maney Publishing, 2014.

Nora, Pierre. "Between Memory and History: Les Lieux de Mémoire." *Representations* 26 (Spring 1989): 7–24.

Novak, Amy. "A Marred Testament: Cultural Trauma and Narrative in Danticat's *The Farming of Bones.*" *Arizona Quarterly: A Journal of American Literature, Culture, and Theory* 62, no. 4 (Winter 2006): 93–120.

N'Zengou-Tayo, Marie-José. "Rewriting Folklore: Traditional Beliefs and Popular Culture in Edwidge Danticat's *Breath, Eyes, Memory* and *Krik? Krak!*" *MaComère* 3 (2000): 123–40.

Ollivier, Émile. *Passages.* Montreal: Le Serpent à Plumes Editions, 1994.

Ortiz, Lisa M. "Re-membering the Past: Weaving Tales of Loss and Cultural Inheritance in Edwidge Danticat's *Krik? Krak!*" Special Issue on Edwidge Danticat, *Journal of Haitian Studies* 7, no. 2 (Fall 2001): 64–77

Ovid. *Metamorphoses.* Translated by Charles Martin. New York: New York Review of Books, 2004.

Paasi, Anssi. "Bounded Spaces in a 'Borderless World': Border Studies, Power, and the Anatomy of Territory." *Journal of Power* 2, no. 2 (2009): 213–34.

———. *Territories, Boundaries, and Consciousness: The Changing Geographies of the Finnish-Russian Border.* New York: John Wiley and Sons, 1996.

Paulino, Edward. "Anti-Haitianism, Historical Memory, and the Potential for Genocidal Violence in the Dominican Republic." *Genocide Studies and Prevention* 1, no. 3 (Winter 2006): 265–88.

Payne, Anthony, and Paul R. Sutton, eds. *Modern Caribbean Politics.* Baltimore: Johns Hopkins University Press, 1993.

Pérez, Celso. "We Are Dominican: Arbitrary Deprivation of Nationality in the Dominican Republic." Human Rights Watch. https://www.hrw.org/report /2015/07/01/we-are-dominican/arbitrary-deprivation-nationality-dominican -republic.

Pierre-Louis, François. *Haitians in New York City: Transnationalism and Hometown Associations.* Gainesville: University Press of Florida, 2006.

Pinto, Samantha. *Difficult Diasporas: The Transnational Feminist Aesthetic of the Black Atlantic.* New York: New York University Press, 2013.

Plummer, Brenda Gayle. *Haiti and the United States: The Psychological Moment.* Athens: University of Georgia Press, 1992.

Popescu, Gabriel. *Bordering and Ordering the Twenty-First Century: Understanding Borders.* Lanham, MD: Rowman and Littlefield, 2012.

Potter, Mark. "Boatload of Haitians Swarms Ashore in Florida." CNN News. http://www.cnn.com/2002/US/South/10/29/haitians.ashore/.

Pressley-Sanon, Toni. "One Plus One Equals Three: Marasa Consciousness, the Lwa, and Three Stories." *Research in African Literatures* 44, no. 3 (Fall 2013): 118–37.

Pyne-Timothy, Helen. "Language, Theme and Tone in Edwidge Danticat's Work." Special Issue on Edwidge Danticat, *Journal of Haitian Studies* 7, no. 2 (Fall 2001): 128–37.

Radhakrishnan, Rajagopalan. *Diasporic Mediations: Between Home and Location.* Minneapolis: University of Minnesota Press, 1996.

Redon, Marie. "Hispaniola." In *The Political Economy of Divided Islands: Unified Geographies, Multiple Polities,* edited by Godfrey Baldacchino. New York: Palgrave Macmillan, 2013.

Robertson, Roland. *Globalization: Social Theory and Global Culture.* London: Sage, 1992.

Rosenblum, Marc R. "US Immigration Policy since 9/11: Understanding the Stalemate over Comprehensive Immigration Reform." August 2011. Migration Policy Institute, https://www.migrationpolicy.org/research/RMSG-us-immigration -policy-cir-stalemate.

Roumain, Jacques. *Masters of the Dew.* Translated by Langston Hughes and Mercer Cook. London: Heinemann, 1978.

Safran, William. "Diasporas in Modern Societies: Myth of Homeland and Return." *Diaspora: A Journal of Transnational Studies* 1, no. 1 (Spring 1991): 83–99.

Sagas, Ernesto. *Race and Politics in the Dominican Republic.* Gainesville: University Press of Florida, 2000.

Said, Edward W. "Intellectual Exile: Expatriates and Marginals." In *Edward Said Reader.* New York: Vintage Books, 2000.

———. *Orientalism.* New York: Pantheon Books, 1978.

———. *Out of Place.* New York: Alfred A. Knopf, 1999.

———. "The Voice of a Palestinian in Exile." *Third Text* 2, no. 3 (1988): 39–50.

———. *The World, the Text and the Critic.* Cambridge, MA: Harvard University Press, 1983.

Sarthou, Sharrón Eve. "Unsilencing Défilé's Daughters: Overcoming Silence in Edwidge Danticat's *Breath, Eyes, Memory* and *Krik? Krak!*" "The Caribbean and Globalization," special issue of *Global South* 4, no. 2 (Fall 2010): 99–123.

Sassen, Saskia. *The Global City: New York, London, Tokyo.* Princeton, NJ: Princeton University Press, 2001.

———. "The Global Inside the National: A Research Agenda for Sociology." *Sociopedia.isa,* 2010. http://www.saskiasassen.com/pdfs/publications/the -global-inside-the-national.pdf.

Sawyer, Mark Q., and Tianna S. Paschel. "We Didn't Cross the Color Line, the Color Line Crossed Us: Blackness and Immigration in the Dominican Republic, Puerto Rico, and the United States." *Du Bois Review* 4, no. 2 (2007): 303–15.

Schiller, Nina Glick, and Thomas Faist, eds. *Migration, Development, and Transnationalism: A Critical Stance.* New York: Berghahn Books, 2010.

Schiller, Nina Glick, and Georges Fouron. "Transnational Lives and National Identities; The Identity Politics of Haitian Immigrants." In *Transnationalism from Below,* edited by Michael P. Smith and Luis Eduardo Guarnizo, New Brunswick, NJ: Transaction, 1998.

Schuller, Mark. *Killing with Kindness: Haiti, International Aid, and NGOs.* New Brunswick, NJ: Rutgers University Press, 2012.

Sciolino, Elaine. "Clinton Says US Will Continue Ban on Haitian Exodus." *New York Times,* 15 January 1993. http://www.nytimes.com/1993/01/15/world /clinton-says-us-will-continue-ban-on-haitian-exodus.html.

Scott, Joan W. "Fantasy Echo: History and the Construction of Identity." *Critical Inquiry* 27, no. 2 (Winter 2011): 284–304.

———. *The Fantasy of Feminist History.* Durham, NC: Duke University Press, 2011.

Segel, Naomi. *Narcissus and Echo: Women in the French "Récit."* Manchester: Manchester University Press, 1988.

Sell, Jonathan P. A. Introduction to *Metaphor and Diaspora in Contemporary Writing,* edited by Jonathan P. A. Sell. New York: Palgrave Macmillan, 2012.

Shackleton, Mark. "Haitian Transnationalism: Edwidge Danticat's 'Caroline's Wedding': A Case Study of Literary Anthropology." *Suomen Antropologi: Journal of the Finnish Anthropological Society* 28, no.2 (May 2003): 15–23.

Shamsie, Yasmine. "Export Processing Zones: The Purported Glimmer in Haiti's Development Murk." *Review of International Political Economy* 16, no. 4 (2009): 64–92.

Shea, Renée. "The Hunger to Tell: Edwidge Danticat and *The Farming of Bones*." *MaComère* 2 (1999): 12–22.

———. "Teaching Edwidge Danticat's 'The Funeral Singer': A Study in Voices." In *AP English Literature and Composition: Close Reading of Contemporary Literature*. Curriculum Module. College Board, 2011. http://apcentral.collegeboard.com/apc/public/repository/cm-eng-lit-close-reading.pdf.

Shelton, Marie-Denise. "Haitian Women's Fiction." *Callaloo* 15, no. 3 (Summer 1992): 770–77.

Shemak, April. "Re-membering Hispaniola: Edwidge Danticat's *The Farming of Bones*." *Modern Fiction Studies* 48, no. 1 (Spring 2002): 83–112.

Sophocles. *Oedipus, the King*. Translated by Anthony Burgess. Minneapolis: University of Minnesota Press, 1972.

Spivak, Gayatri Chakravorty. "Echo." In *The Spivak Reader*, edited by Donna Landry and Gerard Maclean. New York: Routledge, 1996.

Steger, Manfred. *The Rise of the Global Imaginary: Political Ideologies from the French Revolution to the War on Terror*. Oxford: Oxford University Press, 2008.

Stephens, Michelle Ann. *Black Empire: The Masculine Global Imaginary of Caribbean Intellectuals in the United States, 1914–1962*. Durham, NC: Duke University Press, 2005.

Stepick, Alex. "Unintended Consequences: Rejecting Haitian Boat People and Destabilizing Duvalier." In *Western Haitian Immigration and United States Foreign Policy*, edited by Christopher Mitchell. University Park: Pennsylvania State University Press, 1992.

Taylor, Charles. *Modern Social Imaginaries*. Durham, NC: Duke University Press, 2003.

Thiong'o, Ngũgĩ wa. *Globalectics: Theory and the Politics of Knowing*. New York: Columbia University Press, 2012.

Tölöyan, Khachig. "The Nation-State and its Others: In Lieu of a Preface." *Diaspora: A Journal of Transnational Studies* 1, no. 1 (Spring 1991): 3–7.

Torres-Saillant, Silvio. "Tribulations of Blackness: Stages in Dominican Racial Identity." *Latin American Perspectives* 25 no.3 (1998): 126–46.

Trescott, Jacqueline. "Edwidge Danticat: Personal History." *Washington Post*, 11 October 1999. http://www.washingtonpost.com/archive/lifestyle/1999/10/11/edwidge-danticat-personal-history/3d923b6f-c294-4317-989f-98379350e630/?utm_term=.5f320606569a.

Trouillot, Michel-Rolph. *Silencing the Past: Power and the Production of History*. Boston: Beacon, 1982.

Turits, Richard Lee. *Foundations of Despotism: Peasants, the Trujillo Regime and Modernity in Dominican History.* Stanford, CA: Stanford University Press, 2003.

———. "A World Destroyed, A Nation Imposed: The 1937 Haitian Massacre in the Dominican Republic." *Hispanic American Historical Review* 82, no. 3 (2002): 589–635.

Vega-Gonzáles, Susana. "Sites of Memory, Sites of Mourning and History: Danticat's Insights into the Past." *Revista Alicantinade Estudios Ingleses* 17 (2004): 6–24.

Vinge, Louise. *The Narcissus Theme in Western European Literature up to the Early 19th Century.* Lund: Gleerups, 1967.

Walcott, Derek. *The Antilles: Fragments of Epic Memory.* Farrar, Straus and Giroux, 1993

Walcott-Hackshaw, Elizabeth. "Home Is Where the Heart Is: Danticat's Landscape of Return." *Small Axe* 12, no. 3 (October 2008): 71–82.

Wallace, Michele. *Black Macho and the Myth of the Superwoman.* New York: Verso, 1978.

———. *Invisibility Blues: From Pop to Theory.* New York: Verso, 1990.

Walters, Tracey L. *African American Literature and the Classicist Tradition: Black Women Writers from Wheatly to Morrison.* New York: Palgrave Macmillan, 2007.

Walters, Wendy. *At Home in Diaspora: Black International Writing.* Minneapolis: University of Minnesota Press, 2005.

Wasem, Ruth Ellen. "US Immigration Policy on Haitian Immigrants." Congressional Research Service Report for Congress, 17 May 2011.

Wordsworth, William. "I Wandered Lonely as a Cloud." In *William Wordsworth: Poetry for Young People.* New York: Sterling Publications, 2003.

Wright, Michele M. *Becoming Black: Creating Identity in the African Diaspora.* Durham, NC: Duke University Press, 2004.

Wucker, Michele. *Why the Cocks Fight: Dominicans, Haitians, and the Struggle for Hispaniola.* New York: Hill and Wang, 1999.

Yuval-Davis, Nira. *Gender and Nation.* London: Sage, 1997.

Zane, J. Peder. "Edwidge Danticat's Top Ten List." The Top Ten. http://www.toptenbooks.net/authors/edwidge-danticat.

———. *The Top Ten: Writers Pick Their Favorite Books.* New York: Norton, 2007.

Zéphir, Flore. *The Haitian Americans.* Westport, CT: Greenwood, 2004.

Index

CPSIA information can be obtained
at www.ICGtesting.com
Printed in the USA
LVHW110613311018
595455LV00001B/199/P